ABOVE EVERY NAME

The Lordship of Christ and Social Systems

edited by

Thomas E. Clarke, S.J.

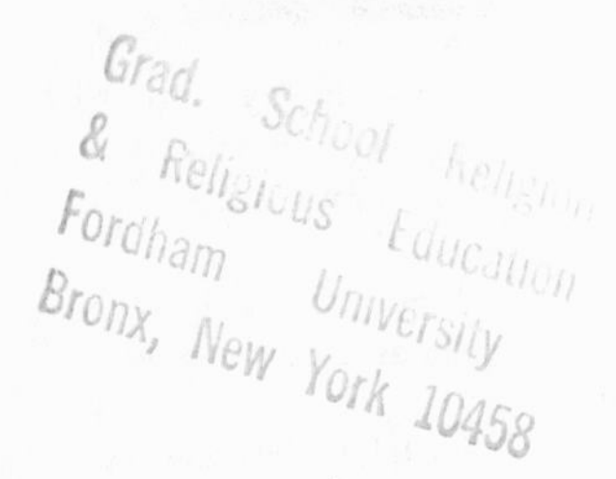

PAULIST PRESS

Acknowledgements
The publisher wishes to gratefully acknowledge the use of material from the following works. J. Moltman, "The Cross and Civil Religion," *Religion and Political Society,* New York, Harper & Row, 1974, pp. 34–35. Lloyd Gaston, *No Stone on Another: Studies in the Significance of the Fall of Jerusalem in the Synoptic Gospels,* Leiden, Brill, 1970, p. 244, and pp. 425–426. Documents of the Catholic Church, unless otherwise noted, are cited according to the translation found in Joseph Gremillion, ed., *The Gospel of Peace and Justice: Catholic Social Teaching Since Pope John,* Orbis Books, 1976.

Library of Congress
Catalog Card Number: 80-82082

ISBN: 0-8091-2338-X

Published by Paulist Press
545 Island Road, Ramsey, N.J. 07446

Printed and bound in the
United States of America

Contents

Foreword

For most people, involvement in social systems is like speaking prose—they have been doing it unreflectingly all their lives. Many of us seem to experience systems, structures, institutions as at best boring, and at worst oppressive. Those who are alert may have the feeling that, within our technological society, deeply cherished values are being subtly eroded by the preponderance of system. Their lives appear fraught with a moral ambiguity which they don't quite know how to dispel. They find no Archimedean point within "the system" (actually a network of diverse and often conflicting systems) which might afford sufficient leverage for a firm stand. And they are all too well aware that, even were they able to escape the world of social system, they would be carrying with them the inner baggage of compromise and confusion, the tools and elements of, perhaps, even worse systems.

"Unhappy humans are we!", they might say, echoing St. Paul's cry of woe (Rom 7:24). "Who will deliver us from this 'deadly embodiment?' " But, if they really wish to respond as Christians, they need to continue with Paul: "Thanks be to God"—deliverance comes "through Jesus Christ our Lord" (Rom 7:25). And they need to join Paul in his lyric celebration (Romans c. 8) of the liberation which has been inaugurated through the outpouring of the Spirit of Christ Jesus. For *every* situation of desperation, Christians have recourse to "the Name above every name" (Phil 2:9), to the power of the One whom they acclaim as Lord, conqueror of all that darkens or enslaves our humanity.

In renewing this most basic of all Christian confessions—that Jesus is Lord—the present volume orchestrates it with a specific motif: he is Lord of social systems, too. It desires to lend Christians support and enlightenment in their struggle to be faithful to their Lord in and through their involvements within contemporary society and culture. How this recourse to Jesus as Lord is to be understood in ways that are not fundamentalist or escapist—such is the burden of our common message.

In ringing the changes on this theme, this product of many discussions at the Woodstock Theological Center picks up the basic affirmations of a previous volume in this series, *The Faith that Does Justice,* as well as the landmark utterance of the Episcopal synod of 1971:

> Action on behalf of justice and participation in the transformation of the world fully appear to us as a constitutive dimension of the preaching of the Gospel, or, in other words, of the Church's mission for the redemption of the human race and its liberation from every oppressive situation.[1]

This book, then, is about the "political" character of Christian faith. It deals with the Gospel precisely from the viewpoint of *power*—the power of systems, good and evil, graced and sinful—and the power of the Lord exercised within, over, through, and sometimes against, various social systems.

Before commending these eleven essays to the interest of the readers, it will be helpful to say a few words about some of the principal terms they will be encountering. There is, first of all, the term *Lord* (and lordship). We have chosen this biblical naming of Jesus the Christ (in preference, for example, to "servant" or "shepherd" or "high priest") because it is expressive of the theme of power, and relates to the conflict between God and his anointed, on the one hand, and on the other, the "principalities and powers" (Eph 3:10; 6:12; Col 1:16, 2:10,15), which is one of several designations in the New Testament for the cosmic forces seeking to enslave our humanity. A major interest in this volume, treated especially in Joseph Weber's essay, is the linking of such mythic expressions of the cosmic aspects of sin and redemption with contemporary descriptions of the positive and negative forces at work in our society. Lordship thus becomes the most germane Christological term for regarding Christian faith in relation to social systems.

The alert reader of the following essays will not miss a certain movement of attention among three distinct but related aspects of this lordship. There is, first of all, what might be termed an anticipatory or "proleptic" lordship, exercised by Jesus himself as he is portrayed in the gospels. He teaches and he heals. He is critical of his own social system, and he begins to form a community which will shape society in radically alternative ways. Inevitably his role as preacher, teacher, wonder-worker, community-builder, brings him into the role of suffering servant. He embraces the human condition even to the cross. This attention to the lordship of Christ as anticipated in the earthly ministry of Jesus has a twofold value; it helps us keep in view the Christian paradox, that power is won through powerlessness, that servanthood is the way to lordship; and it permits the exemplary or paradigmatic role of the earthly Jesus as he appears in the gospels to become a source of light and energy for our own stewardship of earth.

The second phase of lordship which the reader will find here is the exercise of power by the risen Lord prior, in some fashion, to the response of Christians to his rule. It is necessary to note this facet of his lordship if the primacy of God's initiative in achieving his kingdom of grace is to be acknowledged. Lordship in this aspect is no substitute for the initiatives of Christians. On the contrary, when properly grasped it evokes those initiatives. The value of accenting it is primarily in rooting Christian hope not in our own fragile and fallible resources but in the power of God communicated to his victorious Son, our exalted Lord.

Thirdly, we have also attended in this volume to the exercise of Jesus' lordship precisely in and through the mediations of human enterprise, particularly in the form of Christian imagination. There is a genuine sense in which Jesus becomes the Lord today only interdependently with our exercise of responsible stewardship. The acceptance of responsibility for the social systems which make or unmake us as humans is, as Monika Hellwig's essay emphasizes, a Gospel imperative. This third accent helps to preserve us from a hazard which those who speak too glibly of Jesus as Lord are open to—what Dietrich Bonhoeffer called the mentality of "cheap grace," and what

Dorothee Sölle criticizes as a mentality of "substitution" (as opposed to "representation").[2] This accent in our book is the immediate basis for both the challenge and the support that we hope to provide for our readers. The lordship of Christ, without ceasing to claim our absolute obedience, has truly been committed to our care. In this sense the present volume, while not immediately concerned with pragmatic "how to" questions, directs itself not merely to the Christian contemplation of social reality but to its transformation.

That social reality is systemic in character. "Social systems" is the other term of our title which calls for some clarification here. Being for the most part theologians and not social scientists, we did not feel it incumbent on us to get involved in the subtleties and complexities of language touching structures, institutions, systems and the like. Hence the reader should not expect a great deal of either precision or uniformity in our use of such language. We did benefit, however, by the efforts of Philip Land and John Coleman to enlarge our acquaintance with the diverse understandings of relevant terms on the part of economists, sociologists and others. And, with whatever personal variations, we all related positively to the well-known framework of Peter Berger and Thomas Luckmann (summarized by Land in Chapter 9).

Basically, then, what "social systems" means for us is less a thing or complexus of things than a phenomenon or process. When humans act and interact as humans they embody their personhood and relationships— for weal and for woe—in time, space, matter; in, for example, dress, furniture, architecture; in language and symbols; in customs and laws; in economic processes and social patterns; in the overall organization of human life on planet Earth and beyond. In very diverse ways, the family is a social system; so is a business corporation; so is a cocktail party. What helps to make such human creations theologically interesting is that they take on a life of their own, embodying and reflecting us who have projected them, and yet standing in their own right over against us, and—what is theologically even more interesting—profoundly influencing us in our personal and relational life. We have created them, but they in turn create—or deform—us. Though not simply identical with ourselves as persons or with our personal relationships, they remain within the sphere of the human. They are not mere things but precisely human embodiments. As such, they fall within the range of a theological anthropology, that is, of Christian faith in its reflective interaction with all that bears the stamp of the human. They are appropriately viewed as sharing in the sin/grace dialectic so central to the Christian interpretation of history. In fact, all the basic theological categories are applicable to social systems. Christology and soteriology, ecclesiology and eschatology, no less than the moral and spiritual theologies based on them, need to address themselves, if they are to be complete, to the reality of social systems.

The reader will find that the term "social system" is often used without being sharply distinguished from terms like "structure" or "institution." The appeal of the word "system" for us was partly in its broad scope. We desired a term which would not exclude any of the vast variety of societal embodiments of the human. Further nuances and specifications of the term will be encountered in particular essays. So far as we can see, while we have not offered a precise definition of social systems, we have sufficiently, for our purposes, shared a common identification of this crucial aspect of human life which readers will not find difficult to relate to their own experience.

We have just described social systems in terms of *embodiment.* This latter term is analyzed at some length in the essay of Otto Hentz. What we discovered in the course of our project was a cluster of four terms intertwined in their meaning and import: *incarnation, embodiment, sacrament,* and *imagination.* There is no space or need here to develop an analysis and synthesis of these terms, but some brief comments are called for. Incarnation and embodiment are more or less synonymous terms, with the former carrying a more theological and the latter a more anthropological flavor. Together they form a recurring motif. It is fair to say that we were agreed from the first on two assertions: that social systems do represent embodiments of the human—extensions, so to speak, of the human body itself, and so an imprinting of the human image of God on time, space, matter; and, secondly, that the divine intention expressed in the Incarnation of God's Son achieves its fullness *(pleroma)* only to the degree that social systems in fact embody this image of God restored in and through Jesus who is Lord.

The terms "sacrament" and "sacramental" add further connotations to "incarnation" and "embodiment." They bring these concepts explicitly into the sphere of sign or symbol. As the human body is symbolic of spirit, so the extension of the body in social systems manifests the human which it embodies. To the degree that the manifestation is humanizing rather than dehumanizing, it reflects the presence of God and his Christ in human society, and so takes on a certain sacramental character, as the world created by humans becomes "charged with the grandeur of God."

We were quite aware in our discussions that the language of incarnation, embodiment and sacramentality is, like all theological language, risky. History testifies to certain types of incarnationism which invite to passivity and which tend to deify some finite and fallible human institution or structure. Here Francine Cardman's treatment of emperor and Church, as well as Avery Dulles' portrayal of the tensions and complementarity of charismatic and institutional structures within the Church as system, offers helpful cautions.

Similarly, the appealing motif of sacramentality can—once again history testifies—degenerate into a sacramentalism which violates the legitimate dignity and autonomy of the human precisely as human, or misses the basic ambiguity and sinfulness which afflicts every aspect of our pilgrim humanity, not least the systemic.

Still, Incarnation and sacrament, properly understood, avoid and even exclude such distortions. By the Incarnation, as Monika Hellwig's essay manifests, the humanity of Jesus itself is constituted as fully free and responsible for history. And the term sacrament, in its anticipatory connotation (sacrament as sign of a reality that is still future) contains the "eschatological proviso" which precludes a complacent sacramentalizing of the stubbornly opaque reality of social systems.

The term "imagination" in some degree crystallizes these other terms. Its meaning here is far broader than the traditional scholastic concept of "phantasm," and it touches more deeply into the spiritual reality of the person. What it designates is human creativity in its potential for mentally rearranging the elements of experience in order to project new possibilities. Organically linked to the heart (understood as the potential for perceiving and cherishing human values), imagination in this sense stands for human freedom and creativity. From a distinctively Christian perspective, the incarnation implies the healing and recreating of this human capacity for the *novum.* As

Brian McDermott's essay delineates, Jesus himself is paradigm for this creative humanizing of social systems. Imagination and sacramentality have kinship, for it is the exercise of holy imagination upon time, space and matter which renders these reflective of the graced image of God and anticipatory verifications of his kingdom yet to come.

The three parts of the volume will be understood best as three clusters of essays rather than as a linear, textbook development of a uniform message. The general movement of thought is from the person and role of Jesus the Lord *(part one),* to the Church as a distinctive social system *(part two),* and thence to the secular systems which both feel and await his lordship through and beyond the initiatives of Christians *(part three).*

Thus Monika Hellwig introduces the first part and the volume as a whole as she portrays Christology as key to our understanding of freedom, historicity and our human responsibility before God for the kind of social systems we create or tolerate. As Jesus' own human freedom was enhanced, not inhibited, by his unique relationship to the Father, so our human responsibility for society is heightened, not diminished, when his lordship is fully received.

James Walsh, likewise, reflects on engagement in the humanizing of social systems, but from a different perspective and with a somewhat different accent. He shows that the Old Testament, in its preparation of the key terms touching the lordship of Christ, had no truck with the unfortunate separation of religion and politics which has captured many generations of Christians. Kingdom and lordship are directly political categories. Within such a heritage, the message of Jesus could not be heard as directed only at pious, private ears.

What Joseph Weber then makes clear in his essay is that this political struggle for (and against) the kingdom of God is cosmic in scope, and that the victory of Christ the Lord over the principalities and powers both antecedes and demands its own ecclesial fulfillment. The Church, he affirms, is truly Church only to the degree in which it witnesses to what he has done and is doing beyond its agency, in all the systems of the world.

Like the three preceding essays, Brian McDermott's primary focus is the person of the Lord. But he attends especially to the Jesus of history as portrayed in the gospels, and particularly to his exercise of imagination, in the parables that he told and in the parable that he became. Here, he shows, is where Christians will find the basic paradigm for their creative struggle to transform social systems.

As McDermott's essay offered a transition from Jesus the parable to the parabling community, his Church, so John Haughey introduces the more ecclesial stage of our journey by meditating on the eucharistic system of the Corinthian Church, a system blatantly unfaithful to the Pauline insight into the new religious system that was constituted by baptism, Spirit and Eucharist. Twenty centuries later, he suggests, we still fail to take with full seriousness that we *are* the Lord's body here and now.

This theme of embodiment, dealt with by Haughey in a particular case-history, receives more theoretical articulation in the Rahnerian reflection of Otto Hentz. He sees the sacramental embodiment of the divine and the human in Christ as key to our Christian role in social systems. Without venturing a formal theology of Christian family, he does, however, offer a basic framework for dealing with the family as the pivotal social system.

A third ecclesial reflection, by Avery Dulles, takes what is now a quite familiar polarity between charism and institution and develops it precisely from the viewpoint of the Church as social system, and of the lordship of Christ as exercised in and through that polarity. His concluding thesis provides a transition to the third part, for he suggests that the institutional/charismatic tension characteristic of the Church, and the exercise of Christ's lordship over that tension, may be found within all human systems, secular as well as sacred.

Francine Cardman's vignette of the Church/Constantine relationship, which might well have been included in the second part, is placed as an introduction to the third part. Historically it delineates how a secular political structure, the Roman empire, was affected through the ecclesial exercise of Christ's lordship. And, though it does not explicitate the link with present-day efforts to embody the kingdom in particular political systems, its low-keyed message offers a needed caution about the hazards and ambiguities of every such embodiment.

The remaining three essays of the volume deal with three linked aspects of the secular social systems with which Christians and others have to struggle today. Philip Land draws upon the notions of imagination and embodiment in his critical/creative approach to economic system. He finds our present system seriously deficient, and describes the kind of transformation which Utopian Christian imagination is suggesting today. Thomas Clarke likewise draws upon the essays of McDermott and Hentz in a reflection on our present health system. He asks whether and how the lordship of Christ, prefigured in the gospels, can be exercised through the healing touch of a technology that has been transformed through Christian imagination.

Appropriately, the concluding essay, by John Farrelly, deals with the beautiful theme of peace. It parallels for systemic peace what Land's essay has done for economic system, drawing upon a rational theological grasp of the structure of the human to mediate the biblical message of peace to our present world system. The "peace of Jerusalem," which Luke saw as a literal fruit of acceptance of the message of Jesus, thus becomes a paradigm for the peace of the earthly city yearned for in our own day.

As there has been a wide variety of perspectives presented in these eleven essays, so we expect that different classes of readers will make use of the volume in a variety of ways. Those in the ministry of Christian education in its diverse forms—the college or high school classroom, the forum of adult education, popular journalism, and the like, will find here some basic perspectives, insights and materials which, combined with their own skills, can be made available to still wider circles of inquiring and committed Christians. Priests and other pastoral ministers should be helped to develop their own appreciation of the social dimensions of the Gospel, so that their preaching, pastoral counseling and organizational guidance to their local communities in parish or diocese may reflect a deeper appreciation of how involvement in social systems is integral to Christian living.

Similarly Christian activists, as well as those engaged in government and in public interest institutions will, we hope, find both guidance and encouragement for their demanding and often tedious tasks within intractable systems, particularly through the strong affirmation which our volume gives to the importance of their special vocations. And, finally, though our work is intended more to communicate than to advance scholarly research, colleagues in theology and other fields who are concerned with us to rethink their respective areas in the light of recent insights into the societal dimension of the human may here find some stimulus for their own endeavors.

Whoever the reader may be, our hope is to have offered a modest and sound encouragement in support of the current widespread effort to recover the societal or political relevance of the most central of all Gospel confessions: Jesus is Lord.

There remains only to say a word of thanks to Fr. Robert A. Mitchell, S.J., former director of the Woodstock Theological Center, and currently president of the University of Detroit. His presence and his participation in our discussions for almost the full two years of their duration were no small factor in their finally bearing fruit in these pages.

NOTES

1. *Justice in the World* n. 6; Joseph Gremillion, *The Gospel of Peace and Justice: Catholic Social Teaching Since Pope John,* Maryknoll, New York: Orbis 1976, p. 514.

2. Dietrich Bonhoeffer, *The Cost of Discipleship,* New York: Macmillan 1959, pp. 35–47; Dorothee Sölle, *Christ the Representative,* London: SCM, 1967.

Part I
Jesus Christ the Lord

1
Christology and Attitudes Toward Social Structures

Monika K. Hellwig

The Ambivalence of Christians

As Christians we seem often to be caught in an uneasy ambivalence toward the social structures that so largely shape our lives, characters, hopes and identities—an ambivalence in relation to the economy, the disposition of political controls, the juxtaposition of national and international interests, the culture patterns inherent in education and urban planning, the relationships and priorities defined by health-care systems, and so forth. Too often, it seems, we vaguely acknowledge an obligation to good citizenship and responsible stewardship, but then tend to narrow down that obligation to fairly trivial decisions within the *status quo,* as though most of the consequential social structures were simply a given in relation to which we have no freedom and therefore no responsibility.

To express this another way, we call Jesus Savior of the world, and yet we constantly act on the assumption that the world as such (the world of human affairs, the "real" world) cannot be saved but is doomed to perpetuate injustices and oppression, frustrating conditions of work, inauthentic and repressive interpersonal relationships, dishonesty in the conduct of political and economic affairs, ruthless selfishness on the part of sovereign nations, conflicting expectations and destructive values. In our liturgies and our hymns we hail Jesus as Prince of Peace, but in practice we seem to restrict the peace that we expect to find through him to peace of heart or peace of mind, while assuming that nations (including those that call themselves Christian) will continue to make war, to stockpile armaments and to kill for the national interest. We celebrate a feast that names Jesus Christ the King, but we tend rather quickly to invoke the saying that his kingdom is not of this world (Jn 18:36) with an interpretation that limits his kingship to the hearts of believers, the affairs of the Church, or a final judgment that is placed outside history. In practice we often acknowledge no relationship between the kingship of Christ and the allegiances by which public affairs are governed, except a tenuous and indirect relationship through the private conscience of the individual believer within the task that the present order of society has assigned to her or him. There seems to be a basic contradiction in the Christian position when we call Jesus Lord of history and then somehow tend to reduce the history over which we expect his effective lordship to be extended to a tenuous strand of "salvation history" that neatly bypasses the real issues that make or break human lives.

Theological concern over this ambivalence and over the underlying ambiguity in the interpretation of the Christian Gospel is certainly not new. In a general way it has been addressed in the papal social encyclicals over the past one hundred years.[1] In various contexts and for various reasons it has also been of central concern for several contemporary schools of theology, such as the theology of hope of Jürgen Moltmann and Wolfhart Pannenberg, the political theology of J.B. Metz, and the liberation theology of Latin American and other Third World authors.[2] For the most part these theological endeavors have addressed themselves to a re-examination of our conventional eschatologies (concerned with the content of Christian hope) and of our conventional soteriologies (concerned with the process of redemption/salvation). The present essay purports rather to address itself to the relationship between our formal Christology (concerned with whom we understand Jesus to be) and our attitudes and expectations in relation to social structures. The term "social structures," in this essay, stands for those many obvious or subtle predictable patterns of behavior that regulate relationships among individuals or groups, such as who obeys whom, who deals with whom, who owes whom what, who makes which decisions, who enjoys which advantages or has access to which resources and opportunities, and so forth.

Basic to an understanding of the issue under discussion is the fact that the Christian message is the good news of salvation in Jesus Christ, divine Son of God. Jesus is to the Christian the revelation of true man (the truth of what it is to be human) and true God (the truth of what God is like). In what we say and think of him, therefore, we imply an understanding of our own destiny and possibilities, and an understanding of our own relationship to God and to the future. Because our human existence and self-realization are never an isolated private affair but always realized in a multitude of relationships in public and private sectors of our lives, that understanding of our own destiny and possibilities that is implied in our Christology necessarily includes our destiny and possibilities as a people. We imply an understanding of possible and desirable ways of interaction of divine creativity and human freedom which cannot remain in the private sector but always has wider societal repercussions. In other words, whether we care to acknowledge it or not, inasmuch as our Christology interprets what it is to be authentically human and what it is that we may expect of God, it also implies certain attitudes and expectations in relation to social systems and structures. This works, however, in two directions. How we think about the lordship of Jesus Christ influences our attitudes and perceptions in relation to social structures, but the reverse is also evidently true: our previous perceptions of social structures and systems, which we take for granted, predetermine in some measure what the lordship of Christ can possibly mean for us.

This essay intends to explore the social implications logically suggested by various approaches to Christology, and in the light of this exploration to suggest a desirable focus in Christology. Clearly, there are many factors which contribute to anyone's social attitudes. For a Christian, the style and content of Christology is most certainly one of them. However, because other factors do converge on the shaping of social attitudes, it would be foolish to claim a necessary or one-to-one relationship between a particular style or focus in Christology and a particular social stance. Likewise, the Christology a person is able to consider and accept is certainly conditioned by that person's perception of social systems, but also by many other factors. It would be equally foolish to try to establish a necessary causal link from a particular social perception to a particular Christology. All this, however, being granted, there seems to be good reason to look soberly at the intrinsic logic of the various ways we construct our Christologies, in order to ask whether the implications they carry are really such as we would want to endorse when they are made explicit.

Alternate Christological Approaches and Their Social Implications

Among the various ways that Christology is approached perhaps the most pervasive distinction, and certainly the one most frequently cited, is that pointed out by Karl Rahner between a descending and an ascending Christology.[3] These terms have come to be used in varied and quite confusing ways. As applied to the *content* of Christology they are not helpful, because any genuinely Christian account of Jesus Christ must deal with the divine and the human, with God's initiative and with the history of men and women. As applied to the *method* of Christology, however, the distinction seems to be both valid and helpful. Whatever nuances the term may have elsewhere, for purposes of this essay a "descending Christology" is one which takes its starting point in dogmatic affirmations of the divinity and Messianic election of Jesus and moves from there to the consideration of his earthly, historical existence and its meaning for us. Correspondingly, in this essay an "ascending Christology" is taken to mean one which begins with the historical testimonies concerning the man Jesus and with our capacity to enter into his experience by empathy, and which moves from there to a consideration of the meaning of the Messianic and divinity claims made for this man by his followers.

Descending Christologies in the extreme form schematically set forth in the following paragraphs are not found among reputable scholars today, yet they have been influential and appear still to inform much preaching, teaching and Christian piety in our times. For this reason it seems to be important in this volume to consider the implications that flow logically from the extreme positions, even though contemporary scholarship for the most part carefully avoids the extremes and uses ascending and descending approaches in careful complementarity, retracing steps the Christian community has taken in the past and reflecting upon them in a new light.

In a descending Christology, what is important precedes history; the ultimately significant events are programmed or blueprinted in heaven. Jesus is at the center of history, simply because it had to be that way, having been eternally foreordained. The actual course of his life took the path it did because it had to happen this way, having been foreordained. If Jesus is the revelation both of the truly human and of the truly divine, and the course of his life is exemplary, we are presented with a vision of reality in which creative or constitutive decision-making is seen as a divine function whose human correlate is only the choice whether to obey by executing the projected order of things or whether to rebel. Thus there is a certain intrinsic logic by which the perfection of the human is expressed by the acceptance of the *status quo* as divinely willed—a certain inducement to passivity in the structuring of our world, as though we were actors in a drama who must be careful not to deviate from the script, but must put as much expression as possible into a faithful, literal rendering of it. The social implications of a descending Christology seem to tend subtly to include an emphasis on the givenness and predetermination of the right order of things in human affairs.

It would seem, then, that a descending Christology rather easily results in an unquestioning acceptance of the *status quo* as divinely intended as long as the powers of the established order acknowledge that their authority is from God (or at the least, do not disclaim this). However, it should be pointed out that this is also likely to happen in reverse. A church or individual with a strong practical interest in maintaining unquestioning acceptance of the givenness of social structures and systems will find this easy to do, because questions will simply not occur. In this atmosphere, a descending Christology will commend itself as self-evident because it is continuous with the perception of all reality as somehow foreordained independently of human choice and historical developments.

On the other hand, a descending Christology, in its emphasis on the givenness of the order of things, carries a certain logical thrust toward a relativizing of all authority other than that of God. It can very comfortably align itself with a social vision and expectation that includes ultimate accountability to more than human laws, so that even if structures and roles are firmly in place as given, the conduct of all individuals within these roles never escapes the judgment of God as revealed in Jesus Christ.

Nevertheless, it is hardly accidental that the ascending approach to Christology has been invoked in our times by the socio-critical theologies. Simply because it begins with the historical testimonies, an ascending Christology is much more likely to align Jesus with the dispossessed who are the negation of the *status quo.* An ascending Christology tends to a view of salvation as a truly historical dynamic—historical in that it involves the interplay of human freedoms and decisions, and historical also in that it involves the structuring and restructuring of human societies, large as well as small, secular as well as professionally religious.

The social implications of an ascending Christology tend, then, to include an emphasis on the right and duty to question the apparent givenness and predetermination of the right order of things—to question it in the name of the human crucified Jesus who is acclaimed as Messiah and Lord. Ultimately significant events are not seen as blueprinted in heaven but as the outcome of a human struggle of creative and constitutive decision-making by Jesus and others aligned with him, including contemporary believers.

From the Past or from the Future?

Because the influence also moves in the other direction, from pre-existent social perceptions to the kinds of Christology we seek and fashion, Jürgen Moltmann has suggested a different distinction from the descending/ascending one of Rahner; a Christology may be approached from the past or from the future.[4] Who Jesus is, and why we should call him Christ and Lord, may be defined with reference to what is already established (whether in past history or in an a-historical pre-existence) or with reference to a future that is not yet. Clearly this corresponds to two ways of defining social reality—either in terms of what has been accomplished in the past or in terms of a future that is the object of striving. By the inner logic of the situation, the approach to Christology chosen will tend to confirm the existing perception of the social reality. It will in any case have been chosen as the more coherent and credible inasmuch as it expresses the "self-evident" or "common sense" pattern as seen from that viewpoint.

The past/future selection of viewpoint, in practice, seems most often to be dependent on the experience that an individual or community has had of life and society. To experience security and adequate provision and acceptance in the society normally means that one sees the societal structures as stable, the outcome of a satisfactory development. To experience exclusion, contempt, insecurity and inadequate provision, on the other hand, normally means that one has to interpret reality with reference to a better future as the object of hope and effort, and therefore that one has to see the present societal structure as instable because only in process of development. The hoped for future may be envisioned rather uncritically as the outcome of a violent take-over of economic and political power, or as the outcome of an apocalyptic type of divine intervention in which the human cooperation is at most that of waiting, or as something attainable only outside the social structure of the world and beyond death, or as the sum of many individual conversions to brotherhood and stewardship, or as the outcome of a more complex process of conversion of interpersonal relationships and therefore of structures, even the largest and most intricate.

The viewpoint from which a person or a society perceives reality is certainly not wholly determined by immediate personal experiences of inclusion or exclusion, but may be profoundly modified by radicalizing experiences of participation with the excluded in intimate companionship and empathy. Christian traditions of spirituality have rather consistently interpreted the evangelical counsels in such a way as to cultivate such radicalizing experiences, more especially with reference to the ideal of evengelical poverty. Actual identification with the poor, the marginated, the oppressed and the unwanted tends, of course, to a Christology shaped not by reference to what has been accomplished in the past, but by reference to a future hope. However, there is ambiguity in the thrust to look to the future for orientation, for that future may still be understood as an otherworldly future or at least as a future beyond the influence of human effort or creativity. When it is so understood, there is little consequential difference between the logic of a Christology based on past accomplished fact and that of a Christology based on a future fulfillment that is not susceptible of human influence, and might, therefore, just as well be considered as having been accomplished in the past and leaving us no participatory task.

Establishment and Periphery

Because of the foregoing ambiguity in an approach to Christology that is from the future, J. B. Metz introduces, at least implicitly, a different distinction in the approaches to Christology, and in this he is followed by the liberation theologians, Gutierrez, Sobrino and Boff among others.[5] Metz is concerned with "the future in the memory of suffering" and therefore requires a Christology that takes its starting point both in the past and in the future. The distinction that is made by this group of authors is directly and unambiguously related to the theologian's perception of, and attitudes toward, social structures and systems. It is a distinction between a Christology undertaken from the viewpoint of establishment and one undertaken from the viewpoint of a critique of all that is established in the name of the excluded and of the oppressed. Authors who make this distinction claim explicitly or implicitly that the latter viewpoint is necessarily a privileged one among Christians.[6]

Clearly, a Christology from the perspective of the oppressed and the excluded may be an ascending Christology within Rahner's distinction and a future-based Christology within Moltmann's distinction, but it defines itself much more specifically. The claims made by Christians for Jesus as Christ and Lord are seen as essentially and directly, not accidentally or indirectly, concerned with the social structures and systems of the world. Constitutive of the Christhood and lordship of Jesus in such a Christology are a past beginning, a present possibility, and a future consummation (through human cooperation) of the transformation of social structures to eliminate exclusion, oppression and contempt.

Toward a Relational Christology

Unfortunately, a fully coherent Christology along these lines does not seem to have been written yet.[7] This is at least in part due to unsolved problems as to what is legitimate theological method in Christology. This problem points to a fourth distinction which seems to be the most important of all for the questions raised in this volume. It is the distinction between a Christology done from the analysis of the isolated subject and a Christology done from relational categories. It seems to be this distinction that is implied by Edouard Schillebeeckx when he writes that the capacity to make history provides the hermeneutic key to understanding identity.[8] This rather abstract way of expressing the matter might be rephrased: who any person is, is best understood in terms of the difference that person makes, has made or can yet make; who Jesus is, is to be understood from studying the difference he has made, is making and can make to others and to the course of human affairs throughout history.

This contrasts with an approach to Christology which sets it rather within a timelessly constituted world of Greek philosophy than within the historically constituted world of biblical creation and salvation faith. In the timeless perception, God is, because existence is of God's essence, and God is Lord because of the intrinsic infinity and the self-contained, self-sustaining omnipotence that are predicated in the very idea of God. All this can be explained and justified without any reference to creation and history. In other words, God is, so to speak, analyzed as an isolated subject and conclusively defined as such. Something similar is done in the same frame of reference with Jesus. At least since Origen,[9] if not earlier, the major currents of formal Christology define the identity of Jesus within this isolated subject that is God. It is true that Jesus is identified as the Word and then, as the second term of a trinity, is defined with reference to the other two. However, the trinity that is intertwined in the definition itself remains the isolated subject. Within it the Son or Word can also be given complete intelligibility without reference to creation or history. Jesus, like Father and Spirit, is God and Lord because this is intrinsic to his timeless being, even without any reference to creation.

In other words, when the Word enters history in the person of

Jesus of Nazareth, he is already divine Lord because of his pre-existent, a-historically defined identity, and he becomes Messiah (Christ), the universal and definitive Savior, because the divine Lord present in history could not be other than that, no matter what the course of his human history or his impact upon others, as that might be observed. In this perspective, then, a whole Christology can be constructed in which the actual life, death, resurrection and total historical impact of Jesus all appear as accidental. This, though not unusual, would seem to be an entirely false understanding of an "incarnational" Christology.

The social implications of such a Christology would seem to include the underlying assumption that the relation between our acclaiming Jesus as Christ and Lord on the one hand, and the kinds of social structures we form or reform in order to live together in the world on the other hand, is at best an accidental one. There is, for instance, nothing in the structures and social systems, or in our maintaining of them, that could be in contradiction of our claim that Jesus is Lord and Christ, short of explicit ideological opposition to religion in general or Christianity in particular. At the same time, the cruelty, greed or pride of individuals within the system would be seen as evidence that they have not submitted themselves to the lordship of Jesus. In this context, Communism would readily be seen as being in opposition to the lordship of Jesus, because it has officially put itself on record as being against religion. On the other hand, any type of dictatorship, colonialism, structures of economic imperialism, unrestrained capitalistic competition and even slavery would scarcely be seen as contrary to the lordship of Christ except by an indirect route, as being in some way a transgression of a natural law ethic.

The alternate approach, as suggested by Schillebeeckx, is one that seeks to understand the identity of Jesus in terms of his "capacity to make history," which situates itself within the historically constituted world of creation and salvation faith. In this view the transcendent God emerges as Lord because "he brought us out of the slavery of Egypt" and we have experienced in ourselves a transformation into a people which is still in progress, and because, being both compassionate and powerful to achieve his purpose, God is beyond all others faithful to his promises. If we call Jesus the Lord and

Christ in this context, it is because he has brought us out of a slavery analogous to that of Egypt, and we have experienced in and through him a transformation of ourselves into a people which is still in progess, and because he has shown and does show himself both compassionate and powerful to achieve his purpose and divinely faithful to his promises.

In this context, God is God and not irrational fate, Lord and not random chance, not because this can be deduced from something akin to analysis of the isolated subject, but because it can be relationally demonstrated by the impact of the divine on the shaping of human peoplehood (social structures and systems) as well as on the individuals concerned. In this context, we call Jesus divine Lord and Savior-Christ on historical, relational grounds—because of the impact he has had and because of the way human social structures and systems shape themselves in response to him. However, it is quite obvious that not all the structures and systems that shape our lives have in fact come under the dominion of Christ. The Christian claim is that we have experienced enough in our own lives and relationships to know that all structures and systems *can* come under the dominion of Christ and find their perfection in it. The Christian task is one of discernment of where it has happened and where in the present or in the proximate future it can happen, and on the basis of that discernment also a task of cooperation in bringing about the further realization of the lordship of Christ in social structures.

It may at first seem that this is simply another way of making Rahner's distinction between a descending and an ascending Christology, or a more philosophical way of making Moltmann's or J. B. Metz's distinction. But there is something characteristic at stake that cannot be subsumed into any of the other three. It claims the validity (not necessarily the exclusive validity) of a relational approach to understanding and expressing the identity of Jesus within those relational categories in which we can truthfully claim to know something, namely the historical situations in which we participate. Schillebeeckx helpfully expresses this in terms of the "capacity to make history." This really involves a process of reflection that moves between three points: the historical Jesus inasmuch as he can be known or discovered by scholarship; the cumulative effect of Jesus on the human experience and the course of human events thus far, inasmuch as it can be discerned; and the future possibilities of modification of human experience and human expression by the extension of the impact of Jesus and the response to it. This third point is clearly the product of Christian imagination exercised within a participant stance.[10] This approach seems to draw on both of those distinguished by Moltmann and both of those distinguished by Metz, and in choosing an ascending Christology within Rahner's distinction, nevertheless leaves room for an incarnational theology.[11]

Lordship Is a Relational Concept

The earliest Christology of the followers of Jesus appears to have been expressed in the media of stories, images and imposition of titles.[12] Clearly, they were many and experimental. Some faded out of use, some were further developed and some were drastically modified. The title of Lord *(mārê, kyrios)* seems in the course of the Christian centuries to have been more or less swallowed up into the global affirmation of divinity, and this has certainly tended to obscure the fact that lordship is a relational concept. It describes a structure of reciprocity in human relations, a complementarity of roles in which one governs decisions and behavior of another, and the other claims protection and guidance from the first. The complementarity of the roles and expectations is constitutive of lordship.

In the Bible, the notion of lordship, which in itself describes a structure of human relationships, is analogously applied to the transcendent God. As set out in detail in the essay by Walsh which follows, this lordship of the transcendent God is presented as political but distinguished from the modes of dominance actually known. It evidently has two facets. There is a lordship which precedes recognition or consent on the part of the subject. God owns the earth and he owns the people, and he accomplishes his purpose independently of their consent. But there is also a lordship into which people are invited as covenant gift and privilege, and which is portrayed as consequent upon their consent.

The Hebrew Bible constantly gives us hints that while lordship is the privileged model or analogy, the governance of God is not like the dominion of kings, princes and overlords of this world. What seems to be hinted—and this is necessarily a modern interpretation—is that, far from being an alien control, God's government is true liberation of the person, and far from impoverishing and reducing the social structure of the people, it constitutes them truly as a people. This, of course, stresses voluntary reciprocity as a constitutive factor of that specific difference which makes God's lordship unlike the lordships we usually experience.

The New Testament applies the notion of lordship to the person of Jesus and applies it in cosmic dimensions, as presented in detail in the essay by Weber in this volume. The analogy made here is not directly with the kings and lords of the world whose manner of government we know and experience concretely. Rather it seems to be an analogy with the lordship of the transcendent God, distinguished from and defined in opposition to the patterns we observe in the world about us (cf. Lk 22:25–27). Just as there are two aspects to the lordship of the transcendent God so there seem to be two aspects to the lordship which the New Testament and the early Church generally claim for Jesus. In calling for our faith and response, they confront us both with a lordship that is prior to and independent of our response—a kind of ownership of the earth and the people established in the death and resurrection—and with a lordship that is to be co-constituted by our response. The relationship between these two aspects would seem to be of enormous import for Christian attitudes to social structures.

Divine Creativity and Human Freedom

The relationship between the two aspects of the lordship of the risen Jesus—the aspect of the givenness of what is and the aspect of invitation to create the bond that may be but is not yet—seems to be closely linked to the relationship between divine creativity and human freedom. Our Christology, as mentioned at the outset of this essay, is certainly prototypical of our understanding of the relation of human freedom to divine creativity in general.[13] If Jesus is the revelation to us of the truly human as well as the truly divine, if he is the human incarnation of the divine and the divine assumption of the human, if he is the way, the truth and the life and the recapitulation of the human race, then the interaction of divine and human creativity and initiative in him holds a model by which we are to understand what should be the mode of reciprocity of divine and human freedom in other human persons. Jesus becomes the model of relationships to God, other persons individually, the future, and the whole range of human social structures and systems that express the interaction of persons with one another and with their environment.

Four Levels of Understanding

If our Christology is to be a key to all this, there seems to be a number of interdependent levels or aspects in the Christology itself that make it so. There is, *first* of all, our understanding of the relation of Jesus to the transcendent Father. *Secondly,* there is our understanding of the relationship of the humanity and divinity within the person of Jesus. *Thirdly,* there is our perception of the implications of these first two levels for the interaction of the creativity of Jesus with other human freedoms in the redemption. *Fourthly,* there are the social-structural-systemic dimensions of this interaction of freedoms.

If we consider Jesus in the relationship in which the New Testament so frequently shows him, defining his mission and identity in "conversation" with the Father, we have basically two options in interpreting the identity as Messiah and Lord that emerges from the Scriptures. These options are here depicted as somewhat more sharply opposed than they appear in the complexity of real life situations, so that they may emerge more clearly. On the one hand, we could see Jesus' own freedom, will, creativity, initiative, being initially or progressively eliminated as he fulfills to the letter an explicitly revealed blueprint. In his person, then, the plan of the Father would be "perfectly" fulfilled by submission or cancellation of any human plans. This, then, would be the reason for calling Jesus Lord: the elimination of human creativity leaves him the total and immediate embodiment of the will of God.

The logical step to the *third* level above is that we should find our identity and mission as Christians analogously with the identity of Jesus before the Father, that is by eliminating human creativity and initiative and cancelling human plans. The logical step to the *fourth* level above is that in the economy of salvation our task is the implementing or execution of what is explicitly blueprinted in the revelation handed down to us from Jesus as Lord; it may too easily be concluded that the impact on social-structural-systemic dimensions of life of the divine creativity embodied in Jesus as Lord, makes itself felt to the extent that it meets the appropriate human emptiness of historical initiatives and creative or radically critical planning. In other words, social structures and systems may be brought under the lordship of the transcendent God through the mediation of the lordship of Jesus, but this will not be mediated by our critical opposition to or creative reconstructions of structures and systems but rather by our patient acceptance of them as the God-ordained context of our lives. Obviously, the foregoing is proposed as a logical model of the implications carried from one level of Christological understanding to others. Where people actually stand at each level depends on a variety of factors.

There is an alternate way of interpreting Jesus' identity as messiah and Lord. We could see his own freedom, will, creativity, initiative being initially or progressively expanded as he responds to the smothering silence and darkness of the transcendent God by assuming in ever-increasing intensity the gift and burden of freedom. In his person, then, the power and creativity of God are concretely realized precisely because of the fullness of the human expression. It is because his human utterance is no attempt at copying a divine blueprint but is intensely and creatively his own that it is able to mediate the divine silence that is wholly other than it. What makes us recognize him as Lord is not that we are able to look at a divine model with whom to compare him, but rather that we are able to experience the integrating, healing force of his presence in the inter-relationships of human freedoms.

The logical step from this to the *third* level enumerated above, is that discipleship no longer appears as a matter of passivity or mimicry or looking for blueprints. Rather discipleship calls for that kind of dependence which supports increased consciousness and creativity and initiative in yet uncharted directions.[14] The logical step to the *fourth* level is that the lordship of God over social structures and systems mediated by the lordship of Christ, is indeed further mediated by our critical opposition and creative reconstructions of structures and systems. We know the salvific and appropriate nature of our initiatives not because we can point to a blueprint from the past, but because we are able to experience the integrating, healing force of the divine by the impact of our initiatives on the inter-relationships of human freedoms.

However, the *second* level cuts across all this; our understanding of the relationship between the humanity and the divinity of Jesus is crucial in shaping our perception of all that conerns the redemption, and therefore in shaping our attitudes to social structures and systems. If we understand the conciliar statements which culminated in Chalcedon in 451 in such a way that Jesus is seen as a divine person, a pre-existent, fully fashioned reflexive consciousness in a state of consummate freedom that leaves no room for growth, then the New Testament preoccupation with the relationship between the growing human Jesus and the transcendent Father becomes irrelevant. In spite of all protestations about two wills and a number of ways of knowing, we are in fact unable to take Jesus seriously as a human center of decision-making and redemptive creative imagination, such as is described in the essay by McDermott in this volume. Instead, it leaves us with such an impoverished idea of "incarnation," that it leaves no room for the principle of sacramentality or "embodiment," discussed in the essay by Hentz—a principle that has played such an important role in Catholic theology in and after Vatican II. Such an understanding of the Chalcedonian formulations is, however, not uncommon, though it becomes difficult to defend against charges of heresy when one asks in what, then, the true humanity of Jesus consists.

From such a simplistic perception of the relationship of the humanity and divinity in the person of Jesus, the logical steps to the *third* and *fourth* levels discussed above are certainly in line with the former alternative described above. In effect, what is so wonderful and salvific about Jesus in this view is that he is so little human, which makes him so much divine. This would tend to suggest that we, in turn, are more saved and saving if the dangerously unpredictable elements of our humanity, the imaginative and creative capacities to envisage and shape a better world, are held in abeyance so that the divine can activate the proper plan. No one is likely, of course, to express the position seriously this way; it is so stated here by way of drawing the position to its logical extreme.

In fact, few Christians are comfortable with the foregoing position, but most wonder whether the official teaching of the Church since Chalcedon allows them any alternative. It is here that the suggestion of Piet Schoonenberg seems particularly helpful; we can interpret the formulations of Chalcedon in a different way.[15] In the first place, as is well known, the words that have come down to us as "person" *(persona, prosopon, hypostasis)* do not have the modern meaning of reflexive consciousness, but a far more elusive one.[16] Secondly, Chalcedon did, however, clearly intend to insist on the oneness of identity of the human Jesus and the divine Word. Therefore, in our attempt to understand and express a mystery to which we can give no adequate or appropriate utterance, we might begin at the other end, with what we can know, and project images from there to what we cannot really know. To be human is to be a human person, with all that we know by experience and reflection to be involved in that. To call God person, or persons, however, is to use an analogy which we know to be such. Therefore, to speak of the Incarnation of the divine Word in the human Jesus allows of an understanding in which the human person, Jesus, becomes progressively the expression of self-utterance of the divine into the world by the expansion rather than the diminution of his human creativity and personal initiative—the fullest freedom of self-expression and self-realization attained by total dependence on, or rather interdependence with, the divine.

In this understanding, the coincidence of liberated human creativity with fullest possible dependence is brought about precisely by the radical otherness of the two terms, the divine and the human, whereby they could not be in competition with each other, nor could either possibly be swallowed up and annihilated by the other. Moreover, this coincidence is possible only if the Incarnation or the union of the divine and human in one person is not conceived as prior to and by-passing the human freedom, but rather as progressively deepening within the human freedom. In this understanding there is no pre-emption of all decision-making by a divine take-over; there is not, so to speak, a rape of human freedom.

From such a perception of the relationship of the human and the divine in the person of Jesus, the logical steps to the *third* and *fourth* levels become nuanced and seem to lead effortlessly into the realm of our real experience and challenge in the real world about us in the twentieth century, with all the structural complexities with which that world presents us. A Christology in which the human freedom of Jesus enters into the very Incarnation itself, also allows us to see the saving divine power of the risen Christ as entrusted to our creativity and imagination in the same kind of interdependence as described above. At the *fourth* level, this calls for a shouldering of the burden of quite radical freedom and responsibility in critical discernments and imaginative projections for the forming and re-forming of social structures and systems. These are called for, not as additional and risky charitable concerns for those with energy to spare after attending to the living of a good Christian life, but as central issues of the redemption, once we break down the barriers between the profane in which human activity follows its own ways and the sacred where human passivity waits on God's ways.

The Quality of Divine Lordship: Community and Interdependence

In the light of all that has been said, the distinctive quality of divine lordship would seem to appear in the intensity with which it affirms and completes the cooperating freedoms. It is, of course, true of any exercise of lordship or authority, even that of a master over slaves, that it rests to some extent on consent which makes the complementarity possible. However, what is most painfully and universally evident in our actual experiences of that complementarity, is how constantly it rests upon uneasy compromises of ill-considered self-interest, upon fear and greed and sub-personal patterns of persuasion that diminish and distort personal freedom rather than bringing it to fulfillment in community. Hence we come to recognize the distinctive quality of lordship in Jesus in the negation of the ambivalence and destructiveness that mark worldly lordship.

Thus, Schillebeeckx has pointed out[17] nuances that must have been carried by the New Testament affirmation that Jesus is Lord. To declare that God and not Caesar is *kyrios* is powerful but subject to much ambiguity. To declare that the crucified Jesus and not Caesar is *kyrios* is to leave a good deal of that ambiguity behind though, as is so clearly demonstrated in the essay by Cardman in this volume and hinted at in the essays by Dulles and Haughey, the declaration can again be thoroughly obscured by substituting a triumphalist vision of the risen Christ. If it is indeed the crucified Jesus in his apparent powerlessness who is *kyrios,* this not only means putting one's allegiance in another camp but that the whole pattern of complementarity is of a different quality, and that this must carry through all the complex structures and systems in which we are involved.

The Jesus portrayed in the gospels is not in fact what most of us would consider a non-violent figure; he challenges, confronts, makes ultimate demands, polarizes social situations in the most dramatic way, utters sharp value judgments. If we see him as expressing or actualizing the lordship of God in the world in a new way, it is not because he represents that lordship as ineffectual, benignly permissive, renouncing power. It is rather because he so radically challenges our perception of what is power, authority. The Jesus of the Gospel portraits appears not as a threat to freedom but constantly as a threat to false securities for which personal freedom has been bartered away, and as a threat to those uneasy compromises of fear and greed that pass for community structures.

The real meaning of the proclamation of the lordship of Jesus obviously has enormous importance for the Church's task of evangelization. The Church proclaims the two aspects of the "already" and the "not yet"—of the lordship of Christ that exists prior to our acceptance of it and of the lordship that is co-constituted by our acceptance of it. However, if it is to avoid being a triumphalist or merely magical claim, the proclamation that God has made both Lord and Christ the Jesus who was crucified, does have to be explained and justified. Basically, the New Testament justification appears to consist of the changes experienced by the community of the followers of Jesus. Most of these changes seem to be rather directly concerned with the relationships and structures within the community of believers, or with attitudes to and expectations of the structures and authority claims in the world at large.

This suggests that the claim of the lordship that is God-given and independent of our acknowledgement of it rests on the Church's perception of what has been accomplished in the person and freedom of Jesus himself, namely, that he has become a person who is capable of being the cornerstone of the creation still in progress, who is capable of reintegrating the scattered fragments of the human race. (This would correspond to what has been called redemption *in actu primo.*) The claim seems to be that we know out of our own experience that if people respond to Jesus according to his call, things come together in a community fulfillment of genuine inter-acting, inter-dependent freedoms. Jesus is this kind of person because of his own rising above the fear of death and every other sub-personal persuasion, and because of his own growth into independence from false and treacherous claims of authority and community loyalties, and into dependence on God alone as ultimate authority. It would seem to be in his inner freedom of total dependence on the transcendent God and creative ability to act beyond fear, that Jesus has already brought the "powers" under his dominion and conquered the last enemy, death, so that all knees must bend in acknowledgement that the name of Jesus is *kyrios,* Lord (*cf.* Heb 2:14–15).

Implications for Social Attitudes

There are serious implications of the foregoing for the Christian attitudes toward, and expectations of, the micro- and macro-structures of society. If Jesus, and the Church, are indeed the "seed of unity, hope and salvation for all mankind"[18] as suggested, then the Christian concern cannot be limited to the micro-structures of society, such as the family, the parish, the various face-to-face groups in which we interact. Nor is it sufficient to say with regard to the macro-structures, such as national and international economies, governments, cultural alignments, and so forth, that Christ has already conquered the world and dominated the "powers." If the claim for the "already" of his lordship has to do mainly with the capacity for reform and reintegration in him, then faith is expressed in the appropriate action and life style. And if the nature of his lordship has to do with human creativity and imagination in the restructuring of society, then faith is expressed by critical and imaginative engagement with the macro-structures. One may even conclude that the quality of political power that is more attuned to the coming of the kingdom in all its fullness is that which least rests upon the uneasy compromises of greed and fear, and relies most upon community of goals and interests and mutual trust.

NOTES

1. For a collection of the principal documents since *Rerum novarum,* 1891, see Anne Fremantle, ed., *The Social Teachings of the Church* (New York: Mentor-Omega, 1963) and Joseph Gremillion, ed., *The Gospel of Peace and Justice* (Maryknoll, N.Y.: Orbis Books, 1976).

2. See: Jürgen Moltmann, *Theology of Hope* (New York: Harper & Row, 1967) and *Religion, Revolution and the Future* (New York: Charles Scribner, 1969); Wolfhart Pannenberg, *Theology and the Kingdom of God* (Philadelphia: Westminster, 1969); J. B. Metz, *Theology of the World* (New York: Herder, 1969); Claude Geffré and Gustavo Gutierrez, eds., *The Mystical and Political Dimensions of the Faith* (New York: Herder, 1974); and *cf.* John C. Haughey, ed., *The Faith that does Justice* (New York: Paulist Press, 1977).

3. *Theological Investigations,* Vol. XIII (New York: Seabury, 1975), "The Two Basic Types of Christology," pp. 213–223.

4. *Cf. Theology of Hope,* Ch. 3, and subsequent writings.

5. See: J. B. Metz, "The Future in the Memory of Suffering," in J. B. Metz, ed., *New Questions on God* (New York: Herder, 1972); Gustavo Gutierrez, *A Theology of Liberation* (Maryknoll, N.Y.: Orbis, 1978), Ch. 2; Leonardo Boff, *Jesus Christ Liberator* (Maryknoll, N.Y.: Orbis, 1978), especially Ch. 2.

6. *E.g.* J. B. Metz in "The Future . . ." and Sobrino in *Christology* explicitly.

7. The thoughtful attempts by Sobrino and Boff mentioned above themselves admit that they have not yet achieved what they set out to do, namely to elaborate an entire Christology from the perspectives they set themselves.

8. *Jesus: an Experiment in Christology* (New York: Seabury, 1979), p. 19.

9. See *Peri archon,* Bk. I, Ch. II and Bk. II, Ch. VI, available in translation as *On Christian Principles* (New York: Harper and Row, 1966).

10. See the essay by Brian McDermott on the role of the imagination in the ministry of Jesus.

11. For the relevance and importance of this in relation to social structures, see the essay by Otto Hentz in this volume, and for some of the practical and specific implications, the essay by Thomas Clarke.

12. For a helpful schematic presentation of this, see: John Macquarrie,

The Principles of Christian Theology (New York: Scribner's, 1966), Ch. XII, Section 45.

13. This is a favorite theme of Karl Rahner. See, e.g., "On the Theology of the Incarnation," *Theological Investigations,* Vol. IV, pp. 105–120.

14. See Rahner, *Theological Investigations,* Vol. I, p. 162.

15. See: *The Christ* (New York: Herder, 1971), Part II; and more precisely and explicitly P. J. A. M. Schoonenberg, "Spirit Christology and Logos Christology," *Bijdragen* 38 (1977), 350–375, where pp. 360 to the end (including crucial footnotes on pp. 363 and 365) explain his position, answering point by point the objections made by his critics since the first publication of *The Christ.*

16. See Bernard Lonergan, "The De-hellenization of Dogma," *Theological Studies* 28 (1967) 336–351.

17. *Op. cit.,* pp. 56–57.

18. *Lumen gentium* 9.

2
Lordship of Yahweh, Lordship of Jesus

J. P. M. Walsh, S.J.

This essay will try to deal with two questions. First, we will survey the tradition of Israel—the images, institutions, and theologoumena by which Israel lived—in an effort to understand the meaning of the lordship of Yahweh. Second, we will sketch the ways in which New Testament Christology drew on Israelite tradition to articulate an understanding of Jesus; our effort here is to understand the meaning of the lordship of Jesus. What I hope will emerge from the discussion of the first question is that Yahweh's lordship is defined by reference to what we are calling social systems: the whole range of political, economic, social, and other kinds of relationships human existence comprises; that apart from this "political" realm the notion of divine lordship as it is understood in Israelite tradition is without content; and that therefore the terms in which the New Testament writers proclaimed the good news of salvation in Christ have directly—not secondarily or adventitiously or illatively—"political" reference. The discussion of the second question, about the lordship of Jesus, will stress the continuities of New Testament thought with the central concerns of its Old Testament sources, but also indicate ways in which proclamation of Jesus' lordship puts these concerns in a new light. These discussions constitute parts I and III of this essay.

Each of these questions, though, must be examined from a second point of view, that of consciousness or self-understanding. If one accepted ("interiorized") and tried to live by faith in the lordship of Yahweh, what sort of person would he be? If one affirms the lordship of Jesus, what form of self-understanding does that entail? In part, this is a consideration of what is sometimes called spirituality or subjectivity, but I do not mean it to be a study of "religious" attitudes. The separation of the "religious" aspect of human existence from other "aspects," which is the result of a specific process of intellectual change in Western history, is to a great extent the very presupposition of the question this essay deals with. The lordship of Jesus has come to be thought of as belonging to the realm of "religion," a matter of interior, private, spiritual concern, of one's individual relationship to God. It is this dissociation, of "religion" from (let us say) "politics," that I hope to show is unfounded in Scripture and, from the viewpoint of biblical faith, makes no sense. The question, then, to be put to the central biblical givens of the lordship of Yahweh and the lordship of Jesus is this: what does this lordship mean for the believer? What are its consequences for the way we are to imagine ourselves and our world, for how we are to understand ourselves and how we are to act? How does it shape what, in all the complexities of human interrelatedness and in the particularities of being-in-social-systems, we are? This is the question dealt with in parts II and IV of this essay.

I

"Yahweh is king" or "Yahweh reigns": this acclamation, found early in the tradition of Israel (Exod 15:18), is central and originative in that tradition. This kingship is central also, of course, to the proclamation of Jesus; like its Hebrew equivalents *(malkût, mᵉlūkāh, mamlākāh),* Greek *basileia* means both "kingship" and "kingdom." Given the royal associations of the title *'ădōnāy* (cf. *'ădōnî* as a title for a king), it seems reasonable to use "lordship" and "kingship" interchangeably, and so in sketching the meaning of Yahweh's lordship in Israelite tradition I shall follow that usage.[1] The term *imperium,* recently introduced into scholarly discussion of these matters, of course has its own (extrabiblical) history and associations, and has been criticized as being unhelpful,[2] but since in many ways it enables us to gain a fresh perspective on the nature of Yahweh's lordship I shall make occasional use of it.

Israelite tradition spoke of Yahweh's lordship using two sets of terms and images, one derived from the theological discourse of Canaan,[3] the other derived from the realm of ancient Near Eastern politics and international relations. The first set of images identifies the god of Israel as cosmic lord; in the second, Yahweh's lordship is understood as a political lordship (*imperium,* properly so called).

1. *Cosmic Lordship.* Yahweh is the god who presides over the council of the gods, or "sons of El": his "judgment" (on which see below) in the divine assembly is an exercise of his divine kingship.[4] This kingship is celebrated in the imagery of victory over Sea, piercing the Dragon, treading upon the back of Sea, staying his proud waves, and so on: Yahweh is the one who effects *cosmos,* establishing the world, setting up all that is.[5] When he ascends his holy mountain, to be enthroned in the sanctuary or house which is the emblem of his kingship, the gods (doubtless at a feast) acclaim him as king.[6] These age-old themes[7] of creation and divine kingship clearly portray Yahweh as cosmic lord. The language of storm theophany is strictly speaking separable from this complex of motifs, but is for all practical purposes associated with Yahweh as divine warrior, who subdued Sea "in generations long ago."[8]

This rich and suggestive imagery was used throughout Israelite tradition to affirm that the god who had brought Israel forth from slavery and led them to the mountain of his inheritance was indeed the creator of all. The god who, enthroned upon the cherubim atop the Ark, led the armies of Israel against their enemies in Holy War, was cosmic lord. Yahweh "comes" or "descends" or "goes forth" to scatter his enemies in panic by the voice of his thunder or "rebuke." The one to whom the psalmist would appeal to come to his aid was the "rider upon the clouds" who exposes the sources of the sea, and draws the afflicted man out of "many waters."[9] Creation is redemption, and both manifest the kingship of Yahweh.

2. *Covenant Lordship.* Early Israel had no earthly king: "Yahweh rules over us" (Judg 8:23). Israel was bound to Yahweh by a relationship that could be called "love" or "knowing" or "going after" him, or a number of other terms.[10] The vocabulary is that which describes the relationship between a king and his vassal, and in fact the word used to speak of such a relationship—"treaty" or, as it is more commonly translated, "covenant"—is the precise term

for the relationship established at Sinai. It is this covenantal relationship that constituted Israel a people. The polity of early Israel flowed from this. The affiliated "tribes" found the center of their life as a people in the sanctuary housing the Ark, the throne of the invisible covenant lord; the same covenant lord "went out before" Israel in battle, with the Ark as the palladium of his presence. The leaders who exercised authority over ("judged") Israel were men and women whose courage and skill were endowments of Yahweh: "the spirit of Yahweh clothed Gideon" (Judg 6:34); "the spirit of God rushed upon Saul" (1 Sam 11:6)—the Deuteronomistic Historian takes pains to stress the divine charism. Even after the emergence of monarchy in Israel Yahweh exercised his lordship through spokesmen ("his servants"!), the prophets, who designated kings and reproved them for infidelity and (at least in the North) deposed them by divine authority.[11]

Yahweh's covenant lordship, then, constituted Israel and governed their life as a people. It is sometimes said and most often tacitly assumed that the reality spoken of in covenant terms is a religious one: the treaty language is metaphorical. As the language of Canaan was a way for Israel to speak of their god and his saving deeds, by using age-old metaphors whose import was known to all, so the vocabulary of suzerain and vassal, "knowing" and "loving" Yahweh, and the paraphernalia of blessings and curses were attempts to describe the relationship between a god and his people. From this point of view, images from family life, say, or from some other realm of human experience, might have done as well: the reality clothed in images was religious, the God-man relationship. Covenant terms were "ciphers."

Work done in recent years on the emergence of early Israel, however, calls this dissociation of reality and "imagery" into question, and in my opinion deserves serious consideration. Two lines of inquiry converge: the question of the *Ḫabiru/ʿApiru,* and studies of the social world of Israel in the time of the so-called Conquest. What follows is a sketch of this more recent thinking.

Onomastica of early Israel and of Canaan reveal that, to the extent that one can make illations about racial and ethnic identity from names, there was no racial or (in the contemporary sense) ethnic difference between Israelites and the "seven nations" of Canaan. Like the "sons of Israel," the "sons of Heth," the "sons of Ammon," and so on were a "mixed multitude." The commonly held view that Israel was a racially homogeneous people taking over the land of other racially homogeneous nations is based on a modern assumption, anachronistically read back into the biblical language of kinship, about the nature of race and the racial basis of ethnicity.[12]

What, then, distinguished the "sons of Israel" from the Canaanites? It was their participation in the political entity called Israel, a political entity that according to standard views of the time about political legitimacy was anomalous. In the eyes of the nations, the "sons of Israel" were *ḫabiru*. That is, they gave allegiance to no recognized polity, owed no adherence to the obligations and procedures that defined one's status in, say, a city-state. They were without proper political status, citizens of nowhere, like the men who gathered themselves to David when Saul's jealousy had put David into precisely that condition: "everyone who was in distress, and everyone who was in debt, and everyone who was discontented" (1 Sam 22:2).[13]

The nature of this "illegitimate" polity can be seen by contrast with the established political structures, the "nations" of Canaan. These seem to have been oppressive for all but the few at the top: a king and his politico-military elite, possessing a technological superiority in warfare, were able to control a relatively much larger population, whose condition was in effect that of serfs. The king and his bureaucracy ("servants") and army enjoyed a monopoly of trade and commerce, and through expropriation of the fruits of agrarian labor and of the industry of artisans and craftsmen turned the economy of a city-state and its attached lands into an extension of the royal household. The legitimacy this sort of political arrangement enjoyed was conferred by the gods of the nations.[14]

From this point of view, then, what has been called the "peasant revolt" theory of the conquest becomes plausible.[15] The people of the land threw off their subjection to the kings of Canaan and entered into the political confederation, the coalition of the dispossessed and exploited, that called itself "the sons of Israel." They gave their allegiance to the god who had shown himself to be one who hears the cry of the oppressed, who fashions a people by bringing them out of the house of bondage, who redeems them. Since he is a god who cares about right, and who protects the powerless ("the widow and orphan"), the victories he effects for his own are quite accurately called "justices" (*ṣidqōt YHWH,* Judg 5:11). His people overcome the superior might of professional armies though they fight with neither shield nor spear (Judg 5:8).[16] He binds them to himself by a treaty: they are to "love" and "know" no earthly ruler, whose power is founded on the order of things set up by Baal or Dagon, but him only, not going after other gods. And this covenant lord is also cosmic lord: he is the one who establishes the order of things, and who therefore reaffirms or vindicates that order when men defy it: he "comes with vindication" to smite the wicked, the coalition of kings who storm his holy mountain, the nations whose tumult is like the tumult of Many Waters. Thus we see the import of the use of the standard ancient Near Eastern language of creation and divine kingship in speaking of Yahweh and his justices. The covenant lord of Israel is not one god among other gods, engaged in a struggle for dominance; he "judges" in the midst of the assembly of gods, he is the one whose decree is decisive, he is the one who is "God in heaven above and on earth below" (Josh 2:11). The stipulations entailed by, and embodying, the covenantal relationship with Yahweh (the "words" of the suzerain of Israel) are the expressions of the will of the creator of all, a clue to the divinely constituted order of things. If one lives in defiance of that order, he is dooming himself to futility and destruction; if one lives in a spirit of obedience and fidelity, walking in the way laid out in the law, peace and prosperity are the necessary consequences of that choice. The covenant theologoumena of blessing and curse have their foundation in the cosmic lordship of Yahweh: "Vindication is mine."

I hope that this survey of biblical language about Yahweh, set against the background of a reconstruction of the formation of early Israel in its Canaanite world, shows that it is reasonable to take quite seriously the political reference of covenant language. Yahweh's lordship is a political lordship *(imperium),* not a "religious" lordship dressed up in political language. Israel is a people because of their covenant relationship with Yahweh: the relationship constitutes them a people. The institutions of early Israel flow from this relationship. Infidelity to Yahweh entails dissolution and oppression, as the Deuteronomistic History, in its attempt retrospectively to understand the dynamics of the downfall of the Northern Kingdom, insists (Judg 2:11–19; 1 Sam 8). What led to the destruction of Israel was their tendency to live as a nation-state among other nation-states, both in internal affairs (injustice, syncretism) and in external dealings with their neighbors (foreign adventurism, power politics). The confederation of the dispossessed became an economically stratified, would-be imperialistic power "like all the nations round about," walking in the stubbornness of their own hearts. We shall come back to these matters in part II of this essay. (To a great extent, the institution of monarchy was crucial in this decline, but I wish to defer consideration of this aspect of the history and tradition of Israel until later.)

Against this background of the "kingship" of Yahweh we may now consider some terms whose meaning can be understood only if they are seen in the context of the synthesis of cosmic and covenantal lordship we have studied. They are "judgment," "vindication," and "salvation."

Judgment (mišpāṭ)

The word *špṭ* in Hebrew, like the Ugaritic *ṯpṭ*, includes more than the conventional translation, "to judge," indicates. Its meaning can be approximated as "exercise authority," and includes executive, legislative, military, and judicial functions. Hence, whether applied to Yahweh or to the "judges" of Israel in the period of the tribal league, the word indicates an exercise of authority differentiated only by context. The psalmist's plea, "Judge me, O God," therefore is a call for deliverance as well as for a finding of innocence in the face of accusation by his enemies. The *mišpāṭ* of Yahweh is an exercise of his divine kingship, and not surprisingly is associated with creation language (theophany, conflict with Sea, ascension and enthronement). As in days of old he trod upon Sea, so now he will assert his cosmic lordship and "judge." I am not saying that the judicial connotation is absent from the word's meaning, or is even secondary, but that that note—determining, finding for one side and condemning the other—is entailed by the basic meaning of the term.

Concretely, therefore, *mišpāṭ* may be convertible with the terms to be studied now, "vindication" (cf. 1 Sam 24:13, 16) and "salvation."

Vindication (nāqām)

This word, usually translated "vengeance," has been the object of an influential study by George Mendenhall;[17] his somewhat revisionist views have found their way, for example, into the recently published Supplement to the *Interpreter's Dictionary of the Bible, s.v.* "Vengeance."[18] Though some of the evidence for his understanding of the word can be questioned, his analysis remains on the whole suasive. It goes something like this.

A political entity is held together by a shared sense of obligation and accountability, and a willingness to submit to the procedures which structure that obligation. When one cuts himself off from that network of obligation,[19] the authority which is its structural counterpart or embodiment must act, so that the sundered unity or integrity of the political entity may be affirmed, restored, vindicated. When authority moves to sanction this integrity, by dealing with the outlaw, its action has a double aspect. *Vis-à-vis* the offender there is reprisal, retribution, punishment, "vengeance." *Vis-à-vis* the political entity whose existence, in its integrity, the offense threatens, there is the affirmation of the entity and its authority. In this latter aspect, Mendenhall sees the basic meaning of the term *nāqām:* "vindication." The *Sitz im Leben* for use of the word *nāqām,* therefore, is not interfamilial or intertribal blood feuds, but the authority of the state, in the sense described. A suzerain is the one who can say, "Vindication is mine."

It is clear that this theory is attractive to us because we are uncomfortable with the image of Yahweh as one capable of, even delighting in, revenge, but despite this hermeneutical congeniality we should not dismiss the theory out of hand. Mendenhall cites passages from the Amarna letters to show that the term *nqm* is part of the repertory of duties and prerogatives proper to a suzerain, and that a vassal would appeal to his lord to execute *nāqām* in his behalf, but recent work has shown that *nqm* is not present in the Amarna documents, and so the desired unambiguous extrabiblical parallels are wanting.[20]

What is not in doubt, however, is that *nāqām* is reserved to Yahweh (cf. Deut 32:35), already quoted. As "sin" is spoken of in the language of political rebellion (e.g., Hos 9:15), and Yahweh is rejected precisely as covenant lord, so his acting to affirm his justice by dealing with the offender and upholding his faithful ones should be conceived as an affirmation (vindication!) of his divine *imperium.* The term is cognate with the notion, incorporated into the covenant theology, that Yahweh "by no means acquits" the rebel (Exod 34:7). To that extent, we should not sever the word from the political context its attribution to the covenant lord puts it in.

Salvation (yšʿ)

This word has almost the status, in the Deuteronomistic corpus, of a *terminus technicus,* but despite the covenantal affinities it has there,[21] its basic meaning seems to include military victory.[22] That is, it is a term especially appropriate to warfare. The one who saves is the stronger one: a mighty arm, or strength, or horse and chariot brings "salvation" (or does not bring it!). I would argue that the term does not refer in a general way to rescue from some difficulty and is then applied in contexts of peril to the nation or military struggle, but that deliverance from an enemy is a constitutive part of its meaning. Yahweh is the "savior" *par excellence,* and precisely as the warrior god (*'ēl gibbōr,* Isa 9:6; cf. Exod 15:3) who by overcoming Israel's enemies vindicates his justice, keeping covenant *ḥesed.* Thus, it is indeed a theological notion as it appears in Israelite tradition, but rather than softening its military and political overtones that circumstance merely strengthens them.

The list of words studied could well be lengthened, but I hope that the studies given so far will have fleshed out the thesis that a connection with politics and political life is not something that has to be introduced into the language of Israelite tradition resumed in New Testament Christology: it is built into it. Two other exegetical matters deserve some attention, by way of rounding out this sketch. One has to do with the use of these images and terms in prophetic eschatology and, later, apocalyptic. The other is the question of the so-called royal ideology, one of the principal sources for the Christology of the New Testament.

The Day of Yahweh

Without trying to trace in detail the development of this motif from the period of classical prophecy to what has been called proto-apocalyptic, I can sketch its components in such a way as to indicate what, in the second or first century B.C., a Jew familiar with Scripture might have expected to happen to his people; or rather, how he might, in continuity with Old Testament tradition, have imagined the future: what images were available to draw upon.

The "scenario" is already familiar from the above pages. Yahweh, accompanied by a retinue of the Holy Ones, goes forth or comes on the clouds of heaven, with disruption of nature (earthquake, darkening of sun, etc.). He smites the wicked (*rešāʿîm* Greek *adikoi*), or the nations, dooming them to utter destruction (*ḥērem)* as in Holy War; here the imagery of Sea might well be used to speak of Yahweh's foe. The wicked nations will drink the cup of divine wrath (Hab 2:16–17; Jer 25:15–31; Isa 51:22–23); their blood will flow in streams. Yahweh's faithful ones will be vindicated (the "just": *ṣaddîqîm,* Greek *dikaioi*), and will proceed in his train to his holy mountain, there to enjoy the feast of his kingship in the sanctuary where he is enthroned and reigns. (The language of covenantal blessings and curses can be introduced, conflated as it were with the images of abundance proper to the kingdom and the retribution suffered by the wicked, respectively.) This act of divine judgment (*mišpāṭ)* or salvation or vindication will bring about a new creation, following the pattern of the old in its establishment but not to pass away or be subject to the corruption the old creation underwent.

This tripartite scenario—descent, conflict, ascension—is admittedly a reconstruction from images scattered through various writings from various periods of Israelite and Jewish tradition, but it can appeal to early Israelite (and pre-Israelite) imagery for some support;[23] in any case, imagination is synchronic and synthetic. These images are not used univocally, of course. Second Isaiah did not have in mind a decisive event "at the end of days": he was writing oracles of consolation for the Judahite exiles, assuring them that the God who acted before in their history would again bring them with him in his processional way to Zion (Isa 51:9–11; cf. Isa 35:4). He envisioned an imminent event. Later Jewish writings, using the forms of prophecy, made use of this scenario and its imagery in a like attempt at consolation, by putting the travail of the people into a theological context, but (it seems) with a tendency to "eschatologize" more fully: all this would happen in the end of days. Still, against the view of those who see apocalyptic as a flight from history, I would argue that the visions of divine judgment and dreams of the night characteristic of that form of writing were meant not to steel persecuted Jews to their suffering by holding out the hope of an ultimate vindication (whenever that might be) so much as to recall the basic saving truths of their tradition and so put their suffering into a relativizing, theological perspective. In either view, this imagery was as directly political as *samizdat,* or a pastoral letter by the Polish episcopate in 1979 on the lessons to be learned from the admirable life of St. Stanislaw.[24]

In light of what has been said, it seems to me that it would not have been unreasonable for a contemporary of Jesus, hearing his proclamation that the Kingdom of God was imminent, to assume that Jesus was announcing that God was about to "judge" the enemies of Israel and that bloody retribution was to befall the Roman oppressor. It would have been surprising if any other meaning had been taken from his words.

The Anointed of Yahweh

So far we have studied only the complex of images and motifs associated with the kingship of Yahweh, as if the notice in Judges that "there was no king in Israel" had held good through the whole of the Old Testament period. This is not really a distortion of the tradition, however. The theme of divine lordship, both cosmic and covenantal, is not only foundational for the existence of Israel; it was the burden and the legitimation of prophetic activity throughout the period of the monarchy. The aspect of Israelite tradition we have left in suspension until now, the monarchy, stands in tension with that theme, and indeed presents a real theological problem.[25] The anti-monarchic traditions preserved in Jud 8:22–23 and 1 Samuel 8 put the problem into relief. To choose a king for themselves was a rejection by Israel of Yahweh as their king. How avoid the inevitable tendency to substitute the human person of the king for Yahweh, to make him, rather than their covenant lord, the cynosure of the people, to attribute to him the functions of salvation, judgment, vindication? The Deuteronomistic treatment of the "judges" and "saviors" of Israel in the period of the tribal league stressed that the military and political qualities of these leaders came from Yahweh: their power derived from him, and they were properly subordinate to him. But a king?

The "peasant revolt" theory outlined above tends to confirm the historical reliability of the anti-monarchic traditions found in the Deuteronomistic History. In olden times, the ancestors of Israel had known what it was to have a king, and the contemporary kings of Canaan would serve as a caution against introducing the institution into Israel. It would open the door to centralization of power and to tyranny, precisely because it reposed in a man what were divine functions. The logic of "choosing a king for themselves" was ultimately divinization of the king, especially in view of the divine or semi-divine status of kings in the nations round about. To translate literally the Canaanite (Hebrew) idiom, the king was a "son of God" *(bin'ili),* that is, "a divine being."[26]

One need have no ideological axe to grind to insist, therefore, that the institution of kingship created a tension with the constitutive principles and institutions that made Israel what it was. How was this tension resolved? To a great extent, it never was, but we should look at the attempts made to resolve it, in both the North and the South.

The North preserved features of the tribal league, with its normative traditions and ideology, and so kept within some limits the power of the king. The principal instrument of this limitation of power was prophecy, by which Yahweh, the veritable king of Israel, exercised his lordship. The prophet designated and anointed the king; he (or she) gave oracles relative to warfare, by which the Holy War traditons were preserved; he reproved the king for actions and policies that contravened the requirements of the covenant. This fidelity to the foundational norms of all-Israel, whose expression and guardianship were entrusted to the prophets, was indeed the cause of the schism that had led to the founding of the Northern Kingdom: its existence was the product of a conservative reaction to the absolutism of Solomon (1 Kgs 12).

That absolutism would present no problem if it could be construed as simple infidelity to Yahweh, a runaway metastasis of human power, the tyranny Samuel is depicted foretelling (1 Sam 8) as the inevitable result of the people's rejection of Yahweh as king. But it cannot be. It had a charter in the oracle of Nathan to David. It was the result of divine choice, the double election of David and of Zion. The Dynastic Oracle of 2 Sam 7 (Ps 89) in effect removes all limitations from royal power: despite appropriate chastisement, the Davidic king's rebellion against Yahweh would never cause his rejection; of his (the "seed" of David's) kingship there would be no end. Furthermore, the semi-divine status of a Near Eastern king was accorded to the son of David. 2 Sam 7:14; Ps 2:7; and especially Ps 89:27 seem to be attempts to reconcile the ancient understanding of a king as "son of God" with the primacy of Yahweh: the Davidic king is (so to speak) the adoptive son of God, a *bin'ili* in that sense only, and probably along the lines of a suzerain-vassal relationship.[27] The suzerain was to the vassal as a father is to his son. Still, the need to demythologize or reinterpret the notion shows the problem it presented.

In one or two generations, therefore, David and his heir succeeded in introducing dynastic monarchy, an institution one hundred and eighty degrees opposed to what had obtained in the previous two hundred years of Israel's existence.

Yet we should not ignore the other aspect of the Dynastic Oracle. It presents the royal status of David and of his "seed" as a matter of Yahweh's choice, and so legitimizes the House of David, true. But this very choice retains the initiative in Yahweh's hands; he is still the one whose decree is normative. Furthermore, the "father-son" relationship itself implies a subordination of the Davidic king to Yahweh, as does the language of "reproof"[28] for rebellion against Yahweh. And if Psalm 89 asserts that the Davidic king enjoys a share in the very creative power of Yahweh (v. 26, "I will set his hand over Sea, his right hand over River"), the introduction (vv.2–19) to the psalm makes it abundantly clear that kingship is Yahweh's alone, and participation in that kingship is the result of Yahweh's decree, nothing else.

Against this theological and political background, we may understand the import of the portrait of David given in the so-called Court Narrative (2 Sam 9–20). In a word, David is the ideal king because he is subordinate to Yahweh. He is afflicted, and weak, and sinful, but he casts his care on the Lord, and the Lord delivers him. It is this perfection of David—his weakness, in truth—that accounts for the Deuteronomistic Historian's theme of hope and grace in his great historical work, as we shall see below. "For the sake of David my servant": all would not be lost, despite the many and constant offenses of the descendants of David.

If, therefore, the traditions associated with David, the anointed of Yahweh, and with his House forever, tend to absolutize royal power and magnify the one who wields it, the figure of David himself serves as a corrective to that royal ideology. The tension between the lordship of Yahweh and the (derivative!) lorship of the son of David, a tension arising from the tendencies of human power to make itself an absolute, remains a tension; but the surbordination of the Lord's anointed to the one who chose him and swore to him eternal *ḥesed* is, within Israelite tradition, the only way to resolve or at least allay the tension.

We can state some conclusions. Apart from the *sophia/ḥokmāh* Christology found in certain parts of New Testament tradition,[29] the principal terms Israelite tradition afforded for the understanding of Jesus were directly (not metaphorically) political. The apocalyptic scenario itself would only with difficulty, and not at all naturally, exclude any reference to current events in the life of the nation. Whether he was perceived as one who would effect (or through whom God would effect) salvation or redemption or vindication or judgment; whether he was thought of as the anointed of the Lord, the son of David, the son of God (in the sense of Pss 2:7; 89:27; 2 Sam 7:14);[30] whether he was seen in terms of the Kingdom of God or the Day of Yahweh—Jesus would necessarily have been understood as a figure whose existence and activity had to do with political and military transformations in his time.

A consequence of this is that we should avoid the preacher's cliché, "What a tragic misunderstanding of Jesus on the part of his disciples and of the crowds. . . ." The burden of proof rests with those who would evacuate from the language of the New Testament Christology reference to political transformation. It is clear that there was reinterpretation in the New Testament of the elements of Old Testament tradition I have studied here, but we should not simply assume radical discontinuity in their usage, or an *Aufhebung* of them into the realm of "religion."

In a sense, I have approached the question our volume is dealing with by backing into it from the Old Testament. I hope to have shown that, at least so far as Old Testament tradition is concerned, divine lordship is not something unconnected with "social systems." Before we can discuss what the designation of Jesus as Lord means with respect to social systems, however, we must go back over some of the same ground we have just covered, but from a different point of view.

II

The different point of view is this: what was the self-understanding or consciousness of the Israelite that was both expressed in the tradition and shaped by it? How would an Israelite faithful to what his tradition told him about Yahweh as covenant lord and cosmic lord imagine himself and his world, and precisely with respect to the facticity of what we are calling social systems?

As I hope to show in detail elsewhere, this is precisely the question the body of thought we call Deuteronomistic is trying to answer. The book of Deuteronomy represents an attempt to rethink the tradition of Israel in such a way as to inculcate a certain form of consciousness and, in so doing, to show the connections between self-understanding and the forms of political life that embody it, especially with regard to consequences those forms entail. The parenetic mode of Deuteronomy itself indicates that the purpose of the book is not so much to lay down norms of behavior as to address the human subject in terms of *being* such and such. The book is trying to elicit a fundamental option, one that springs from an awareness of who Yahweh is and what Israel is; this awareness, basic to everything else, is a matter of having certain things at the center of one's consciousness. "Remember"; "do not forget"; "set your heart to . . ."; "your eyes saw . . .": the parenesis aims at forming the reader's consciousness. The well-known passage Deut 6:6–9 uses the device of *merismus* to indicate the necessity of maintaining a certain consciousness in all circumstances ("in your sitting at home, in your going on the way, in your lying down and in your getting up"), both in private and in public life ("on the doorsteps of your house and in your gates").[31]

What is this consciousness? At the heart of human selfhood, according to Deuteronomy, is a relationship to Yahweh. It can be spoken of as "knowing," "obeying" (or "hearing"), "serving," "fearing," "going after," "cleaving to," or "loving" Yahweh, and if these terms without exception are derived from the realm of politics and treaty relationships[32] Deuteronomy wants to retrieve for them their full interior or psychological sense. In his fundamental self-understanding, one is to be wholly centered on Yahweh. He is the covenant lord who loves and chooses Israel and keeps his oath to their fathers,[33] and who bestows on Israel goods not earned but freely given.[34] Israel's relationship to Yahweh, then, is not grounded in what Israel does, not in any quality of theirs,[35] nor in any claim they might have to being in the right.[36] To know this God is to acknowledge that the good things of the land are his gift—to know him, therefore, as giver of gifts. The good things (bread, grain, wine, oil) are thus relativized and made, as it were, byproducts of human efforts; effort itself is to be seen within the horizon of Israel's relationship to Yahweh.[37]

This fundamentally shaping relationship to Yahweh is put into strong relief by contrast with an alternative source of self-understanding, "going after other gods," being assimilated to the nations round about. The "other gods" are those which represent and legitimize as absolute values the good things of the land, fertility of womb and field, survival. Central to this form of self-understanding is reliance on one's own efforts, as entitling one to wealth or victory, as the source of one's achievement, or as proof that one is "in the right": one deserves to eat and be satisfied.[38] Thus "forgetting" Yahweh in the pursuit of good things on one's own terms and as central to one's existence, one lives in the "stubbornness of his own heart": whatever does not fit into this project simply does not count; what one has set his heart on has absolute value, excluding all other considerations, even the covenant imperatives of justice and compassion.

This way of understanding oneself and the world has inexorable consequences. Human effort springing from infidelity to Yahweh is doomed to futility: it runs directly counter to the way the cosmic lord has set things up, and so inevitably entails the kind of "systemic contradictions" that ensure its reversal. The effort to guarantee survival leads to injustice and want at home, and invites foreign invasion with the corollaries of siege, famine, disease, anarchy, defeat, enslavement, and exile. To choose to go after the gods of the nations is to choose evil and death. The covenant curses are a reflex or byproduct of the fundamental option of idolatry. The covenant blessings are a reflex or byproduct of the fundamental option of fidelity, in one's basic self-understanding, to the covenant lord who loves and brings out of slavery, who is faithful and bestows gifts irrespective of merit.

Blessing and curse, then, are to be understood not as reward and punishment[39] but as consequences of one form of self-understanding or the other, as that is lived out in the life of the people. Deuteronomy is a theology of the relationship between self-understanding and politics. It is true that the book itself does not provide the middle term between fundamental option and ultimate consequences, namely, the ways in which (if the anachronism may be allowed) "works righteousness" embodies itself in exploitive and destructive forms of relationships, domestic and foreign, and "love" of the covenant lord as the *unum necessarium,* by relativizing all other goods, permits relationships and social systems characterized by equity, justice, and reverence.

In fact, Deuteronomy seems more interested in the works of self-absolutization and self-seeking than in the concrete ways covenant "love" might be embodied, and that points to what the purpose of the book might be. It is not a timeless, contextless disquisition, but a tract for its times, bearing the marks of the tragic collapse of the North and the history of injustice, idolatry, and power politics that led up to it. Where did it all go wrong? This is the question the book is trying to answer; more accurately, the question is: what were the spiritual and historical dynamics in the nation's life that had as their ultimate logic the nation's undoing? How can Judah avoid the same fate? To answer this question, a political theorist of a later age might well explore thematically the relationships between national consciousness, spiritual identity, values, and so on, and the social systems that embody that consciousness, and trace the consequences of one form of self-understanding over against another, as those might involve systemic contradictions, on the one hand, or be grounded in a clear-sighted cosmic realism, on the other. What the Deuteronomist does, in fact, is to evoke the day when Israel had the opportunity to live its life in the land in integrity, abundance, and peace; when the future lay before Israel as *tabula rasa,* and all was bright promise. The Deuteronomist has Moses set forth the stark option: if you choose to be this sort of people, and live in this way, these will be the consequences; if you choose the opposite, you choose these consequences. Choose. At one stroke, the discourse lays bare the dynamics of the fate suffered by the North and, by the nostalgic regret at opportunity forever lost that must have been aroused in the seventh-century reader as well as the conversion of heart the parenesis is meant to effect, offers the promise that Judah's future can be salvaged still. What might have been can still be.

Deuteronomy is therefore both explanatory and parenetic. So is the Deuteronomistic History (Dtr), which serves as a kind of demonstration of the thesis presented in Deuteronomy. In its redaction of traditional materials and its addition of framing commentary, Dtr draws lines of connection between the syncretism fostered by the royal houses of Israel and Judah, domestic injustice (expropriation, social inequities, perversion of judicial process), and the foreign adventurism that invites invasion and exile, and traces these back to the people's failure to be what they are called to be, both by their infidelity and by the kings' wickedness. The strand of the History that Cross has termed Dtr sees the only promise for the (still salvageable) future in the promises made to David.[40] This emphasis on David should not be understood as the effusions of a court *flack,* or the sycophantic manipulation of Josiah or some other scion of the Davidic line, but as a pointed way of particularizing, in the seventh-century political context, the central Deuteronomic imperative to reliance on and fidelity to Yahweh: the Davidic king is the repository of hope for the future if that king is like David—trusting in Yahweh, not taking matters into his own hands, not identifying his personal fortunes with those of God.[41] The king who does rely on his own power and the strength of his own hand will bring disaster; so, Saul, Absalom, Adonijah prove unsuitable, though they seem to be men of parts ideally qualified to exercise royal power. David in his weakness and sinfulness knows that it is Yahweh who is Israel's lord, and is subordinate to him.[42]

From this sketch of the rethinking of Israelite tradition that we call Deuteronomy and the Deuteronomistic History, we see that the counterpart to the lordship of Yahweh is a subjectivity or consciousness wholly centered on Yahweh as suzerain, judge, and vindicator. Because he is "God in heaven above and on earth below," and "there is not other," obedience to his judgments leads to blessing. A consciousness shaped by concern for survival and the anxiety-provoking illusion that wealth and "salvation" come from one's own efforts, on the other hand, entails systemic contradictions in the life of Israel that necessarily bring about their own undoing: curse. The portrait of David and the hope reposed both in the promises made to him and in the form of kingship he embodies underline the connection between subordination or obedience and the good of the people. The Deuteronomic corpus might be called a study in the lordship of Yahweh and social systems.

As an exercise in political theology, the Deuteronomistic corpus takes what we might call a macrocosmic approach. Its retrospective interest and parenetic intent look to the life of the nation, and application to individual cases of Deuteronomic categories leads to the futile and presumptuous bromides of Job's comforters: the book of Job can usefully be read as a polemic against this sort of procedure.[43] Though the strongly marked dualities of Deuteronomic thought accord well with the prophetic categories of the "just" and the "wicked,"[44] it offers no strategies for one caught in the toils of injustice and oppression, at least directly. One who lives in a polity whose governing principles are those of idolatry and infidelity, and who tries to remain faithful to the covenant lord and his judgments, will likely find himself a victim: Naboth is the parade example. A latter-day Naboth will derive little consolation from having the historical dynamics of his plight explained to him; he is suffering on the "microcosmic" level. The parenesis of Deuteronomy is aimed not at the "just" one who finds himself victimized but at the "wicked" who do the victimizing; and the inevitability of doom for the wicked likewise is meant to turn them from their violent ways, not to comfort those they oppress.

What, then, is the poor man, the just one, to do? The central datum of Israelite tradition is that Yahweh hears the cry of the oppressed, that his judgment *(mišpāṭ)* is just, and that his Day means vindication for the victim, destruction for the wicked. One persecuted, therefore, is to entrust his cause to Yahweh of Hosts, and if his plea, strenuously insisting on the rightness of his case, sounds to our well-bred sensibility more than a little sanguinary in tone, the depth of feeling involved expresses faith in the centrality of justice in the divinely appointed scheme of things, and faith as well in the *ḥesed* of the God of justice. To give way to despair or indifferentism (by making one's own the sentiment of the fool, that God does not see, or care[45]) is apostasy. To play vindicator, on the other hand, is to supplant Yahweh as "judge," and is equally infidelity to the covenant lord. Paradoxically, this kind of self-help—taking matters into one's own hands, appointing oneself enforcer of cosmic law—is subject to the Deuteronomic critique: one who allows his own grievances to become central to his self-understanding and so hardens his heart as to "go in his own way" has in effect embraced the spirit of self-absolutization and reliance on one's own power that is the wellspring of injustice. It is idolatry.[46]

This is the awkwardness built into the tradition of Israel, then, that fidelity to Yahweh requires both a passion for justice—nonnegotiable, uncompromising, not to be rationalized away—and the willingness to wait upon the Lord. Absent the first, Yahweh is reduced to the status of the gods of the nations round about, a mere legitimator of an unjust status quo. Absent the second, Yahweh is rendered otiose: one effects his own *nāqām*. In a sense, then, the question asked above is misplaced. What is the oppressed just one to do? He is to cast his care upon the Lord. If we first look for strategies (what is one to *do?*), our attention is misdirected.

We see this in the book of Daniel, not only in the stories of how in olden times God sustained the Jews who, even in the face of strenuous royal efforts to make them apostatize, remained faithful to ancestral ways, but especially in the apocalyptic vision of chapter 7. The writer tries to communicate an understanding of what is happening to the people by imaging the future that will come out of present persecution, and he does this by going back to the foundational images of Israel's existence. Yahweh will judge—indeed, has already passed judgment—and that judgment means destruction for the persecutor. It also means that dominion *(exousia)* and sovereignty are conferred on the faithful people. This outcome is assured: the judgment takes place in solemn session of the heavenly court; the human figure in whom the faithful see themselves and God's intentions for them has access to the judge of all.[47]

III

I hope to have indicated how Israelite tradition always includes a reference to what in this book we are calling "social systems": that Yahweh's lordship is nowhere envisioned apart from the context of the life of the nation, of economic and political relationships. Even the Deuteronomic theology, which seems to be the most interior or "spiritual" or "religious" body of thought in the Old Testament, represents a meditation on the causes of political collapse, and on the conditions of the possibility of peace, abundance, and comity. Apocalyptic itself grows out of political oppression, and answers the agonized political question with an exuberant re-imaging of the divine *mišpāt.*

If we are attempting, then, to establish the relationship between the lordship of Jesus (or, more generally, the Christology of the New Testament writings) and social systems, asking as it were about the meaning of the word "and" in the title of this volume, the question we are addressing betrays the influence of the spiritual and intellectual changes that have set modern Western thought at odds with the world view of late biblical Judaism and the New Testament writings. The alleged secularization of political life that is the legacy of Western political thought is founded on hidden absolutes, involving a vision of the human good and of human nature for which claims are tacitly made that can only be called "cosmic," and having the status of what has come to be called "religion." Principalities and powers are at work in modern social systems.

That said, we can sketch some of the ways in which New Testament Christology draws on the tradition of Israel to understand Jesus, and then in the light of our previous discussion indicate what that understanding implies about social systems.[48]

1. Jesus is portrayed as the faithful one *(ḥāsīd),* the just man persecuted by the wicked, the innocent man whose blood is shed, who is vindicated by God.[49] The scandal of his rejection and execution is thus put into perspective by assimilating him to various Old Testament figures who rely on God to sustain them against their faithless enemies: God's fidelity is shown in Jesus' resurrection and exaltation.

2. We can take this one step further. The specific note of New Testament Christology, corresponding to the shameful circumstances of the death of Jesus, is the insistence on how he was reckoned among the wicked. Central to Paul's argument in Galatians 3 in his use of Deut 21:23, "Cursed is everyone hanged upon the tree" (cf. also 2 Cor 5:21). The figure of the servant of Yahweh is Isa 52:13–53:12 underlies this tendency of New Testament Christology, but in the New Testament writings there seems to be a heightening or radicalization of the paradox, playing off the well-established categories of the just and the wicked. This is seen especially in the Synoptics' depiction of Jesus' identification with sinners, in his table fellowship with them, in his baptism, in the struggle in the garden (if the cup is taken as the cup of wrath), and especially in his parables: the *dikaios* is excluded, or excludes himself, from the kingdom, the sinner is welcomed to the feast. The apocalyptic expectations are both fulfilled and reversed: fulfilled, because the cup of wrath is indeed drunk, and justice is fulfilled in the fate visited upon the one condemned; reversed, because the tidy duality of "just" and "wicked" is transcended. Jesus does not cling to what is rightfully his, but so identifies with sinners that he suffers the destiny of the wicked. Gracious, self-emptying love leaves behind (subsumes but transcends) strict reckoning of desert and merit. The "justice" that is based on consciousness of being in the right must reckon this kind

of love to be *adikia,* injustice. It is in the cross, the instrument of the criminal's death, that God's justice is seen.

3. "God has made both Lord and Messiah this Jesus whom you crucified" (Acts 2:36). From what we have just seen, it is clear that the exaltation of Jesus is not only the vindication of God's faithful one, but the conferral of lordship precisely on the one condemned as sinner, the one "cursed of God." Here again, there is continuity with the tradition of Israel, in the sense that the divine function of *mišpāṭ* is conferred on a man. As with the Davidic king, the anointed of Yahweh, there is a share in the divine kingship.[50] The Synoptic title "Son of Man," despite all the difficulties involved in its understanding, surely underlies the attribution of *exousia* to Jesus.[51] But the *novum* is that this divine authority belongs to "this Jesus whom you crucified," the obedient one who is not only obedient to death but to death on the cross.[52] Justice is established by the one who calls into radical question received ideas of justice.

4. But Jesus is not only the instrument of divine *mišpāṭ,* he is *kyrios.* There is no doubt that this title[53] puts Jesus "on a par with" God,[54] and identifies Jesus as being (to anticipate later dogmatic formulations) of divine nature, as sharing in godhead. It must be stressed that the one of whom this title is predicated is the one who was obedient to death on the cross: this emptying, and refusal to cling to what was his, has cosmic implications, according to the hymn preserved in Phil 2:6–11, in that the celestial, earthly, and chthonic powers—the rulers of the present age, which purport to guarantee a divinely instituted order of things—acclaim as "lord" him who overturns their authority. As Yahweh is cosmic lord, so now is Jesus. The power that establishes the fundamental law of the universe,[55] the law of justice, and vindicates that law, is now revealed as powerlessness, obedience, and gracious love.[56]

IV

If we speak of "interiorizing" what New Testament Christology proclaims, or having our self-understanding shaped by faith in the lordship of Jesus, we are really speaking of a gift, of something that God does, and that is to make us share in the sonship of Jesus. God gives this gift because he wishes to subject all things to the Son, to recapitulate all things in Christ, to bring about a new heaven and a new earth. From what we have seen it should be clear that this transformation of all things has to do with people having enough to eat, and living in peace—every man under his vine and under his fig tree—and being happy. It has to do with freedom from oppression. In a real sense, it has to do with what cannot be imagined except in general terms and by negation of the multiple ways human sinfulness devises to be destructive.

So if God makes us sons and daughters of him, configured to Christ, that is not to be understood apart from the overall divine purpose. Yet it is worth considering this aspect of the divine action in itself, both because it indicates the nature of the transformation in human affairs God is effecting, the establishment of his kingdom, and because we naturally ask, What does this mean for me? What am I to do?

Let us consider, then, the duality (or at least pairing) found in Mark 1:14–15. Jesus proclaimed that the kingdom was near, and he called upon people to undergo *metanoia.* The proclamation looks to what was happening in the realm of public events: the lord of all was going to establish his justice. The *metanoia* called for was to take place in view of what God was doing, and as various parables show it had to do with the proper readiness to take in and act on that divine action. In effect, *metanoia* means to be able to believe in and rely on the power of God that was proclaimed to be at work. It therefore means a transformation of people in the way they imagine themselves and their world, so that they attend to the mighty work God is doing, and become part of it, and are judged by it.

Now Christian spirituality and theology has concentrated on the personal dimensions of *metanoia* (and often has tended to understand it individualistically), elaborating the ways God works in the soul by assimilating the Christian to Christ in faith, hope, and charity. More recently, political theology and the concerns of liberation theology, especially as they have been brought to bear on Scripture, have tried to de-privatize the Christian proclamation,[57] and this had led in some quarters to a discomfort with the traditional concerns just mentioned. Oppositions are drawn between "activism" and "piety." Here, I think, the notion of *metanoia* can be helpful.

At the heart of what God did, and does, in Christ is the imperative—the gift—of interior transformation. This is irreducible to the macrocosmic aspect of the establishment of the kingdom. It is not the whole story, but neither can it be bypassed. Yet (again) *metanoia* is transformation in view of the cosmic transformation God is effecting. If I am to be configured to Christ, that is not something that is apart from or stands over against this making all things new. If I am given the gift of affirming faith in the lordship of Jesus, it is a faith in the one whose lordship subdues the powers which, left to their own devices, legitimize an unjust status quo. *Metanoia* means the ability to see that all human institutions stand under the judgment of God's justice, and that that justice has been revealed as something that goes beyond rights and wrongs strictly reckoned. It means living in fidelity to the God of justice, who in gracious love chooses to be servant. It means being like the one who seemed to be straitened and overcome by the Powers but was in reality free. It means accepting servanthood, since servanthood embodies the power of God, who makes all things new, and is itself a transforming agent. *Metanoia* is a politically subversive force. It entails a No to injustice, a refusal to be defined by the structures of the established order (especially, mirror-image-fashion, by simple negation of them). But it takes the form of a love that does not reckon wrongs and rights, is incapable of judgment, forgives. It leads us to drink the cup and undergo the baptism Jesus accepted. It enables us to imagine a world whose social systems provide opportunities to take the form of a servant, not as a strategy for effecting social change (that will happen, but it is not the point) or as calculating the political effect of one's servanthood (that effect is God's work), but because that is the way which Jesus calls us to go, following him, and he is Lord.

NOTES

1. For the sake of clarity we should note here that the title *kyrios* attributed to Jesus by the early Church represents the divine title *'ădōnāy* (cf. below, n. 53). It does not represent *melek,* "king." To this extent, speaking of the "lordship" of Yahweh in the context of a study devoted to the lordship of Jesus may create some confusion.
2. See Delbert Hillers in *Catholic Biblical Quarterly* 40 (1978) 90.

3. And the ancient Near East in general: (cf. Thorkild Jacobsen, "The Battle Between Marduk and Tiamat," *Journal of the American Oriental Society* 88 (1968) 104–108. The discussion of Frank M. Cross, *Canaanite Myth and Hebrew Epic* (Cambridge, Massachusetts: Harvard University Press, 1973), pp. 3–194, is basic to an understanding of the language and imagery of Canaan and of its incorporation into Israelite tradition.—Canaanite texts are cited by reference to A. Herdner, *Corpus des Tablettes en Cunéiformes Alphabétiques* (Paris: Imprimerie Nationale, 1963), abbreviated as *CTA*.

4. On the divine council, see Ps 82:1 (cp. CTA 15.2.11); Ps 89:6–8; Deut 32:8–9; 1 Kgs 22:19–22; Isa 6:1–12; Job 1:6). See Cross, *Canaanite Myth and Hebrew Epic,* pp. 177–181, 183, 185–186 on the divine council in Canaanite lore; pp. 186–190 on Yahweh and the divine council in Israelite tradition.

5. The imagery of victory over Sea is usually invoked in contexts dealing with the exodus or other acts of redemption: Isa 51:9–11; Ps 77:17–20; Isa 17:12–13; 27:1. For contexts where creation itself is in view, cf. Ps 29:10; Job 9:8; 26:11–13; 38:8–11. The connection with divine kingship could not be clearer in Ps 89:6–12. The imagery of conquering Sea/River carries with it reference to the establishment of *cosmos,* since that seems to be the burden of the notion of divine kingship in the culture of Canaan: what made the stories of Baal's victory over Sea and over Death "mythic" to their pre-Israelite auditors is precisely the life-and-death question they answer, whether the lord of fertility and life would prevail over the forces of chaos and desiccation. These stories can be read conveniently in the translation of Michael D. Coogan, *Stories from Ancient Canaan* (Philadelphia: Westminster, 1978), pp. 86–115, a translation of *CTA* 1–6.

6. Exod 15:17–18; Ps 29:1–2; Ps 89:6–9. The connection of the "house" with kingship is basic to the episode in *CTA* 3–4 (Coogan, *Stories,* pp. 94–104). Cf. also 2 Sam 5:11–12. For the feast, cf. Isa 25:6–9, and the grim transformation of the motif in Zeph 1:7.

7. I mean the term in the sense used by A. B. Lord, *The Singer of Tales* (Cambridge, Massachusetts: Harvard University Press, 1960), pp. 68–98. We can speak of a "pattern," not in any Jungian or myth-and-ritual sense, but simply in the sense of a well-known story line, where conflict with and victory over Sea is followed by ascension of the mountain enthronement, etc., as it is preceded by the theme of preliminaries to conflict ("going forth," "descending," "coming").

8. Cross, *Canaanite Myth and Hebrew Epic,* pp. 147–177, especially pp. 155–163.

9. Among myriad texts, see Num 10:35–36; Ps 68:2; Ps 18:2–20; Ps 69:1–3, 15–16.

10. Cf. below, n. 32.

11. Delbert Hillers, *Covenant: The History of a Biblical Idea* (Baltimore: Johns Hopkins, 1974) offers an excellent survey of covenant and its links with other institutions in Israel.

12. George E. Mendenhall, *The Tenth Generation* (Baltimore: Johns Hopkins, 1974), pp. 27–28, 144, 152–153, 188–189, 220–226; and "The Hebrew Conquest of Palestine," in *The Biblical Archaeologist Reader 3* (ed. Edward F. Campbell, Jr., and David Noel Freedman; Garden City, N.Y.: Doubleday, 1970), pp. 110–120, especially 117–119.

13. Mendenhall, *Tenth Generation,* pp. 122–141, and references there to the standard works of Bottéro and Greenberg; "Hebrew Conquest" 105–107. Manfred Weippert, *The Settlement of the Israelite Tribes in Palestine* (Studies in Biblical Theology 21; London: SCM Press, 1971), pp. 63–102, shows the complexity of the "Ḫabiru/Hebrew" question.

14. Mendenhall, *Tenth Generation,* pp. 142–153, 221–224. (Cf. 1 Sam 8:11–18).

15. See Walter Brueggemann, "Trajectories in Old Testament Literature and the Sociology of Ancient Israel," *Journal of Biblical Literature* 98 (1979) 161–185, especially 163–168.

16. Michael D. Coogan, "A Structural and Literary Analysis of the Song of Deborah," *Catholic Biblical Quarterly* 40 (1978) 143–144, 165–166, rightly warns against trying to reconstruct the details of a particular battle on the basis of what we find in the Song of Deborah. Poetry works by metonymy: the phrase about "shield and spear" typifies the situation of early Israel. Cf. the Song of Hannah, 1 Sam 2:1–10, for the same emphasis.

17. "The 'Vengeance' of Yahweh," *Tenth Generation,* pp. 69–104. Mendenhall's understanding of "vindication" is of a piece with his notions about the *ḫabiru,* political legitimacy *(ṣedeq),* covenant, and other concerns recurring in his writings; given the systematic interrelations of these ideas, an argument for his understanding of *nāqām* might almost be made (as the Scholastics would say) *ex convenientia.*

18. J. E. Lindsey, "Vengeance," *IDB Supplement* (ed. Keith Crim; Nashville: Abingdon, 1976), pp. 932–933.

19. "Cuts himself off," that is, in a radical way that calls into question the integrity and even existence of the political entity. Not every violation of law does this, and which offenses are thought to constitute fundamental "withdrawal" (to use Mendenhall's term) is a matter that varies from one political order to another.

20. Except in the Sefire Inscriptions, III:11–12, 22. See the forthcoming study by Wayne Pitard, "Amarna *ekēmu* and Hebrew *nāqām.*" Pitard shows that the word Mendenhall reads as a form of the root *nqm* is simply Akkadian *ekēmu* "to remove." Mendenhall argued (*Tenth Generation,* p. 79) that the Canaanite scribes used forms of *ekēmu* but were actually "using it in a way which corresponded to West Semitic *NQM,*" since *ekēmu* never means "rescue," as the Amarna forms in question do. Pitard demonstrates that the Akkadian word does have that meaning, and that the Amarna passages are not really evidence for the meaning of the root *nqm.*

21. Yahweh "saves" Israel, or raises up a judge or "savior" to save Israel, from the hand of their oppressors. Deut 20:4; Judg 2:16, 18; 3:9, 15,

31; 6:14, 15, 36–37; 7:2, 7; 10:12; 13:5; 15:18; 1 Sam 4:3; 7:8; 19:19; 11:3; 14:6, 23, 39; 17:47; 19:5; 2 Sam 8:6, 14; 23:10, 12; 2 Kgs 6:27; 13:5; 14:27; 19:19, 34.

22. Deut 20:4; Josh 10:6; Judg 2:16, 18; 3:9, 15, 31; 6:14, 15, 36–37; 7:2, 7; 8:22; 10:12, 14; 12:2, 3; 13:5; 15:18; 1 Sam 2:1 (cf. the parallelism with swallowing enemies); 4:3; 7:8; 9:16; 10:27; 11:3, 9, 13; 14:23, 45; 17:47; 19:5; 23:2, 5; 2 Sam 3:18; 8:6, 16; 10:11, 19; 19:3; 23:10, 12; 2 Kgs 5:1; 13:5, 17; 14:27; 16:7; 19:19, 34. The root *yš‘* does have a generalized sense of "helping" or extricating from some difficulty in Deut 22:27; Judg 6:31 (?); 1 Sam 10:19; 14:6 (?); 25:26, 31, 33 (where it is a question of redress); 2 Sam 23:5; 2 Kgs 6:26, 27. Deut 28:29, 31 probably have a military connotation.

23. Cf. above, n. 7. Lars Hartman, *Prophecy Interpreted* (Coniectanea Biblica New Testament Series 1; Lund: Gleerup, 1966), tries to establish apocalyptic patterns inductively, pp. 50–70.

24. See Klaus Koch, *The Rediscovery of Apocalyptic* (Studies in Biblical Theology 22; London: SCM Press, 1972), especially p. 131.

25. Jon Levenson, "The Davidic Covenant and Its Modern Interpreters," *Catholic Biblical Quarterly* 41 (1979) 205–219, would nuance this view. But see the article of Walter Brueggemann cited above, n. 15.

26. On the divine nature of kings, see Henri Frankfort, *Kingship and the Gods* (Chicago: University of Chicago Press, 1948). "Sons of El" means "members of the genus 'god' ": Cross, *Canaanite Myth,* pp. 45–46. This usage of "son" should not be taken as indicating paternity or kinship; it is the partitive usage familiar from (for example) Amos 7:14.

27. See 2 Kgs 16:7, and Philip J. Calderone, *Dynastic Oracle and Suzerainty Treaty* (Manila: Ateneo de Manila University, 1966).

28. 2 Sam 7:14; cf. Prov 3:12.

29. See James M. Robinson, "Jesus as Sophos and Sophia: Wisdom Tradition and the Gospels," in Robert L. Wilken (ed.), *Aspects of Wisdom in Judaism and Early Christianity* (Notre Dame, Indiana: University of Notre Dame Press, 1975), pp. 1–16.

30. Cf. Martin Hengel, *The Son of God* (Philadelphia: Fortress, 1976), pp. 44–45.

31. The parenetic or hortatory intention of Deuteronomy is seen not only in the discourse of the first eleven chapters but even in the laws of chaps. 12–26. The laws often are followed by a motivating clause: 13:3b, 5b, 10b, 17b–18; 14:2, 21a; 23b, 29b; 15:10b, 15; 16:12a, 20b; and so on. The specific commands and prohibitions are always put in the context of what Yahweh has done for Israel, the people's experience, the identity they are called to. In not a few cases, the laws themselves seem not so much to aim at regulating behavior as to inculcate a spirit which should inform behavior: be the sort of person who. . . . Cf., for example, 22:6–7.

32. W. L. Moran, "The Ancient Near Eastern Background of the Love of God in Deuteronomy," *Catholic Biblical Quarterly* 25 (1963) 77–87.

33. 4:37; 7:6–8, 12; 10:15.
34. 6:10–12; 8:12–17.
35. 7:7–8.
36. 9:4–6.
37. 8:17; cf. Judg 7:2.
38. When Monika Hellwig in this volume argues against a Christology that sees "Jesus' own freedom, will, creativity, initiative being initially or progressively eliminated as he fulfills to the letter an explicitly revealed blueprint" and that accordingly conceives us, as disciples, "more saved and saving if the dangerously unpredictable elements of our humanity, the imaginative and creative capacities to envisage and shape a better world, are held in abeyance, so that the divine can activate the proper plan," we of course recognize this as inauthentic. The Incarnation does not diminish human potentialities but liberates them. Yet to insist on the centrality of human freedom and creativity—the capacity to "make history"—can easily lend itself to a kind of "works righteousness," which sees our human dignity and fulfillment as consisting in the capacity always to be in control, to achieve maximum predictability in all aspects of our life, to shape nature and events according to what we freely choose as the good. It is not this capacity to be in control that constitutes our humanity but the capacity for reverence, appreciation, wonder, "thanksgiving." See George Grant, *Technology and Empire* (Toronto: Anansi, 1969), who shows how the Liberal tradition mediates an understanding of man *(sic)* as one who (to borrow from Deut 8:17) says in his heart, "My own power and the strength of my own hand have gotten me this wealth."
39. Klaus Koch, "Gibt es ein Vergeltungsdogma im Alten Testament?," *Zeitschrift für Theologie und Kirche* 52 (1955) 1–42, shows how the almost universally accepted notion of divine punishment is simply not found in the Hebrew Old Testament. Israelite thought rather takes the line that "as one sows so one reaps": one's deeds themselves entail certain consequences. His analysis seems to me convincing.
40. "The Themes of the Book of Kings and the Structure of the Deuteronomistic History," *Canaanite Myth,* pp. 274–289.
41. Cf. 2 Sam 15:24–26; 1 Sam 25:26, 31, 33, and Mendenhall, *Tenth Generation,* pp 94–95, 100.
42. 2 Sam 16:12 (LXX), and cf. Ps 132:1, *'unnôtô.*
43. See Cross, *Canaanite Myth,* pp. 343–345.
44. Mal 3:18.
45. Isa 29:15; Jer 12:4; Ezek 8:12; 9:9; Ps 10:11–14; 14 (53):2–3 (English 1–2); 33:13–15; 73:11; 94:7; Job 22:13; cf. Exod 2:25.
46. Cf. n. 41 above.
47. The "access" *(mahl^{e}kîm)* to the heavenly court granted the high priest Joshua in Zech 3:7 surely is of a piece with the vision in Daniel 7; cp. the *eisodos* of Hebrews 10:19.

48. The fourfold progression that follows is by no means meant to correspond to any sort of development in early Christology, nor is it meant to be a typology. It is simply an expository device.

49. For example, Jer 26:15 seems to be echoed in Matt 27:25; Wis 2:18 in Matt 27:43; and so on. See John R. Donahue, *Are You the Christ?* (SBL Dissertation Series 10; Missoula, Montana: Society of Biblical Literature, 1973), pp. 71–77, where the use of Ps 27:12 and Ps 35:11 in Mark 14:56–59 is studied. These examples could be multiplied indefinitely.

50. Ps 89:26; with Mark 6:49 and parallels, compare Job 9:8 (LXX).

51. Dan 7:14 naturally comes to mind when we read in Mark 2:10, "That you may know that the son of man has authority [*exousia*] . . ." since both Greek versions of the Daniel passage depict *exousia* being conferred on the "one like a son of man." The difficulties and complexities of the "son of man" question are set forth and clarified by Joseph A. Fitzmyer, "The New Testament Title 'Son of Man' Philologically Considered," in his *A Wandering Aramean* (SBLMS 25; Missoula, Montana: Scholars Press, 1979), pp. 143–160.

52. See the comments of Ernst Käsemann on the "interpretive insertion" of the words "death on a cross" (*thanatou de staurou:* better, perhaps, "a cross-death") in Phil 2:8, in "A Critical Analysis of Philippians 2:5–11," in Herbert Braun et al., *God and Christ: Existence and Province (Journal for Theology and the Church* 5; Tübingen: J. C. B. Mohr/New York: Harper & Row, 1968), pp. 75–76. The centrality of "cross" in New Testament thought emerges from the survey of the use made in the New Testament writings of Deut 21:22–23 done by Max Wilcox in his article " 'Upon the Tree'—Deut 21:22–23 in the New Testament," *Journal of Biblical Literature* 96 (1977) 85–99.

53. The various views of the meaning and provenience of the *kyrios* title in New Testament Christology are conveniently summarized by Joseph A. Fitzmyer, "The Semitic Background of the New Testament *Kyrios*-Title," *A Wandering Aramean* (n. 51 above), pp. 115–142, especially pp. 115–117. Against those who see the origin of the title in the world of Hellenistic pagan religion, Fitzmyer shows that it reflects a divine title in both Greek and Aramaic, used in the Palestinian Jewish and, later, Palestinian Jewish-Christian world. Martin Hengel puts the matter thus: " . . . statements in the Old Testament in which the inexpressible divine name . . . was used, were now transferred directly to the *Kyrios Jesus.* Paul can already give Joel 3.5, 'Everyone who calls upon the name of the Lord will be saved' . . . , as the basis for the key acclamation ['Jesus is Lord *(Kyrios)*']" (*The Son of God* [n. 30 above], p. 77).

As to the meaning of the title when applied to Jesus, Fr. Fitzmyer concludes from a careful survey of New Testament usage that it "was first applied to Jesus of the parousia and that the general extension of it brought about the gradual retrojection of it to other phases or states of his existence, even to that of his earthly mission" (p. 129).

54. Fitzmyer, "The New Testament *Kyrios*-Title," 131. The phrase "on a par with" is used in the sense of "sharing in some sense in the transcendence of Yahweh," and is carefully chosen to indicate that this "is meant in an egalitarian sense, not in an identifying sense, since Jesus was never hailed as [*'abbâ*]." This language is used so as to avoid a certain inexactitude that crept into scholarly discussion of this matter, a confusion between *Gleichsetzung* and *Identifizierung* (cf. p. 142, n. 90), and also, as it seems, to bypass the anachronism (from the New Testament point of view) of categories like "essence" and "nature," terms which it took Christian tradition hundreds of years of theological reflection to introduce into Christological discourse.

That it is hardly unthinkable that divine status would be attributed to a man in Jewish thought is seen from the discussion of Hengel, *The Son of God,* pp. 46–47, where he adduces titles like "prince of the world" and "the little Yahweh"(!) attributed to "Metatron" in III Enoch, and the interpretation of Akiba of the thrones of Dan 7:9: one is for God and the other for David (i.e., the Lord's anointed). See also Hengel's discussion of the figure of Michael-Melchizedek (pp. 80–81): " . . . even in Palestine itself, the Essenes of Qumran in their eschatological exegesis could transfer Old Testament passages, the original text of which clearly meant God himself, to a mediator or redeemer figure near to God. . . . The kingdom of God is identical with that of his vizir."

55. Col 1:15–17; Eph 1:10; 3:9–11.

56. Mark 10:42–45; Luke 22:25–27.

57. José Porfirio Miranda, *Marx and the Bible* (Maryknoll, New York: Orbis, 1974) is an especially important book. See my reviews in *Theological Studies* 36 (1975) 825–826, and *Cross Currents* (1978) 110–112. Also, John Howard Yoder, *The Politics of Jesus* (Grand Rapids, Michigan: Eerdmans, 1972).

3
Christ's Victory Over the Powers

Joseph Weber

The affirmation of Jesus Christ as Lord of one's personal life can be understood by most Christians. One's faith is lived out in one's daily, personal life. It makes a difference in how a person experiences and understands life. Christians also can usually understand that Jesus Christ is Lord of the Church. In the community of the Church this lordship is celebrated in worship and prayer, and responded to in obedience. Can the Christian also say that Jesus Christ is Lord in such a way that he is Lord over the structures of the world? Christ exercises his lordship in the world through the Church, but is he also to be affirmed as Lord in the world apart from the Church? Because his name is not named in the world and because there is nothing witnessing directly to his lordship in the world, there is a tendency in the Church to limit Christ's lordship to the life of the believer and to the life of the Christian community. Such a limitation has often resulted in a severe reduction of the relevance of Christian faith. If Jesus is only Lord of my personal life or only Lord of the Church, how can Christian faith be relevant to the great political, economic and social issues confronting humankind? The thesis of this essay is that Jesus Christ is indeed Lord of the world and it is from this lordship that Christian faith gains its significance for the economic, political and social issues confronting human life throughout history.[1]

To ask theologically the question of whether Jesus Christ can be understood as Lord of the world does not imply that his lordship over the structures of the world is evident or knowable apart from the Church. The confession that Christ is Lord over the structures of the world is a confession of the faith of the Church. It can be made only from within the Church. However, this confession does say something about the world in distinction from the Church.

There are two basic reasons for examining the meaning of the confession that Jesus is Lord of the world. The first reason is to understand better the Gospel itself. There are tendencies in our churches to limit the Gospel to the believing individual. Some Christians confess that Christ died for their personal sins and stop there. Some say that Christ comes to them in their personal experience and frees them or integrates their life. He is their Lord. But how is he their Lord? Can this personal reality of faith be understood apart from how Jesus Christ is Lord for others, for the Church and for the world? When one reads New Testament passages such as Matthew 25:31–32, 28:18, and Mark 14:62, one discovers that the first proclamation of Jesus as Lord affirms his lordship not just over individuals, but over the whole cosmos. Therefore, in order to understand the fullness of faith we must understand what it means to say that Jesus is Lord of the world.

The second reason for examining the nature of the lordship of Christ over the world is to understand what this means for the life of the Church in the world. Has Jesus Christ made any difference in the world? If we can truly and faithfully confess Jesus Christ as Lord, does not this confession compel a new understanding of Christian responsibility for the structures of the world? If the eschatological hope of the Church is that in Jesus Christ God has acted to bring about his will for his creation, then the Church is not an end in itself, but is the real sign of what God has done and is doing in Jesus Christ for all of the world.

The Structures of the World and the Principalities and Powers

Before we can explain the meaning of Jesus Christ's lordship over the world, we must make clear what is meant by the word "world." In the common usage employed until now in this essay, it means the total unity of nature and culture which is the matrix of all human existence. In this sense, the Church is also part of the world. Sociologically, one can only regard the Church as another institution in the world. Theologically, in its own self-understanding, the Church is understood as either in some way apart from the world or as a unique reality in the world. It is not just one other institution in the world, where the world is defined as the total unity of nature and culture.

This common usage, however, is not the usual understanding of the world in the New Testament. From the standpoint of New Testament theology, two aspects of the use of the word "world" need to be observed. The first is the world as God's creation (Acts 17:24); it is the totality of all that is created (Jn 1:10; 1 Cor 3:22). To speak of the world as creation is a confession of faith: its beginning and its end, its meaning and its purpose are not inherent in the world. God is its creator. However, God's rule over all creation is not unambiguously affirmed in the New Testament. God as "Lord of heaven and earth" (Matt 11:25) is not said to exercise his rule over the world directly, fully, and unambiguously. The final rule of God is always the object of eschatological hope.

God's sovereignty is not exercised unambiguously in the present world. The second aspect of the world, then, is the world as *kosmos,* as fallen creation, the place of darkness where the evil powers exercise their authority. In Apocalyptic Judaism this ambiguity of God's reign is expressed by the concept of two ages. "For this reason the Most High made not one world but two" (2 Esdr 7:51). This world waits with eager longing for the coming world, but at the moment is the dominion of Satan. Such a twofold understanding of "world" is part of the background of Jesus' ministry and is taken over into the thought of the early Church.

Jesus and the New Testament Church have no speculative interest in the demonic powers that control the present world or age. They are not subjects in themselves which the Christian writers discuss. These demonic powers serve only within the drama of salvation. Both Jew and Gentile would have some understanding of what a reference to being subjugated to the demonic forces was meant to convey. Such an understanding of the world as subjected to demonic forces, or fate, or astrological powers was based on the common experience of alienation, helplessness, and political disintegration of the peoples of the time. Within early Christianity the understanding of the world under the principalities and powers, under God's judgment, and in need of redemption reaches a terminological clarity in the letters of Paul and in the gospel of John. In both Paul and John the world is not the place of the unambiguous rule of God, but it is the fallen world, the old age under the power of Satan, the place where God's judgment is to take place (1 Cor 3:19; 5:10). This use of *kosmos* has its roots in Apocalyptic thought (1 Cor 2:8: "rulers of this age," 1 Cor 7:31; 2 Cor 4:4; Rom 3:19; Jn 8:12). Christ comes into this world, the place of darkness and the locus of God's judgment (Jn 7:7; 12:30). God's good creation has been perverted and subjugated to Satan. There is no speculative answer given in the New Testament to the question of how this came about or why God has allowed it. The New Testament is not interested in the demonic in any theoretical way. Rather, the demonic powers are relevant only within the divine drama of Christ's victory over them.

The terminology used to name the demonic forces is quite varied: principalities, lords, gods, angels, demons, spirits, elements, Satan and the devil. (See Rom 8:38; 1 Cor 15:24; Eph 1:21; Col 1:16; 2:10, 15; Jn 12:31; 1 Cor 2:6, 8; 2 Cor 4:4; 12:7; Gal 4:3, 9; Rev 12:7–9; Mk 1:23; 3:22, *et al.*) The names all refer to the same reality. They are all expressions of the power of Satan.[2]

Although the names given to these demonic forces are personal, the main emphasis is on their power. They express collectively the power of Satan. They threaten and pervert creation as it was intended by God. In 1 Cor 15:26 Paul says that death is the last power to be destroyed. The demonic as the harbinger of death brings distortion and chaos into creation.

The demonic is not an abstract force that can be separated from human existence or from the social and political structures of the world. The demonic forces exist in and through structures. They enter human existence in such a way as to be inherent in human existence. In the exorcism narrative in Mark the demon entered a human being, causing the disruption of life (Mk 1:23; 9:21). The ultimate meaning of the exorcism is eschatological: the power of God establishes his kingdom against the demonic which has distorted his creation. The same motif is found in the controversy stories in Mark's gospel. Jesus is opposed by the Pharisees and by the authority of Herod, who see him as a threat to the established order of their power (Mk 3:6). In Mk 2:1–12 Jesus' healing power and his authority to forgive sins are seen together. Jesus' ministry is one of healing and restoring existence to what God intended in his creation. His ministry meets resistance on the part of the Pharisees, Herodians, and finally of the powers in Jerusalem because such a ministry is a threat to their power. One can see that the demonic is expressed in mindsets, in religious institutions, as well as in political power structures. The role of Satan in the course of this opposition to Jesus is clearly expressed by Luke: "Then Satan entered into Judas Iscariot . . ." (Lk 22:3). The whole passion narrative is placed in this perspective. The relationship between the demonic powers and historical events and structures is apparent in 1 Cor 2:8: "None of the rulers of this age understood this; for if they had, they would not have crucified the Lord of glory." Most exegetes agree that the term "rulers of this age" refers to the demonic powers that brought Jesus to the cross, so that Paul is not referring directly to the Roman authorities. Yet Paul knew that Jesus' death was an historical event perpetrated by Jews and Romans. The demonic acts in and through historical structures, distorting them into instruments of death.

In 1 Thess 2:16 we learn that Satan has twice prevented Paul from coming to the Thessalonians. Paul does not inform us of the specific instances, but Satan uses events and structures to prevent the spread of the Gospel.

Paul's understanding of the Law profoundly illustrates how the demonic can pervert God's intention for his creation. The Law was given by God as an order serving life. It was good and holy. Now, however, it has been perverted by the power of sin. What was intended to serve life, has become a means of death and a curse (Rom 7:1–3; Gal 3:13). Structures of creation which were intended by God to serve life are used by the demonic forces to bring death.

In Revelation, Chapter 13, Satan in the form of the dragon gives his power to the beast, the Roman Empire. The second beast in 13:11 is the embodiment of that very power given to the first beast allowing it to exercise its deception. Through great signs it draws all humans to it. Satan acts through the structures of the world, deceiving humankind. The structures that are originally intended by God are not evil in themselves, but become evil under the influence of the principalities and powers.

This language about the principalities and powers is, of course, profoundly mythological. However, the New Testament is not interested in mythological speculation. It is interested in the drama of salvation. The mythological language is used to expose the demonic reality embodied in human existence and in the structures of the world.

> When the principalities penetrate the world and the circumstances of human life in order to exercise their power through them, they thereby conceal themselves in the world and in the everyday life of mankind. They withdraw from sight into the men, elements, and institutions through which they make their power felt. To seem not to appear is part of their essence.[3]

The language of sociological description cannot get at the reality of the demonic. To seem not to appear is the essence of the demonic. The function of mythological language is to unveil the demonic reality that penetrates the *kosmos* and corrupts human existence. It exposes the terror and alienation that are common to all humankind. The demonic is not simply the disobedience of human beings or the experience of alienation. It is not essentially psychological, but has an objective quality. We can point to elements in social structures that correspond to what the New Testament exposes as demonic. For instance, in an analysis of American technological society Herbert Marcuse has written:

> Under such conditions, decline of freedom and opposition is not a matter of moral or intellectual deterioration or corruption. It is rather an objective societal process insofar as the production and distribution of an increasing quality of goods and services make compliance a rational technological attitude.[4]

Can one not say that the apparent rationality of technological civilization is leading us to a breakdown in order and meaning and therefore closer to death? The great irony is that the conscious intention of such an attitude is to create greater productivity and improve life, while at the same time there is concealed the desire for self-affirmation and for greater profits. One must understand the demonic character of technological societies within a dialectical process.

In his essay Father Land has pointed out the dialectical character of social structures. They grow out of the nature of the human to form a world with language, symbols, and structures. These structures come to have then a reality of their own as they are objectivized and become autonomous. They then are internalized and shape the humanity in which they originally had their basis. Examples would be gender roles, values concerning the nature of the family, the state, positive law, order-defining economic structures, etc. In this dialogical process one can see how the demonic is both personal and objective. The demonic does have a *sui generis* quality which is rooted in structures, institutions and historical situations. "So then it is no longer I that do it, but sin which dwells within me" (Rom 7:27).

The Lordship of Christ over the Principalities and Powers

The earliest Christology of the Church is the identification of Jesus after the Easter event with the Son of Man.[6] Embedded in the trial scene in the gospel of Mark is a saying that combines Daniel 7:13 and Psalm 110:1. Jesus' exaltation is proclaimed. He is already the Son of Man. As exalted Son of Man he is the one coming to execute judgment. It is important to note that in both Daniel 7:11–13 and Psalm 110, God's defeat of his enemies is mentioned. "Sit at my right hand, till I make your enemies your footstool . . ."[7] Christ's exaltation is the beginning of the eschatological drama that leads to the establishment of God's reign over his creation. In this earliest Christology Jesus is proclaimed not primarily as the Lord of the Church, but as the Lord of the whole cosmos who will execute God's judgment over his enemies.

The eschatological proclamation of Jesus' lordship after the Easter event is in continuity with the ministry of the historical Jesus. Jesus interpreted his exorcisms as the eschatological sign of the coming of the Kingdom of God (Lk 11:20). He understood his ministry as an entering into the strong man's house, binding him, and thereby destroying Satan's power (Mk 3:27). The Easter event is the vindication of Jesus' struggle against the demonic during his earthly struggle. Jesus' exaltation raises his struggle in proclaiming the coming of the Kingdom of God to a cosmic level. He is established now as the king of the kingdom which he proclaimed as the Kingdom of God.

In the earliest *kerygma* the full meaning of Christ's exaltation was not realized. However, under the influence of the experience of the Spirit, which Ernst Käsemann calls enthusiasm,[8] and the unexpected success of the Gentile mission, the Church develops its understanding of the meaning of Christ's lordship over the enemies of God. Jesus is acclaimed Lord (*Kyrios*) in opposition to all other claims to lordship (1 Cor 8:6–16; Phil 2:11). The fundamental centrality of this understanding of Christology is evident in the use of Psalm 110 throughout the New Testament (Mk 14:62; Acts 2:34; 1 Cor 15–27; Eph 1:20, 22; Heb 1:13).

The interpretation of the exaltation of Jesus as the victory over the demonic powers reaches its climax in the great hymns of the Hellenistic Church. In the pre-Pauline hymn quoted in Philippians 2:6–11, Christ enters into the realm of this world which is where humankind is held enslaved. He shares human slavery and even dies in giving himself for humankind. His coming and dying break the power that the demonic holds over humanity. God exalts him and his lordship is proclaimed to all the demonic powers who must now bend their knees before him. Clearly, Christ is regarded as not just Lord of the Church but of the whole world.

The gospel of Matthew ends with an enthronement scene. It is not a resurrection appearance scene, but the manifestation of Jesus' exaltation: "All authority in heaven and earth has been given to me" (Matt 29:18). Jesus' exaltation is the basis of the mission of the Church: "Go, therefore, and make disciples of all nations" (Matt 28:19). We can observe from these texts that the mission of the Church is not to establish Christ's lordship in the world, but to witness to his lordship as already established by God.

In passages such as Col 1:15–20; Phil 2:5–11; and Eph 1:20–22, it appears that the lordship of Christ has already been fully established, although it should be noted that the victory even in these hymns is not evident in the world. These passages most likely are liturgical in origin. As doxological expressions proclaiming the lordship of the exalted Christ over the cosmos, as celebrated in the

Church, these passages must necessarily be compared with other passages more closely related to Jewish Apocalyptic where one finds an eschatological reservation (see especially 1 Cor 15:25–26). The final victory is assured, but not yet made fully manifest. The battle still rages. The world is the place of the great struggle between Christ and the principalities and powers. The victory over the demonic is assured, indeed has already begun, but the demonic can still exercise its power (Rev 12:11 –12).

Obviously the world is not under the lordship of Christ in any way that is unambiguously apparent to humankind. The language of the New Testament is not descriptive of things as we see them empirically.[9] The confession of Jesus Christ's lordship over the world is a doxological expression of the faith of the Church—the community which acknowledges and lives already in a new reality. The world is still a place of disobedience and struggle, but there is now a fundamental difference. Christ is reigning as king over the world (*basileuein,* 1 Cor 15:24). The Church now lives in the world on the basis of this kingship. It lives in the eschatological reality that the seer expresses in Revelation 11:15: "The kingdom of the world (*kosmos*) has become the Kingdom of our Lord and of his Christ, and he shall reign for ever and ever."

The Lordship of Christ and the Life of the Church in the World

The hope of the Church is not just a hope for the future. It is founded on the decisive change that has already taken place in the world through Christ's victory over the principalities and powers. The principalities and powers have no future; therefore they can have no ultimate claim upon us. In the baptismal preface to the hymn in Colossians 1:15–20 the Church confesses that "he has taken us out of the power of darkness and created a place for us in the Kingdom of the Son" (Col 1:13). The Church is the new creation which lives in the Kingdom of the Son. It is directly under the lordship of Christ (see the essay by Father Dulles). But the Church knows that this new creation is intended for the whole of God's creation. It is a *pars pro toto* and only when it understands itself in relationship to all of creation does it truly understand itself. Therefore, the first responsibility of the Church to the world is to be the Church. The watchword of the Oxford Conference of 1937, not long before the tragic outbreak of World War II, was "let the Church be the Church."[10] Such a slogan did not mean that the Church was an end in itself, but that the Church exists in and for the world as the sign of the new creation. The Church is the sign in the world of Christ's victory over the principalities and powers, making known even to them that their power has been taken away. ". . . that through the Church the manifold wisdom of God might now be made known to the principalities and powers in the heavenly places" (Eph 3:10). Because the Church is an obvious threat to the principalities and powers, it is under continual attack. The principalities and powers exercise their power through social and political structures and historical situations, which means that the struggle in which the Church is to be involved is not an abstract theological struggle, but a struggle involving all the social, political, and economic structures of the world. Because the Church is the sign of Christ's victory over the demonic powers it belongs to its very nature to be under attack—usually either by direct persecution or else by subtle forces of adjustment and acculturation which wish to make the Church essentially innocuous. The world rejects the proclamation of the Church that Jesus Christ is Lord because the world is the place where the demonic powers are still trying to exercise their power. The time of the demonic powers, however, is limited. Their fight is one of desperation (Rev 12:12). The primary mission of the Church, therefore, is not just to remind the world of moral principles, or to evangelize individuals, or to assure its own institutional life. Rather, the Church is engaged in a struggle against the demonic in order to proclaim and in order to be a sign of Jesus Christ's lordship over the whole world.[11] The Church is called by God to live in the world as if it were already fully God's renewed creation (Col 2:20–21).

Fundamental to the Church's life in the new creation are the sacraments of baptism and the Eucharist. Baptism is not just a sacrament of the regeneration of the individual. In baptism the Christian, through Christ's death, is removed from the realm of the demonic and enters into the new creation. It is the actualization of the new creation in the life of the Church in the existence of every believer. When one is in Christ through baptism one is a new creation (not a new creature) (see 2 Cor 5:17).[12] The sacrament is not to be understood in terms only of personal salvation, but in terms of God's claim upon all of his creation through the lordship of Christ.

In the celebration of the Eucharist the Church manifests itself as the sign of the new creation. The lordship of Christ is proclaimed and the demonic is rejected (1 Cor 10:21). What happens in the Eucharist is not the celebration of a cultic act in an isolated sacral place, but the celebration of Christ's lordship over the world. Those who celebrate the Eucharist affirm the lordship of Christ and reject every political, economic and social structure that manifests the demonic. If there is not justice and love in the community celebrating the Eucharist, the Church does not discern the body of Christ (see Father Haughey's essay in this volume). The greatest profanation of the body of Christ in the Eucharist is not cultic, but the lack of justice and love in the Christian community. St. Paul admonishes the Christians in Corinth because in their celebration there are divisions, lack of concern for the hungry, and a drunken disregard of the concerns of others (1 Cor 11:17–21). One cannot celebrate the Eucharist and practice injustice in social, economic or political structures. If the Eucharist is the celebration of the lordship of Christ it denies all other claims of lordship, be they economic, social or political. In this sense, then, every Eucharist is acutely political. In celebrating the Eucharist the Church rejects the claim of the principalities and powers which they exercise in many and subtle ways in the structures of the world.

Because the Church knows that the structures of the world are ultimately under the lordship of Christ, the Church lives in the world as in the new creation. It struggles in the world against all the forces that pervert structures. It has responsibility beyond its own institutional life for the life of the world. I have been using "Church" in this essay to mean the new eschatological reality of the people of God, the body of Christ, the community that consciously lives under the lordship of Christ. From a sociological viewpoint the Church is also, of course, a social institution among other institutions. The Church does witness in the world as institution and does exercise its influence as an institution, but it cannot be understood as being fully the Church if it is identified only as a social institution (see Father

Dulles' essay in this volume). The responsibility of the Church is not to impose its institutional life upon the world. Such an undertaking would make the Church into just another institution with its own power claims. The lordship of Christ is not imposed upon the world through the power of the Church as an institution. The Church is a sign of the lordship of Christ in the world and a witness to what the world is called to be by its creator. Although the final victory of Christ will be manifest at the end of time, the new creation is being actualized in this world through the reign of Christ who is putting all of the creator's enemies under his feet. In this sense the Church is an instrument of Christ's reign: not in itself defeating evil, but being used by Christ in its life and witness as an instrument of his victory (see Rom 16:20). Where genuine humanity is called forth, where life conquers death, where structures are freed to express God's intention for humanity, there the Church must be involved because every relative expression of justice and love realizes the eschatological lordship of Jesus Christ.[13]

Jesus Is Lord

How does the Church discern, in the structures of the world, where the lordship of Christ is being exercised and the demonic is being defeated? It is important to remember that *Jesus* is Lord. The exaltation of Jesus to be Christ and Lord is God's vindication of his loving, courageous and sacrificial ministry which led to his death on the cross. God did not bring about the new creation in a triumphalistic power play, but through sacrificial love. It is Jesus, the son of Mary and Joseph, the one who invited sinners and tax collectors to eat with him, the one who proclaimed good news to the poor, the one who refused to accept the status quo and who did not join the Zealots in violent opposition to Rome, the one who endured in love to the end—this Jesus is the Lord. His way of love is reflected even in the great mythological hymns of the Hellenistic Church. In Philippians 2:7 we read that Christ emptied himself and became a slave—a slave to the demonic forces whose defeat is manifest at the end of the hymn in Philippians 2:11. Although the hymn describes the drama of salvation in mythological terms, it has its roots in the life of Jesus—a life of service and sacrifice that led to his death. The Gospel memory of the life of Jesus served as a basis of the Church's discernment of how the lordship of Christ is operative in the world.

Jesus made it clear that structures are all relative and are not ends in themselves. They are to serve humanity. He radically reverses the meaning of the Law (Mk 7:15). He invites the ritually unclean and the tax collectors to eat with him. Such an invitation is a radical reversal of the religious values of the Pharisees, causing them to oppose Jesus (Mk 2:15–16; Matt 1:18–19). He disobeys the Sabbath laws in order to serve human lives (Mk 2:27). In a disputation with the Pharisees Jesus rejects the casuistry in the marriage laws that allowed a husband simply to divorce his wife. A divorce in Jesus' society put a woman into a precarious social and economic situation. Jesus affirms marriage by referring to the creation narrative. Marriage is to serve the humanity of God's creation; it is not an end in itself (Mk 10:29). Both marriage as an institution and the laws about marriage are to be tested by whether they serve humanity. A sign of the demonic is when structures and institutions implicitly claim to be ends in themselves. If the tendency of the demonic is to "withdraw from sight into the men and elements and institutions through which they make their power felt," then we must refrain from any direct identification of what is with the will of God (see Rom 1:24, 26, 28). Jesus rejects the claims of the religious and social structures of his time to express the will of God. He relativizes them in light of the eschatological reality of the Kingdom of God.

Paul writes: "For you know the grace of our Lord Jesus Christ, that though he was rich, yet for your sake he became poor" (2 Cor 8:9). As in Philippians 2, there is here a description of the great drama of salvation where Christ enters the poverty of the world. Such a description of poverty in mythological terms can only be convincing if it has its root in the poverty of Jesus and his ministry to the poor. Jesus did not make an ideal out of poverty, but he made clear that the poor are the special object of God's concern. The poor are able in a unique way to appreciate the eschatological mercy of God (see Lk 16:19–31). They do not attempt to establish their own power over creation. This tradition is reflected in the name Christians in Jerusalem applied to themselves: "the poor" (Gal 2:10; Rom 15:26).

Jesus commanded a man to sell all and to give to the poor (Mk

10:21). He proclaimed good news to the poor: "Blessed are you poor, for yours is the Kingdom of God" (Matt 11:5). "But woe to you rich" (Lk 6:20, 24). The poor are blessed because they have not used power structures to gain their own good. Jesus' relation to the poor must be seen in the context of the exploitative structures of Palestine under Roman occupation. In Jesus' time the rich were becoming richer. Taxes were a great burden and there was over-population.[14] Jesus' ministry was not just to isolated spiritual needs, but had direct relevance to the economic, political and social structures of his society. His lordship now is a lordship for the poor and the oppressed and a judgment against the rich (see the special role of the poor in Luke's gospel: 14:13, 21; 4:18; 19:8–9).

In relationship to the political structures of Palestine under Roman occupation, Jesus neither advocated a passive acceptance nor a violent resistance. The proclamation of the Kingdom of God was not directly a political program. Jesus cannot be identified with the Pharisees, who ordered life as they found it with the interpretation of the Law. He cannot be ranked among the Essenes, who withdrew from social responsibility in protest, waiting for a final act of God at the end of time. Jesus did not support the resistance fighters, who tried to overthrow Roman occupation in hope that then the Kingdom of God would be established. Jesus did not resort to physical violence to destroy structures.

Among his disciples were both a tax-collector and a resistance fighter (Matt 10:3; Lk 6:15). Because the Kingdom of God was already being realized in his ministry, Jesus invited others to live in this reality. Jesus' proclamation and action allowed and invited people to live in the world as a new creation. He invited and thereby allowed humans to be as God intended them to be. Thereby, he initiated a new ethos, a specific way of being in the world and with others, a gracious and courageous celebration of the presence of God. Celebration means a total response of the human community as an act of thanksgiving for what God has done. This celebration is more radical than a political program because it means a continual disruption of the demonic to make room for the new creation in the world. The ethos of this celebration is the joy and freedom gained through Christ's victory. Yet the joy and freedom are known through suffering love.

The cross defines both the life of Jesus and the life of the post-resurrection community. In Mark 14:62 the Son of Man is exalted, but it is the same Son of Man who suffered. The cross is not just a way station to the exaltation, but remains the sign of exaltation in the world. It is the place where the demonic is being defeated. Suffering love is the way of the people who confess Jesus as Lord (MK 8:34). The great hymm of victory in Philippians 2:5–11 is used by Paul to call the community to love and humility. After the defeat of the principalities and powers by Christ is asserted in Colossians 2:15, there follows a section calling for a life of freedom from the elemental spirits of the universe, which has been achieved through Christ's death. In Christ's death we also die to the demonic (see also Gal 6:14). The cross is the sign of the exaltation of Christ, which defines the life of the Church in the world. The world has been freed from the principalities and powers through the sacrificial suffering of Jesus on the cross, who as exalted Lord does not cease to be the Christ crucified (1 Cor 1:23). Jesus' life and death are the paradigms for the Church's life in the world (see the papers of Fathers Clarke and McDermott, who concentrate especially on Jesus as paradigm).

The eschatological hope in which the Church lives because of Christ's victory over the principalities and powers is a hope for all of the world. The Church as the new creation is the sign that this new creation is intended for all the world. The lordship of Christ is exercised both in the Church and in the world. Both live in the light of his victory over the principalities and powers. From this standpoint of faith it does indeed make sense to speak of Christ's lordship over social structures. Fundamentally, this is a doxological confession: it is what the Church celebrates, what it proclaims, that from which it lives. However, the lordship of Christ says something about the world and calls for the Church's responsibility in this world. The world is shown what it really is by the obedience of the Church which has the courage to live in the world as the new creation under the sign of the cross.

NOTES

1. To put this concern into a different terminology one can say that the biblical vision of redemption applies to all of creation. An order of redemption cannot be clearly separated from an order of creation. It is not biblically sufficient to assert God's sovereignty over the world only through God's providence. It is God, the Holy Trinity, Creator and Redeemer, who is sovereign over the whole world.

2. Heinrich Schlier, *Principalities and Powers in the New Testament* (New York: Herder and Herder, 1961), p. 16.

3. *Ibid.*, p. 29.

4. Herbert Marcuse, *One Dimensional Man* (Boston: Beacon Press, 1964), p. 48.

5. Lordship in this essay is not restricted to the title *Kyrios,* but includes all the Christological titles that express authority, power and rule.

6. See Ferdinand Hahn, *The Titles of Jesus in Christology* (London: Lutterworth Press, 1969), pp. 28–34; and Heinz Eduard Toedt, *Der Menschensohn in der synoptischen Ueberlieferung* (Guetersloh: Verlaghaus Gerd Mohn, 1963), pp. 207–212.

7. Hans Conzelmann, *Outline of the Theology of the New Testament* (New York: Harper & Row, 1969), pp. 68–76.

8. Ernst Käsemann, *New Testament Questions Today* (Philadelphia: Fortress Press, 1969), p. 124.

9. "For the Hellenistic Church, therefore, Christ's dethroning of the principalities and powers is primarily a heavenly event which has not yet become known everywhere on earth, not yet everywhere verified, still awaits completion and, for this reason, obligates the earthly community to mission." Käsemann, *op. cit.,* p. 128.

10. See Nils Ehrenstrom, "Movements for International Friendship and Life and Work," in *A History of the Ecumenical Movement 1517–1948,* Rouse and Neill, editors (London: Society for Promoting Christian Knowledge, 1953), p. 591.

11. "For a monumental struggle against the powers of darkness pervades the whole history of man. The battle was joined from the very origins of the world and will continue until the last day, as the Lord attested." Vatican II, "Pastoral Constitution on the Church in the Modern World," par. 37.

12. To translate the Greek word *Ktisis* here as "new creature" would miss the cosmic scope of the language used by Paul, which has behind it the Apocalyptic conception of two ages: "The old has passed away, the new has come." See Rom 8:19–23, where the same word is used for creation. See also Gal 6:14–15.

13. "Earthly progress must be carefully distinguished from the growth of Christ's Kingdom. Nevertheless, to the extent that the former can con-

tribute to the better ordering of human society, it is of vital concern to the Kingdom of God." Vatican II, *op. cit.,* par. 39.

14. Gerd Theissen, *Sociology of Early Palestinian Christianity* (Philadelphia: Fortress Press, 1978), pp. 33–46.

4
Power and Parable in Jesus' Ministry

Brian O. McDermott, S.J.

One of the trickiest issues in any discussion of social structures and their transformation is the problem of motivation. What motivates someone to get up and act in a creative and fruitful way vis-à-vis the social structures which encompass us? How are people touched so that they discover resources and energies which empower them to stick with it, once they have begun to be engaged in the struggle for a more human world? For the Christian, the question is even more pointed. In what ways can believers draw on their faith for motivation to think, feel and act in a socially responsible manner, and in a manner which opens up horizons beyond those of self, family, or intimate friends?

People, Paul Ricoeur assures us, are not motivated by direct appeals to their wills, but by experiencing their imaginations being touched by someone or something that excites them into hoping and acting. Taking this hint seriously, this essay will explore in a modest way the relation of Christian imagination to the social fabric of our lives, by exploring how Jesus, the center and basis of Christian faith, was an imaginer, and how that imagining touched the social structure of his day.

In the first part of the essay, I shall explore how Jesus expressed his imagination in naming his Father, evoking the symbol of the kingdom and speaking in parables. Jesus' parabolic deeds, which are rooted in his relation to his Father and to the kingdom he symbolized, will be treated in the second part. Finally, in Part III I shall offer some reflections on Christian parabling in our own time.

When I use the term "imagination" in this essay, I am referring to that affective, emotional, intellectual and volitional center of ourselves where are generated our hopes and desires, a lively sense of possibility and a feel for alternatives. Biblical writers would probably have been satisfied with the term "heart." But "imagination" suggests the relation of the person to felt possibilities, to new and better futures, to alternatives that quicken one's energies when they are recognized and owned.[1]

I. ABBA, KINGDOM, PARABLE

In the ninth chapter of the Acts of the Apostles (v 21) we read how, after his conversion, Saul stayed awhile with the disciples in Damascus and then began to proclaim Jesus as Son of God. People are amazed, for this is the very man who "worked such havoc in Jerusalem among those who invoked this name." Christians are here described as those who invoke the name of Jesus as Son of God, Christ, Lord. Indeed, the New Testament makes it evident that the invoking of this name and this name invoked are both fraught with power.[2]

Stretching back as far as Genesis and moving up to the likes of Paulo Freire in our own day,[3] people have been intrigued by the depth of power that can reside in the human ability to name. We Christians can look at the story of Jesus as partly a story of one who names with power. And this, I suggest, is one privileged path of access to Jesus' imagination as it lived in relation to social structures.

Jesus' Abba-experience

From the center of his life, Jesus called his God "Abba." Jesus invoked his God in terms of unparalleled intimacy and reverent audacity. If we can trust those scholars who see this use of "Abba" in direct address to the God of Israel as peculiarly characteristic of, and perhaps original with Jesus, then, in this word, this name, we stand before the mystery of his heart, mind and affection.[4] The ability to be open to such a thoroughly human and original experience is ultimately due to the Father's own involvement in Jesus' life through the power of the Holy Spirit. For while it is true that God the Father is the ultimate source of all authentic religious experience, this holds true in a special way for Jesus. There is no adequate human mediation of God in Jesus' life, unlike the situation in the lives of Christians, who find in Jesus the adequate mediation of the mystery of God. Jesus is, finally, alone with the Father. Yet, on the other hand, Jesus' experience of God was not simply a privately mediated experience either. Mary and Joseph, townspeople and teachers, and, in a privileged way, the Hebrew Scriptures, nourished Jesus' sense of God in ways we cannot trace or define. Nor do we need to. Yet the "stories of God" which Jesus heard from those who loved him and knew him as son of Mary and Joseph, fostered his developing sense of the kind of relationship with the Holy Mystery into which he was being invited. Thus, Jesus *learned* to imagine God. Not in the sense that he pictured the Invisible One, but in the sense that his mind and heart were touched and enlivened by the love and life-experience of others to trust his own experience. He could grow in a solitary experience of Yahweh precisely because the roots of his religious experience grew deeply in the soil of his own religious past, incarnated in the love of Mary and Joseph and the stories of God they told him. "Abba" as a direct invocation of God says both aloneness and rootedness. The invocation of God which Mary, Joseph and others expressed in the presence of the growing child nourished in gradual and deep ways the extraordinary sense of intimacy which was Jesus' alone. Their imaginings of God nourished an almost scandalous imagining of God by the son of the carpenter.

In invoking God as Abba Jesus evoked a world as well, or better, a world was evoked for Jesus. In response to the Father's initiative in his life, there developed within Jesus' imagination a symbol: the Kingdom of God. Having its roots in the Old Testament prophets and in apocalyptic literature, this symbol became the center of Jesus' ministry and concern. Invoking the Father he evoked the symbol which shaped that ministry. For the Kingdom of God, as preached by Jesus, was not so much a teaching, or a program, or a concept, but rather a symbol—God's powerful action as king and the state of affairs that power would effect. Recent research has stressed the point that Jesus' speech and action did not simply indicate a different reality, the kingdom, somehow "out there," but that Jesus' message was bearer of the reality spoken of. Word and deed were symbol, not mere sign, of the reality evoked; they shared in its life.[5]

As Jesus was grasped by the symbol of the Kingdom of God (for it grasped and shaped him as much as it was engendered in his imagination), it was the action of God that would usher in a world of right relationships, when God would come into his own as king. This kingdom or reign was a future event which was already coming to pass in Jesus' own proclamation and ministry. Apparently Jesus did not imagine time as we modern Westerners do, in linear fashion; rather he imagined God's time for the world as both present and future—as some scholars put it, God's future reign occurring in Jesus' present as an anticipation of its yet to be consummated fullness.[6]

From Abba-experience to Kingdom

What is the relationship between Jesus' Abba-experience, that is, his invocation and naming of God as Abba, and his symbolization of God and world in terms of kingdom? In the New Testament texts we cannot find many verses which expressly relate this invocation with this symbolization.[7] Yet the centrality of this metaphor and this symbol in Jesus' experience and public life allow one to suppose that in the mental and affective life of Jesus they were closely bound together, nourishing one another throughout his ministry. Indeed, the intimacy, familiarity and authority expressed in the direct invocation of his God as Abba was probably the personal basis in Jesus' own life for his preaching of the reign of God.[8] Not that the latter symbol proceeded from the Abba-experience in some logical fashion, but in the sense that the experience of God as Abba gave Jesus, in the depths of his spirit, the courage and the capacity to envision God's reign as near in a way which was novel, compelling and radical. For scholars can show that the ways in which the New Testament reports Jesus' employment of the symbol of kingdom, and the very frequency with which he used it, have no parallels in the Old Testament or the intertestamental period.[9] The experience of God gave birth to naming God Abba and that naming empowered him to imagine God's kingdom in this new way.

The more profoundly we name someone from the center of our lives the more the invocation is the expression of participation in a presence. A naming, in the sense of an invoking, is a metaphoric response to a presence and reality in which we are invited to share. It is this fundamental depth-dimension of the naming process that allows us to see the connection between the Abba-experience and invocation of God by Jesus and the way Jesus experienced God's Kingdom. And his ministry suggests to us that the symbol of "God acting as king" in Jesus' life engendered concrete hopes and wishes for his fellow Jews and beyond. For he invited others to participate in the reality of the symbol and to taste the energizing life of the symbol—the kingdom that was "at hand," "in your midst," coming, yet, in some real way, already at work, effectively present.

The Parables

The gospels themselves aid us in our effort to appreciate the influence the Abba-experience and the symbol of the kingdom had on Jesus' imagination. For in those parables which can be traced back with some assurance to the pre-Easter Jesus we find the metaphoric enlargement of the kingdom-symbol, as Jesus confronted particular people in particular circumstances and desired to express what kingdom meant in those circumstances. Empowered and encouraged by the experience which allowed him to name God "Abba," and to symbolize the kingdom, Jesus spoke to them in parables.

Scripture scholars are impressed by the use of parables in Jesus' ministry, for they do not have, in their original form, any counterpart in rabbinic or other Jewish literature.[10] Whereas other writers in Jesus' religious milieu employed stories or "parables" in order to illustrate or exemplify some truth of the Law, Jesus spoke in parables as the only really appropriate way in which the reality of the kingdom could be expressed. Thus, to enter into the parable is to enter into what "kingdom" is all about.[11]

For instance, by means of the parable of the Samaritan, Jesus conjured up a world in which the accursed half-breed, "worse than a Gentile," acts as neighbor to the Jew, when Jewish authority-figures fail him (Lk 10:29–37). The Jew in need accepts the ministrations of the Samaritan (thus delaying the coming of the Messiah, according to some rabbis!) and this act of welcome is as novel and revolutionary as the Samaritan's offer of help. In telling this parable Jesus touches the imaginations of those who are listening to him and offers them the chance to develop a new body of images which can subvert their segregated faith and rigid religious habits. He does not teach a doctrine of good neighborliness; rather, he fleshes out a world which the religious sensibilities of his hearers are invited to make their own. The telling of the parable is of short duration, and the event which takes place between Jew and Samaritan is a passing occasion, but the power of the parable resides in its symbolic capacity to portend a world in which the enemy is the compassionate one, and one's "colleagues" reject one. Racial and religious typifications break open, the myths of "Jew" and of "Samaritan" are cracked and new pathways of life under God's rule open up. Shared assumptions die, or are at least invited to die, that new life may arise between individuals and classes of people.[12]

In the parable of the unforgiving servant (Matt 18:23–35) Jesus compares the kingdom to a king dealing with a subject. The servant is freed of a debt that runs into the millions and is not able to dismiss in turn a hundred-dollar debt owed him. The overwhelming mercy shown the servant clashes with the servant's sense of his due and confronts the hearers of the parable with a world in which mercy is the ultimate principle of coherence. As Eta Linnemann has pointed out, we are accustomed to view mercy as an exception against a background of established rights. We are merciful when we forsake our rights. But the parable seems to suggest a universe in which mercy is the ordinary thing! No defense or apology or explanation of this is offered. And the prospect is dizzying! Would our world *be* coherent if mercy were its ultimate principle, fleshed out in all human actions? But the parable neither asks nor answers such questions, but rather challenges the listener to live as though the world is founded on mercy. Which it is.[13]

In the parable of the dishonest steward, who "adjusts" the amounts owed to his master and so wins favor with both the debtors and the master, Jesus may well be letting us in on his sense of humor.[14] For in this parable the Kingdom of God is compared to a situation in which someone apparently acts as a rogue and, in a deed of enlightened self-interest, enters into his master's favor by "taking the bull by the horns"! Such initiative, in the face of impending doom, is admirable in the eyes of the master.

If "taking the bull by the horns" is a dimension of kingdom-reality, so too is the experience of its utter gratuitousness. The person who is most likely to appreciate that gratuitousness is the one who lets himself be lured into the world suggested by the parable of the vineyard workers (Matt 20:1–16). Those who worked all day and those who worked for one hour receive the same wage. There is no logic here. Nor is it sheer arbitrariness. It is, indeed, an incalculable act by which the householder gives *the very same thing* to all the laborers. To experience that as good news rather than as an affront to the American sense of fair play is to begin to taste what God's kingdom is all about.[15]

I spoke above of the possibility that Jesus showed his sense of humor in telling the parable of the dishonest servant. It has been pointed out by Scripture scholars that Jesus' comparison of the kingdom to a mustard seed might also be a clue to a humorous dimension of his imagination as well (Matt 13:31f.). In the Old Testament the great cedar of Lebanon, sheltering birds in its branches, is taken to be an apt image for the great kingdoms of Mesopotamia and Egypt, and for the messianic kingdom. But Jesus, with a sure and gentle touch, transmutes the image. For him the apt image of God's Kingdom is the ordinary mustard shrub and the tiny seed from whence it springs.

This employment of the image of mustard seed and shrub is a marvelous example of ironic imagination.[16] The expectations of his listeners are turned upside down, as the image suggests a kingdom that cannot be measured by what is mighty in this world. Jesus is telling us something fundamental and structural about the occurrence of the kingdom within history: the small, quantitatively insignificant beginning which is the mustard seed can become, by some wonderful transformation, the disproportionately large mustard *shrub* that is able to "shelter the birds of the air." This metaphor, so upsetting, in a humorous sort of way, to the ordinary religious sensibility, is a telling sign of Jesus' entire life and ministry, for Jesus is the kingdom come among us in the form of concealment, lowliness, irony, and poverty; the parabler imagines the kingdom under the sign of parables which are as practical as they are simple.

II. Jesus' Parabling Through Action and Passion

Jesus' deeds are yet another way in which he gives his imagination a body. Here, too, we find a pattern of naming and evoking a world, where the naming is an exercise of power.[17] In his confrontation with the demonic powers of his day, as Joseph Weber's essay shows, Jesus was engaged in a conflict of structural, even cosmic proportions. Yet each conflict is played out in a particular situation in relation to specific people. Most expressly in his exorcisms, but in all his acts of healing and forgiving as well, Jesus was anticipating in finite but thoroughly concrete ways, the shape of the kingdom that was coming.

Struggle with the Powers

In the very first chapter of Mark (vv 21–28), Jesus is engaged in this struggle of naming and of exercising power. Mark has already indicated that Jesus called his first disciples and taught in the synagogue with *exousia,* and now that teaching extends itself into an act of physical and spiritual liberation. The rebellious power which is enslaving the poor man names Jesus, in an effort to bind his power—"I know who you are—the holy one of God!" Here the demon is trying to domineer by naming, but Jesus silences him and in turning compassionately to the needy man, allows him to experience the reality of the kingdom in the form of (relative) wholeness and health. Naming here is an act of domination, but it is countered by an act of compassion, whereby Jesus exposes himself to the reality of the other and commits himself to his cause.

Later in Mark, Jesus does compel the powers enslaving a man to utter their name—"Legion"—and thus binds the dehumanizing force at work in the person (Mk 5:1–13). Jesus "gave the word" and the unclean spirits left him at once. In the contest of naming it is "Jesus, Son of God Most High" shrieked forth by the enslaving power and, "What is *your* name!" authoritatively called for by Jesus. Binding the demons, Jesus realizes in a partial but concrete way the meaning of the kingdom-reality he is preaching, and the Abba-experience of Jesus is opened to participation by one who was a "half-human" of unclean spirit. "To speak a true word is to transform the world."[18] And having spoken the true word Jesus capacitates the broken man to enter into authentic relation with himself and others.

Exorcisms and healings are not the only ways in which Jesus acted parabolically. In calling Zacchaeus down out of his tree, so that he could dine with him (Lk 19:1–10), Jesus acted out the conferral of the eschatological blessings—the blessings of the end time—and did this in relation to a toll collector (Quisling). Jesus dined with sinners and prostitutes as well. The practice of eating with sinners under the sign of the kingdom he preached was one of the most characteristic activities of Jesus. Each time he did it, it was an acted-out parable of forgiveness. A world-reversal occurred for those who, shocked and scandalized, beheld such goings-on. Through such a lived-out parable Jesus makes the kingdom-symbol come alive so that those who welcome his message can participate in the reality of the symbol. The participation is a fragmentary experience—partial, finite, a passing interchange—but it *is* a share of the blessing of the kingdom—in a situation in which Jesus' Abba-experience is shared with others in the symbol of the kingdom. By his action, Jesus blesses sinners, prostitutes and tax collectors, for they accept Jesus and his compassion for them. Jesus' naming them "blessed" arises out of his exposure to their reality and their possibility before God. They moved his innards to compassion for them (Matt 9:36).

But this vulnerability has another moment to it. Besides naming demons and by deed exorcising them, in addition to eating with sinners and so enacting the kingdom reality, Jesus calls the scribes and Pharisees "hypocrites," and grieves for them in true prophetic fashion. In the gospel accounts it is clear that this naming is not a labelling, a defense mechanism, nor is the grieving simply a reaction, but a true response in which he allows himself to be affected by those who close themselves to him. This naming and this grieving are at once an act of strength, an act of understanding, an act of self-exposure and of servanthood. The conflict and pathos are not merely personal, they are not restricted to a few individuals who misread Jesus, but are a passionate conflict between Jesus and the structures of this world which would quench the Spirit.[19]

When we name, to the depth we do so, to that depth we hand ourselves over. The powers of this world—larger than synagogues, Pharisees, scribes, Herodians—penetrated into Jesus and tried to lord it over him. By naming truthfully Jesus exposed himself to the powers he was combatting. "He emptied himself, and took the form of a servant, and was found to be in human likeness" (Phil 2:2–11).

Jesus the Parable

In the end, the one who called God "Abba," the one who preached the kingdom and told parables and enacted them in powerful deeds, became himself the parable. The world-reversal which he imagined and invited others to taste, he had to undergo himself. The very life which generated the parables had to submit itself to the truth of the parable. His vulnerability became complete—if we are to believe Mark's account of the crucifixion. Somehow Jesus came to realize that the coming of his Father's kingdom required his full exposure to the powers inimical to the kingdom, the powers which rejected the world-reversal that Jesus lived and spoke of. The partial and powerful anticipations of that kingdom which Jesus worked were not enough. The power which was Jesus' had to be surrendered to the Father through a "being handed over" so that the Father's form of power might effect the kingdom. The naming of his opponents and his grieving over them is shown to be a loving exposure to their (false) power and deadly numbness out of obedience to the Father.[20]

Thus Jesus' passion and death offer a parable of the coming of the kingdom which, while not in the slightest trivializing his deeds of power in healing and confrontation, throws those deeds onto a completely new and revolutionary plane. In conflict with the "powers of this world," and having tasted the full powers that were his in the Father, Jesus allowed those foreign powers to "lord it over him" in full obedience to the Father and in the strength of his Abba-experience. We do not need to think that Jesus' understanding of the kingdom was always a uniform one. From the beginning of his ministry Jesus sought to proclaim the kingdom in word and deed. Yet the inauguration of his public ministry coincided with the death of John the Baptist. That awareness, coupled with his intimate knowledge of the Hebrew Scriptures, could not help but shape his imagination of the kingdom as one that involved suffering. As his Galilean ministry ran into increasing opposition, Jesus was faced with the question, What is the power that can accomplish the reality of the kingdom? The deeds of Jesus were finite—healings, exorcisms—whose results, both exterior and interior, could well have been passing; that was out of Jesus' control. The reign of God was an event, an act which was proper to his Father, and yet what Jesus did was crucial to that coming. Day by day, he needed to discern when acting on his part was appropriate, and when passivity, or better, becoming subject, out of faithful love for his enemies, to the power that warred against the kingdom, was the better avenue to the kingdom that was to come.

Jesus dies. He dies with the Name on his lips—if we may believe Mark the Evangelist—although the same evangelist suggests by his use of Psalm 22:1 that Jesus had to surrender even his own habitual Abba-experience in that final invocation of the Name. He died denuded of everything but the Father's Name on his lips. Stripped of his habitual religious experience, Jesus cried out to God in bare trust in his invisible, impalpable presence.[21]

Jesus Named in Power

Jesus was heard for his obedience. Not in the sense that one iota of the real depths of passion and death were by-passed, but he was heard through and in the very dying and death. When the followers of Jesus began to experience him as alive in the glory of his Father and in the Spirit's presence and power when they were gathered together in Jesus' name, they recognized that Jesus' final impotence was embraced by the Father's faithful power.

The one who invoked the Name, who preached the kingdom and who spoke in parables of word and deed now became himself the Name. People began to invoke Jesus' name, to call upon him in powerful metaphors: Son of God, Christ, Son of Man, Lord, and to find that such invocation and naming expressed their deepest experiences of the Spirit in their midst.

What experience or experiences gave rise among the early Christians to this imagining of Jesus, this new understanding of him in and through metaphors from their own religious traditions?

There were those believers who had known the pre-Easter Jesus, who had been given to see the Risen One and who experienced the power of the Spirit when acting in Jesus' name. Such a one was Peter. Others did not know the pre-Easter Jesus, but received revelation of the Risen and Exalted One and knew the power of his Spirit in their lives. Paul is the prime example here. Still other early Christians invoked the name of Jesus simply because of their faith in the Apostle's preaching and because of the power of the Spirit at work in their lives. To invoke Jesus as Lord, for these people, was to express a relationship to Jesus, God and the Spirit in a way which could only be expressed in such a packed metaphor.

In invoking Jesus as Lord, early Christians expressed the revolutionary experience they underwent whereby they came to realize that in and through the death and resurrection of Jesus the kingdom which Jesus preached, parabled and thus anticipated had come to pass. The world reversal which Jesus, in particular ways and in specific circumstances had invited his listeners to enter into, had entered, through Jesus' activity and fate, into the world, and had affected the world and all people to their roots—the end time was clearly begun, the world was liberated and the powers that alienated humans from each other, themselves and God were contained. This appreciation of the lordship of Jesus ruled out two ways of imagining the kingdom. On the one hand it could not be imagined as something effected simply by dint of human effort, even the human effort of Jesus. Each of his healings, each of his parables, was a partial anticipation of the kingdom reality, but only that. The sum of them did not equal the kingdom reality, while, on the other hand, they were, in truth, participation in that kingdom for Jesus and those who were open to him. But the final impotence of Jesus before God and his opponents gives the lie to any interpretation of the arrival of the kingdom which would conceive it as the simple arithmetic of human efforts, however Spirit-inspired. God effected, once and for all, the inauguration of the kingdom.

An equally misguided way of perceiving the manner of the kingdom's inauguration imagines it as coming to the world independently of human initiative and effort, apart from our "best (or all too human) constructions." The particular actions of Jesus, as well as the preaching in parables, were as necessary to the Father's plan to inaugurate the kingdom as Jesus' death and resurrection. Jesus' deeds and words were the parable of that reign, and all that Jesus was, did and said was both called into radical question in the crucifixion *and* raised in the power of the Spirit. Both the activity and the vulnerability of Jesus were submitted to the power of death but, more radically and effectively, to the power of divine life which came into its own through and in the life and death of Jesus.[22]

In acknowledging Jesus as their Lord, the Christians stood open to the same influence ruling their lives, and in that recognition they experienced themselves as *koinonia,* as a community under one Lord, the first fruits of God's kingly activity in Jesus.

III. The Christian as Parabler

We did not have to go to anything peripheral in Jesus' ministry to learn how he was involved with the structural fabric of life. The preaching and the enactment of the kingdom in word and deed were the mode in which Jesus effectively touched and influenced the structural dimension of our world. To be sure, Jesus' ministry was, to a large extent, a personal ministry, one which involved him with individuals. Yet in the preaching of the kingdom Jesus was evoking a whole new world of relationships. The kingdom as preached by Jesus was not a concept, or a program for social and political change, but a symbol possessed of transformative power for those who let themselves be addressed by its promise of a new way of perceiving and imagining reality and its possibilities.

When Jesus spoke of the kingdom it was not accidental that he did so symbolically, because God's reign, his act of reigning in our world, can only exist in the mode of symbol. Jesus lovingly invited people to enter into the power of the symbol, to get the feel of the world he was evoking by participating in its life. Habitual ways of perceiving and acting were overturned, and new pathways of human life together opened up.

The relation of Jesus to the structures of his day was grounded most radically in his naming of the Father, his preaching in parable and deed the Kingdom of God and in submitting himself to the parable's dynamism of world-reversal in obedience to the Father. The following of Jesus, through the gift of the Spirit, calls for a similar commitment in the life of the Christian: that he or she be parabler, and obedient to the Gospel even unto the darkness of pain and death.

True and False Naming

Saint Paul is firmly convinced that the Christian is invited and empowered by the Spirit to share in Jesus' Abba-experience. The freedom to call—with one's life—on God as "Father," to dare or accept anything because one is rooted in the power of God's intimate love, has its source in Jesus, and so we can name Jesus as well, calling upon him, in the Spirit, as Lord and Christ. The power to name God and Jesus is given to Christians at the center of their lives, making everything possible to the one who believes.

But not everyone who says, "Lord, Lord" will inherit the kingdom of heaven. Not everyone who names Jesus with *the* name or who calls on God as Father is truly in touch with the reality of kingdom. The naming can proceed from one's false or sinful self, or the naming can be directed to an idol or a pseudo-Jesus. The naming can be ineffective because it does not express a double self-exposure: exposure to the disarming and empowering love of God for the one who names, and exposure to the world which the namer indwells. The naming of Jesus, the calling him Lord, is authentic to the extent that it is an act which expresses our vulnerability to God and neighbor in their otherness and proximity.

The one commandment is twofold, love of God and love of neighbor, and the act by which the Christian names God as Father or Jesus as Lord involves letting oneself be touched in mind, heart and affections by one's neighbors in their gritty reality. This does not mean, of course, that every prayer of ours must include explicit reference to our neighbor. But it does suggest that even the most God-centered prayer needs to expose us, in the further unfolding of our lives, to the neighbor.[23]

But this is not enough. The act of naming is an empowering act, an act which allows us to share in God's peculiar power, when it is allowed to be as well a disarming act, that is to say, an act by which we allow the Spirit to disengage us, bit by bit, from the massive "givenness" of everyday reality, where that everyday reality is counter to the kingdom. This disarming of one's familiar world is the work of the Spirit in our lives, and the Spirit can do this in an effective way by encouraging us to draw close enough to the neighbor that we experience his or her world. My everyday world can shield me from both the contingency of my world (it need not be this way) and the world of my neighbor. My allegiance to my world can be shaken in a fruitful way by the experience of another to whom I have drawn close in compassion.

Only a growing openness to the concrete love of God for me can encourage me to stay with this disarming process, to stick it out, as assumptions and patterns of perception get called into question. But the naming of Jesus as Lord calls for the ever more authentic naming of the world we indwell, with the increasing empowerment and vulnerability which that naming entails.

Parabling and Social Structures

In addition to being a namer, the Christian is called to be a parabler as well. Parable in word, but especially in deed, is one of the ways in which the ordinary Christian can participate in the coming of the kingdom. A consideration of the meaning of "social structures" may help to clarify the importance of parable as a way of influencing the social fabric of our lives.

The world of everyday is a world of relationships, mutual expectations and roles which shape the way in which I perceive reality and sense the possibilities inhabiting my given world. Our lives together are built on repetitive actions which we can confidently expect from others and ourselves. The world is a world, to a great extent, because in most ways it is a reasonably predictable place to inhabit. When the postman arrives on my porch at about eleven a.m. every morning, I expect to hear the doorbell ring four or five times in quick succession as he places the mail behind the screen door. If, instead of that he should take out from his mail pouch a can of yellow paint and begin painting the door frame (which does need the services of a painter), I would be bemused, indeed. If at the same time I would notice my rather shy and retiring next door neighbor, a Harvard Business School student from Peoria, coming out of his house wearing all the finery of a Maori warrior, my consternation would increase. And if the automobiles on my busy street started cruising at an altitude of four feet, the fine-mesh network of repetitive and predictable activities which make my human life possible would seem to be unravelling at crippling speed!

Roles and Institutions

The breakdown of natural laws is, of course, a final touch, for it would be quite sufficient to experience the breakdown of the ordinary social patterns that make up human life together to feel the world totter beneath one. The social fabric of our lives arises from repetition of behavior and the typifications which arise from such repeated behavior. Not only do I expect a certain kind of behavior from the man who, each day, arrives at my front door at about eleven a.m., but I have a fairly clear idea of what it means to be a postman, quite apart from this particular fellow. I know what the *role* of postman is. And the notion of role brings us to the heart of institutional life.

> Institutions are embodied in individual experience by means of roles. . . . *All* institutionalized conduct involves roles. Thus roles share in the controlling character of institutionalization. As soon as actors are typified as role performers, their conduct is *ipso facto* susceptible to reinforcement. Compliance and noncompliance with socially defined role standards cease to be op-

> tional, though, of course, the severity of sanctions may vary from case to case.[24]

The institutional order is represented by roles. This happens in a twofold way. A judge, for example, when he acts as a judge, represents that role, but, in addition, he represents the judicial order. "Only through such representation in performed roles can the institution manifest itself in actual experience."[25]

If the function of role is this crucial to institutional life, then a pivotal place at which the power of the kingdom can affect social structures is on the level of the performance of role. This can occur when someone, or a group of persons, begin to perceive themselves in an altered role which is more in consonance with the imperatives of the kingdom.

In a certain Latin American country, a judge may perceive himself as a functionary of the legal system whose role consists in adjudicating small claims according to norms which are, on a common sense level, fair and equitable, but who decides cases involving the right of assembly according to the special agenda of the secret police. If that judge, by whatever route he comes to it, begins to recognize that his handling of these two types of cases makes a mockery of justice, particularly when he enters back into the ideals which once led him into being a judge, he might sense an invitation to judge in a different way a case involving citizens who assembled in public to protest the torture of another citizen. An act like this would not change the state, and it certainly would bring upon his neck the wrath of other judges and the secret police. Many people would say that such an act was futile, "a parable in the void." What resources would he draw on to make such an act? It might be a new surge of concern for some basic human ideals, or the deep and refreshing quickening of spirits he experiences because of a glimpse of a new society. Perhaps he, for the first time, realizes what his Christian baptism means in his adult life for himself and others. But the odds are woefully stacked against him and he knows it. His cause seems as fragile as his own person, weighed in the balance with the powers arrayed against him.

But we do not have to appeal to such a dramatic example to talk about stacked odds. The individual Christian in the United States often has a quite modest, indeed depressing, perception of his or her role in the political and social scheme of things.

Parabling Opportunities

But the opportunities for "parabling" are usually close at hand. Teachers in a city school system can decide to perform their role as people who are concerned with the development of individuality and social awareness in the pupils, rather than as functionaries who simply convey information to or demand conforming behavior from those entrusted to their care. A teacher can express through an entire pattern of activity that education is a process of personal appropriation in a social context. The dominant cultural values of individualism, competitiveness and material success can be challenged by the teacher's modeling of a profoundly different view of how things can be.

A family in a suburban neighborhood can express an ecological sense in the way they treat their property and goods that can "catch" with others in their area, so that a sense of stewardship develops among them. One or several persons in an area threatened by speculating real estate brokers can marshal people and help them come to a sense of community when panic is about to strike because of rumors that a family of a different race may move in and "lower the property values."

Community organizers have found that a hitherto politically impotent block in the inner-city has come into a sense of its human dignity and political power when it has learned ways of getting its voice heard in City Hall. Role-parabling can be "contagious," leading to a sense of community that fosters and expresses the empowerment of people in their personal and social identity.

Organizations such as "Common Cause" try to elicit citizen support by suggesting that the common efforts of concerned citizens can effect change by appealing to the ideals and the enlightened self-interest of legislators. Participation in an enterprise such as Common Cause is much less dramatic than the heroic decision of the judge, but is it wrong to consider such participation parabolic of the kingdom? This is not to suggest that an agenda or program of a group such as Common Cause is identical with the kingdom! But at a certain time and place in our political history it can well be that striving for a government which is more open in its workings and more responsive to the needs of its constituents can be, in a partial but real way, an activity which gives expression to the desire for right relationships which the symbol of the kingdom evokes. Common Cause is no more able to save than is Datsun, and people can take part in such an effort from a whole spectrum of motives, but the introduction of a bit more equity in the workings of government can improve the social context within which we live, and so can transcend in its effects the shoddier motives of people. (Even the steward who "adjusts" the debts of his master has a role in the coming-to-be of the kingdom.)

Christian faith allows one to imagine in a distinctive way both the deed of the judge and the deed of one who, with others, works in modest and steady ways for political reform. The efforts of a Christian to change for the better the political and social fabric of his or her world bear the same signature as the deeds of anyone else, insofar as those deeds can be, and usually are, marked by multiple levels of motivation as well as an unclear future. There is a profound degree of uncertainty about the future of any just or loving deed, once performed. We simply cannot control the effect or influence of our actions. But Christian faith offers, as well, a powerful resource for those who choose to let themselves be engaged in the construction of a more just society: the image of the just deed, sullied perhaps on some level by selfishness, finding its future *not only* in the ever-widening arena of human affairs, where others can undo it or contradict it, but also in the hands of the God whose passion it is to establish his kingdom as the only finally authentic home for the *humanum.* This way of imaging the just deed, which embraces both the cross and resurrection of the crucified, is not the private imagining of the Christian for his or her just deed. The Christian imagines it, hopes for it, for all those who engage themselves for the sake of the *humanum.* An atheistic judge or a reformist private citizen of no recognizable religious coloring is embraced by this imagination.

But having said this, a corrective is necessary. For this way of expressing it could lead us to separate the deed from the doer. Yet the kingdom God has committed himself to is not a kingdom of good deeds, burnished and consummated, but rather a community, a people, and it is to persons that the kingdom is addressed and to them that it is coming. The parabler, and not the parable by itself, is the route through which the kingdom approaches and influences our world. And just as the doers of justice must hand over their deeds and intentions to the ongoing flux of history, so they must hand themselves over to the uncontrollable. This way of dying, which embraces agents and their deeds, is the form in which the kingdom can exercise its power in history. This experience can be a nameless one, or it can be, as it is for the Christian, final surrender to the Name, of all that one is most passionately engaged in.

World-reversal and Mustard Seed

Whenever the world-reversal which is the kingdom occurs, in real but partial ways, that world-reversal is like the mustard seed. No matter whether we are speaking of an event of world-historical significance, or a just deed done in secret. The kingdom does not flatten out the events in our history so that they are all of equal weight, but, on the other hand, in relation to the kingdom, those events are mustard seed-like. The kingdom pervaded the crucified one at the point of his total impotence, so that in the resurrection Jesus the Crucified became the kingdom in person. The mustard seed of his life, his ministry, his invocation of the Father, his speaking in parables, and even his dying a very lonely death, was reversed by the Holy Mystery of God, transformed into the mighty tree of life, sheltering our best, and even less than best, endeavors from a final victory of the power of sin and death.

That mighty tree of life, the Kingdom, is present and effective in our world through the Church, the community of believers who confess the lordship of Christ and act in his Spirit.

NOTES

1. Paul Ricoeur, "The Image of God and the Epic of Man," in *History and Truth* (Evanston: Northwestern University, 1965), pp. 126f: "The imagination has a metaphysical function which cannot be reduced to a sim-

ple projection of vital, unconscious, or repressed desires. The imagination has a prospective and explorative function in regard to the inherent possibilities of man. It is, *par excellence,* the instituting and constituting of what is humanly possible. In imagining his possibilities, man acts as a prophet of his own existence. . . . The imagination, insofar as it has a mytho-poetic function, is also the seat of profound workings which govern the decisive changes in our visions of the world. Every *real* conversion is first a revolution at the level of our directive images. By changing his imagination, man alters his existence."

2. See, for example, Acts 3:6.

3. Gen 2:20; Paulo Freire, *Pedagogy of the Oppressed* (New York: Herder and Herder, 1970).

4. Cf. Joachim Jeremias, *New Testament Theology: The Proclamation of Jesus* (New York: Scribner, 1971), pp. 36f., 61–68.

5. Cf. Norman Perrin, *Jesus and the Language of the Kingdom: Symbol and Metaphor in New Testament Interpretation* (Philadelphia: Fortress, 1976).

6. For example, Wolfhart Pannenberg's title essay in *Theology and the Kingdom of God* (Philadelphia: Westminster, 1969), pp. 51–71.

7. A primary example, of course, is the "Our Father": Lk 11:2–4; Matt 6:9–13.

8. See James D. G. Dunn, *Jesus and the Spirit* (Philadelphia: Westminster, 1975), pp. 37–40.

9. Jeremias, *op. cit.,* pp. 31f.

10. Jeremias, *The Parables of Jesus,* 2nd. rev. ed. (New York: Scribner, 1972).

11. John Dominic Crossan, *In Parables: The Challenge of the Historical Jesus* (New York: Harper & Row, 1973), pp. 19–22.

12. *Ibid.,* pp. 57–66. It is important to note that "priest" and "Levite" stand not only for individuals but for a whole socio-religious order. The parable is about persons and structures.

13. See Eta Linnemann, *Jesus of the Parables. Introduction and Exposition* (New York: Harper & Row, 1966), pp. 105–113.

14. Dan O. Via, *The Parables: Their Literary and Existential Dimension* (Philadelphia: Fortress, 1967), pp. 155–162.

15. *Ibid.,* pp. 147–155.

16. John Dominic Crossan, *The Dark Interval: Towards a Theology of Story* (Niles, IL: Argus Communications, 1975), pp. 93–96.

17. "Naming" here is, of course, quite different from the invocation of the Father. But they are clearly connected.

18. Freire, *op. cit.,* p. 75.

19. Jon Sobrino, S.J. *Christology at the Crossroads: A Latin American Approach* (Maryknoll, Orbis, 1978), pp. 50–55. Walter Brueggemann prefers to see Jesus grieving in true prophetic fashion in the "woes" addressed to his opponents, rather than denouncing them from outside themselves, as it

were. This grieving for them in their numb and dead condition would be Jesus' way of staying faithful to his enemies as they actually were and at the same time seeking to subvert their hatred, fear and effort to control him. See Brueggemann's *The Prophetic Imagination* (Philadelphia: Fortress, 1978). For a brilliant exploration of Jesus' relation to those rejecting him in terms of inclusive representation see F.J. van Beeck, *Christ Proclaimed, Christology as Rhetoric* (New York: Paulist, 1979), Chapter 11.

20. *Ibid.,* pp. 201–209.

21. Walter Kasper, *Jesus the Christ* (New York: Paulist, 1976), pp. 118f.: "[On the cross] Jesus experienced the unfathomable mystery of God and his will, but he endured this darkness in faith. This extremity of emptiness enabled him to become the vessel of God's fullness. His death became the source of life. It became the other side of the coming of the Kingdom of God—its coming in love."

22. "For Paul . . . the one who is risen is the one who enters into his kingdom. But the cross does not therefore become the way to that kingdom or its price. It is rather the signature of the one who is risen. He would have no name by which he could be called were it not the name of the crucified . . . No one has ever been able to talk about the one who is risen without meaning an ideogram for the overcoming and transfiguration of the world (i.e., a cosmological and anthropological ideology) unless the one who is risen remains the one who was crucified and is as such proclaimed as Lord." Ernst Käsemann, *Perspectives on Paul* (Philadelphia: Fortress, 1974), p. 56f.

23. See the fine reflections of Jon Sobrino, *op. cit.,* pp. 169–175.

24. Peter L. Berger and Thomas Luckmann, *The Social Construction of Reality: A Treatise in the Sociology of Knowledge* (Garden City: Doubleday, 1967), p. 74.

25. *Ibid.,* p. 75.

Part II
The Lord and the Church

5
Eucharist at Corinth: You Are the Christ

John C. Haughey, S.J.

I would like in this essay to make several claims about the significance of the Eucharist for our study of Jesus as Lord of social systems. The first claim is that the behavior of Christian communities at their eucharistic assemblies can exemplify Jesus' lordship over social systems. Depending on several factors to be discussed in this essay, these assemblies can begin the process of bringing his lordship to realization and can also be indicative of the manner in which this realization comes about.

This claim assumes that besides being looked at as a sacrament, the eucharistic action of the Christian community can also be examined as a social system. The eucharistic assembly qualifies as a social system in all the senses in which we use that term in this volume. For starters, it is a social projection of commonly internalized values of the participants. This projection does not take place *de novo* each time but takes place in view of and in terms of the "givens" or objectivities that have accrued and become traditional: the ritual, in a word. It is composed of many things such as customs, formal prayers and creeds, material elements, role specifications and doctrinal positions. The assembly's behavior, in other words, has to be to some extent routinized and systematized. But it is also the action of free people, not automatons. The "givens" are not alien to the worshipers but have been created by the value projection of previous generations of believers. If the ritual is congenial to the worshipers, it will continue to have a kind of existence of its own insofar as it aptly expresses the beliefs of contemporary believers. It will undergo modifications insofar as their values or beliefs come to be modified or internalized differently. In brief, the eucharistic celebrations of Christian communities correspond to all the prerequisites of the meaning of social system as we are using that term in this volume. Any inquiry, therefore, into the particulars of the lordship of Jesus over social systems, should be enlightened by his lordship over this particular social system.

A second claim I would like to make is that a profound insight into the theology of the question addressed by this volume has already been sketched out in a very schematic way in several of Paul's comments on the Corinthians' behavior at their eucharistic assemblies, especially 1 Cor 11:17–34. This text is a cameo of the Pauline insight into the relationship between Jesus and the particular social system that was generated by the community of those who believed in his presence in the Eucharist. In the language of this volume we can see that Paul faulted the Corinthians on all three levels of social system: the externalization of their belief, their understanding of the "givens," and their internalization of those "givens." Defective perception of the mystery of the Lord's presence in the community led to defective internalization, and, in turn, to deficient projection or social behavior. It matters little which level we focus on, the liturgy, the beliefs and ritual or the interiority—the success of the Christian enterprise was in jeopardy in Corinth. While the social system of the eucharistic assemblies was generated out of belief, that belief was defective. Once defective belief was projected, it became deficient behavior which weakened the possibilities of any local, social realization of the lordship of Jesus. The consequences of this were grave in Paul's mind. As author of the most venturesome claims about the lordship of Jesus in the New Testament, Paul clearly felt the absurdity of those claims when he saw that this lordship was not coming into realization in the local assemblies of believers. Were he to use contemporary slang, he would have lamented: "if it hasn't got it there it hasn't got it."

I would like to make a third large claim for the subject matter of this chapter. The age old problematic of Christology, a problematic that continues in the modern era, has been concerned largely with the question of how Jesus can be both divine and human. Paul's question was slightly different or an important variation: how can Jesus be both risen and here or himself and us, so to speak? While the Christian community has always confessed its belief that head and members are somehow one, the theological treatment of this question has ordinarily been peripheral to Christology and central instead to ecclesiology. For Paul, however, the many and the one were central to his Christology. By contrast, the favorite object of inquiry of traditional Christology has been the metaphysical constitution of the individual Christ.

This individuation has had happy and unhappy results. It has forced the Christian community in the course of its history especially in its doctrinal and theological developments, to look deeply into the riches of the person of Christ. The uniqueness of this mystery, however, is not fully treated until the social component which is an intrinsic and constitutive aspect of Christology is included in the treatment. So many '-ologies' have been developed in Christian tradition that pressure has been off Christology to do so. Valuable specializations such as eschatology, soteriology, missiology, etc., have profoundly developed the Christian community's understanding of the many aspects of the faith life which it lives. But theological specialization has also produced a negative yield insofar as it fails to capture the unitary insight which so captivated Paul the apostle. The texts I will deal with in this article recall the unitary insight into the Christ mystery and hence give a pristine view of the question asked by this volume.

But there is a corollary to my claim that Christology has spent too much of its time and energy on an individuated Christ. Could the relative inattention given to the question of how he is many and we are he, be due to a poverty of experience? If there is little or no experience of being members of one another in a whole which is his sacred presence, there will be little interest in formulating this experience theologically. Such experience would produce a burning desire to understand and articulate theological treatises and doctrinal formulations. One conclusion that could be drawn, if one agrees that the social aspect of the mystery of Christ has not been well articulated in the Church, is that this experience has been and still is quite meager within its communities. This suggestion does not originate with me, but goes all the way back to Corinth and Paul.

THE CORINTHIAN ASSEMBLIES

These are three rather large claims. In the rest of this essay I would like to give some of the reasons why I make them. For the most part, I will argue to their validity from Paul's ideas about the Eucharist, the Body of the Lord and the community's mission in the Lord.

Two things are worth noting about the Pauline letters before getting to the specific matter of the essay. One is that Paul never undertakes to articulate a formal Christology. His incredibly profound insights into the person of Jesus come out almost as asides as he addresses the pastoral situations with which he is confronted. He articulates an understanding of the Christ mystery only insofar as he is forced to find "answers" to the problems that arise as that mystery takes hold in the believing communities of the Mediterranean world.

Secondly, Paul's way of approaching the problematic of our volume would not have been first to define what a social system is and then try to see how Jesus' lordship relates to it. Paul's imagination worked the other way around. The lordship defined the reality in question. It was already accomplished for Paul. This Lord "was in all, working through all and over all" (1 Cor 8:6). But for those who were in conscious union with their Lord a new creation was only slowly dawning. They were a part of it, conspirators in its realization. What was not of this creation belonged to what was passing away. Death throes, therefore, mixed with birth pangs. The social systems being born in the new creation were so new that they were redefining what had been. Paul busied himself naming this newness.

At the heart of Paul's contribution to first century Christianity's Christology is his understanding, already implicit in his Damascus experience, that the person of Christ is inextricable from the present community. Paul's introduction to this collective person and personality was as abrupt as it was harsh, but once he stopped persecuting that Jesus, he became a primary instrument in the edification of this Jesus-presence in the many cities to which his mission brought him. Paul believed that Jesus would live and move and have his being as Lord locally if the community that was being drawn into the Christ mystery lived out the baptism by which each of its members was transformed. These communities were the only empirical and tangible evidence that the Christ still existed and was drawing all things to himself. But the mission would fail if the whole reality of the Christ presence was not being lived. And it was not being lived because only part of the mystery was believed. *He* was believed in but not according to the manner in which he was present, namely as head conjoined to members.

Corinth is a case in point. When informed of the pattern of behavior that had developed at Corinthian eucharistic celebrations, the Apostle to the Gentiles was appalled. He was appalled because what God had joined together, namely his Son and those who believed in him, "man had pulled asunder" (Mt 19:6). Paul's admonition in 1 Cor 11 addresses the indissolubility of the union between head and members. Their behavior toward one another indicated that the participants had not grasped the fact, the intimacy or the import of this union. Corinthian Christians were giving evidence that they had not been fully converted to the kind of behavior that baptism had called them to and empowered them for. The superficiality of their conversion was evident, not so much in their belief in Christ, which was unmistakable, as in their behavior toward one another. They did not believe that each of them was a member, an instance of the Christ reality. If they had, they would have seen that their behavior toward one another was sacrilegious.

Paul looked upon eucharistic assemblies with an imagination permeated with the power of faith. Those whose imaginations were not so fired either because they were non-believers or because they were unaware of the radical nature of the Christian calling, saw in these eucharistic assemblies only acts of worship of God in Christ. Paul went much further and saw these moments as times when many individuals were being further fused into a single reality, a "new man." In the process, individuals were becoming truly members of one another. To see people, to see oneself, as a member of a whole or as members of one another meant a surrendering of the individualistic self-understandings previously held.

Damascus was the moment at which this experience of the whole Christ began. For Paul, it never ended. He only slowly began to feel like a member among members. We can trace the gradual development of the vision of the relationship between Jesus and his followers in the Pauline epistles. It is not until the captivity epistles, for instance (Colossians and Ephesians), that the headship of Christ becomes an explicit theme. The body theme also does not begin in his writings until he addressed the Corinthians. Paul's imagination, fueled by his faith and his love for Christ Jesus, gradually submitted all issues to this slowly growing vision. The social vision began to absorb the usual ways of seeing people's relationships to one another and God. The vision developed with the practice and experience of communality in his ministry.

Without doing violence to the process at work in Paul, one could say that all social systems were being reconceived by him in terms of the vision consuming him. According to information received by Paul from Corinth, however, the social systems which operated there before the advent of the Christ mystery were having great effect in shaping the features of the social systems being generated by those who supposedly had Christ as their inspiration. The old creation was determining the new creation. In the old systems there were divisions—"Jew and Greek, male and female, slave and free." This was not to be so in the new creation, "for you are all one in Christ Jesus" (Gal 3:27).

More specifically, Corinth was notorious throughout the entire Mediterranean world for its ethnic antipathies, its exploitation of women, its rapaciousness, its catastrophic economic inequalities. It was a symbol of what Paul called the works of the flesh. From the flesh, according to Paul, proceed "hostilities, bickering, jealousy, outbursts of rage, selfish rivalries, dissensions, factions, envy, drunkenness, orgies, and the like" (Gal 5:19–20). But to his dismay these were the qualities that were beginning to appear in the social behavior of the Corinthian eucharistic assemblies. ". . . When you come together it is not for the better but for the worse. When you assemble as a church there are divisions among you . . . each one goes ahead with his own meal and one is hungry and another is drunk" (1 Cor 11:17–21).

ON DISCERNING THE BODY

Traditionally there have been two ways of focusing on the passage in question (1 Cor 11:17–34), which have tended to distract the minds of the readers from its import. One of the usual ways of missing the point has been to hear Paul chastising the Corinthians for being selfish and self-indulgent in their conduct toward one another. Doubtless this point is in the text. But when accompanied with the other traditional tendency, namely focusing on the question of the real presence of the Lord in the Eucharist, the depth of Paul's insight is lost. This insight: the Corinthians' behavior made it obvious that they were "not discerning the body" (v 29). Does the body referred to here by Paul mean the eucharistic species in isolation from the body of head and members which was being built up through the Eucharist? Paul could hardly have been upset about the believers not discerning the Eucharist, since their very getting together was unmistakable evidence of their reverence for and intention to be nourished by the sacrament. A deeper probing of the text is necessary.

One way of answering the question about what "discerning the body" means is to look at the whole text as a unit. The whole is broken into three parts—the problem (vv 17–22); the normative tradition (vv 23–25); then (vv 26–34) Paul's warning and recommendations. By so doing, one can immediately see that the context is Paul's concern about the divisions, factions and selfishness of the members of the Church. But his concern was with something far more serious than selfishness. A speculative position had been developed within the Corinthian communities that he was anxious to eradicate. A nascent gnosticism[1] was developing in Corinth which had some portion of the community of believers verticalizing and spiritualizing their faith in Christ. This had as a consequence a certain despising of the fleshy, tangible corporateness of the sacred presence which made them a people. More specifically, Paul finds evidence of this incipient gnosticism in the way many of the Corinthian Christians esteemed "knowledge." What he had preached, by contrast, was love. "Knowledge puffs up but love builds up" (1 Cor 8:1).

There had developed in the Corinthian communities many who reveled in the fact that they were "free to do anything" (1 Cor 6:12). Hence they would take meats sacrificed to idols and eat those meats with a good conscience. While Paul concurs with their perception he does not agree with their conclusion that they could proceed as if the meat's purity were the whole issue since they were scandalizing those whose consciences had not attained to this degree of knowledge and freedom. He severely reprimanded those who chose to live according to their perceptions and consciences notwithstanding the scandal they were causing to their brethren. In acting individualistically, they failed not only in love, but also showed themselves lacking in the key knowledge that they were to be conscious of, namely that they were members of one another in Christ. "Let no one seek his own good but the good of his neighbor" (1 Cor 10:24).

While Paul and the whole subsequent moral tradition of Christianity would contend that the only legitimate actions one can undertake are those which are in harmony with one's conscience, he is quick to point out that this does not mean that every action which one's conscience can justify should be undertaken. He introduces the notion of the community and that which upbuilds the community because for him the individual in the deepest part of himself or herself has become a member of that community. Member-behavior goes beyond individual integrity. Paul instructs: "Take care lest this liberty of yours somehow become a stumbling block to the weak. For if anyone sees you, a man of knowledge, at table in an idol's temple, might he not be encouraged if his conscience is weak, to eat food offered to idols? And so by your knowledge this weak man is destroyed, the brother for whom Christ died. Thus, sinning against your brethren and wounding their conscience when it is weak, you sin against Christ" (1 Cor 8:9–12).

The speculative position which when full blown could be identified as gnostic also bred an attitude in Christians about their bodies or the physical aspects of their being. Paul goes right to the core of this tendency when he cites the case of intercourse with prostitutes and the false attitudes some entertained about this. "Do you not know that your bodies are members of Christ? Shall I therefore take the members of Christ and make them members of a prostitute? Never! Do you not know that he who joins himself to a prostitute becomes one body with her?... But he who is united to the Lord becomes one spirit with him" (1 Cor 6:14–17).

The speculative error provoking this exhortation was the assumption that whatever involved the bodily could be counted of no importance because Gnosticism believed it was part of that which was passing away. If the physical constitution of human beings would not endure in eternity, the functions and actions relating to the body such as eating and intercourse had no spiritual significance to the gnostic. Hence, if one were to undertake an act of fornication with a harlot, there would be no negative spiritual consequence of that. Paul, by contrast, indicates that by such activity the whole being of the individual is defiled. For Paul, the body signified the whole person. The body is the whole self fully choosing its direction.[2] The emphasis on the resurrection "of the body" in Paul and early Christianity stood foursquare against this error.

There was another dimension to this gnostic tendency that was peculiarly tempting to the Christian. The doctrine of the indwelling Holy Spirit was easily twisted into a way of spiritualizing the meaning of the Christian religion. Hence, if one were open to the Spirit, one became spiritual. Being one with the Spirit began to mean to some Corinthians not only that a special kind of knowledge accrued to particular individuals but also that they were free of relationship to the flesh. Paul himself could have been one of the sources of this misconception since his doctrine about the flesh (*sarx*) is complex and polyvalent. In some instances the flesh, in Paul, is part of the human constitution. In others, flesh is a law, a dominion which many are under and which leads to death.[3]

But what is germane here is that being free of their own flesh, these "spiritual" Christians could also be free from the social flesh or from real incorporation into the body of Christ which Paul preached to them. There was no real corporeality to their membership in Christ. They had been incorporated, in effect, into a metaphorical body, or into a spiritualized realm which they had to have proper knowledge of but did not need to serve in any real way.

This was certainly not Paul's view. Paul understood that the whole person, body and spirit, came under the sway of the Lord's Spirit and the entire person, body and soul, was involved in obeying and serving the Lord. Not involved as an automaton or as a solitary individual but involved as a member of a larger reality, people so intimately related that the image of an organism is not amiss. The Spirit animated this collectivity through every member of the whole. But the only evidence that any part was in fact under the sway of the Spirit was that member-behavior issued from the person rather than the behavior of an individual in isolation from other individuals. "The Body of Christ is the realm into which we are incorporated with our bodies and to which we are called to render service in the body, i.e., total service, service which embraces all our different relationships to the world."[4]

The effect of being in Christ and under the influence of his Spirit has ramifications even for those who are not formally members. An example of this Pauline thinking: the unbeliever who is married to a believing Christian and who desires to continue in commitment to this spouse, is made holy through this spouse. Their children too. "For the unbelieving husband is consecrated through his wife and the unbelieving wife is consecrated through her husband. Otherwise your children would be unclean, but as it is they are holy" (1 Cor 7:12–14). How could this be except that in some way the whole being, body and spirit of the one who was in Christ, was the carrier of the holiness of God and could transmit the effects of their redemption to those to whom he or she was bound in love. Paul, of course, did not confine the efficacy of being in Christ to the domestic realm, but saw the political ramifications of this new force operating in Christians as capable of affecting all social systems. But these transformations would have been rendered innocuous if the gnostic tendencies had been allowed to flourish.

The organicity and virtual physicality of Paul's insight about being under the lordship of Christ Jesus through the Spirit is well attested to in the particular passage we are examining. Immediately after warning them that "anyone who eats and drinks without discerning the body, eats and drinks judgment upon himself," Paul makes what could be taken as a rather crude allegation: "That is why many of you are weak and ill and some have died" (vv 30–31). Paul certainly cannot be criticized for spiritualizing the meaning of the body of Christ! He is alleging that sinful or anti-social or non-member behavior in some members has physical effects on that body. To act non-organically has physical consequences on individuals—weakness, illness and death. Could he mean this? According to his anthropology, he certainly could. In the old creation with its social systems, death reigned. Not to be truly incorporated into the new creation and into this primary instance of a new social system, the eucharistic community, made one prey to all the evils that affected the human condition outside of Christ and before his saving act.

But these dismal consequences to Christians are intended by the

Lord of the Church to issue ultimately in an eternity of well-being for them. Hence Paul goes on: "But when we are judged by the Lord we are chastened so that we may not be condemned along with the world" (v 32). If he did not love them he would not have chastised them. Since he did love them and incorporated them into his own body, he would save them from condemnation by allowing them to taste the effects even in their bodies of their unworthy behavior toward one another.

The judgment theme in this passage and elsewhere in Paul is profound but we will touch on it merely in its connection with the sacraments.[5] By baptism one escapes the ultimate judgment of God. By undergoing baptism one is acquitted of all the sins for which one was guilty. Incorporation into the Christ mystery involves cleansing, propitiation, and atonement. As long as one chooses to live within this mystery, one is not subject to the judgment which can condemn. To be in Christ makes one in this age a participant in the age to come where there is no condemnation. With baptism there is faith, which provides the light to avoid falling back under the reign of sin and judgment. By faith one is capable of making right judgments. Right judgments acted upon keep one from falling back into the condition in which one is judged by God.[6]

It need not have been so. "If we judged ourselves truly, we should not be judged" (v 31). Paul is exhorting his colleagues in the faith to self-judgment or reexamination of themselves lest they fall under judgment. Their sin was not a lack of faith in Jesus. It was an erroneous judgment. They were in error about who they were, because they were wrong about who he was now. Their belief was in a disembodied Jesus. They believed in one not bodied the way he said he would be.[7] For the error to be seen the non-organicity of the body had to be felt by its effects.

The content of the self-examination called for by Paul is liturgical and social. In verse 28: "Let a man examine himself and so eat of the bread and drink of the cup." There is no indication in the text that these liturgical actions in and of themselves were being performed unworthily. His concern as the whole passage indicates is with the blindness and poverty of the social interaction. In verses 33–34: "When you come together to eat, wait for another . . . lest you come together to be condemned."

THE STRUCTURE OF THE EUCHARISTIC MEAL

The reason why there are two aspects of this self-examination can be seen more clearly if one recalls the structure of the passage and the nature of these early eucharistic celebrations. There was the communal meal (at least supposedly communal) called the agape. This was sometimes enclosed within the formally sacramental actions of blessing the bread before the agape and the wine after it and then partaking of both. Apparently this was the order in Corinth.[8] Paul specifically castigates the Corinthians for their behavior in the agape part of the "synaxis." He employs the sacred tradition he had received about the Last Supper as the norm for judging their behavior especially at the agape moment of the celebration.[9]

The Apostle to the Gentiles names the meal's two parts with one name, the Lord's Supper, and upbraids the Corinthians for dichotomizing the one celebration. In the agape moment they were eating their own meals as if they were not attending the Lord's Supper. "When you meet together it is not the Lord's Supper you eat. For the eating, each one goes ahead with his own meal, and one is hungry and another is drunk" (vv 20–21). At the same time, they conveniently sacramentalized the second part of the evening while allowing their pre-member, unconverted unsociability to be evident in the first part. By so doing, Paul laments, they "despise the Church of God and humiliate those who have nothing" (v 22). Those who had nothing, for whom they did not wait (v 33), were probably the slaves whose time was not their own and whose arrival was contingent upon their being freed for the night by their owners.[10]

One of the ways Paul evaluates the Corinthians' behavior is to remind them of the nature of what it is they are doing. He presents to them the tradition, the "givens" that are meant to form the character of their celebration. Verses 23–27 form a unit. By means of this pre-Pauline liturgical tradition, Paul teaches anew the normative moment, the historical Lord's supper, which they ignore or transgress under pain of eating and drinking condemnation unto themselves. At the heart of this supper are the so-called words of institution. Jesus took bread into his hands on this night, gave thanks and broke it saying: "This is my body for you. Do this in remembrance of me" (v 24).

The authors of the new Anchor Bible commentary on this epistle make several important textual observations about both uses of the neuter demonstrative *this.* They are surprised that the traditional interest has been with the *is* rather than with the *this.* "It has been almost unanimously agreed that "this" refers to bread; so the sentence is understood to read, "This bread is my body."[11] They go on to observe that it was, therefore, inevitable that verse 29 on "not discerning the body" should have come "to refer to recognizing that the bread is not mere bread but is in some sense the presence and actual body of Christ."[12] They hope to cast doubt on these assumptions. To this end they make several observations. First, it should be admitted that there is no clear referent for either "this." Second, both of these neuter demonstrative pronouns must be taken together in order to understand what they are referring to. Third, their referent can hardly be construed by a single thing like bread. Fourth, neither "this" can refer to bread since the gender of the demonstrative is neuter while bread is masculine in Greek. Fifth, in Paul's writings the neuter demonstrative usually refers to a clause, phrase or an implied idea if not to a neuter noun. So the authors turn to the second "this." They conclude, after analyzing the Old and New Testament usage of "Do (*poieite*) this," that in similar usages "this" is commonly used to refer to a call to the whole action of table fellowship which, of course, included the distribution of bread. This fellowship was to be enjoyed at a special kind of meal, namely, a memorial observance such as Passover or Purim. By putting all of this information together, they conclude that Jesus is saying to his disciples something like: "your fellowship at this meal in remembrance of me is my body for you." The commentators are sure that the particle of food alone is not being called the body of Christ. "If Paul had wanted to convey that idea, his regular usage would have been to write, 'This bread is my body'; note 'this bread' in verse 26, where reference to the body is pointedly missing."[13]

If this line of textual reasoning is followed, the implications are notable. Jesus would be bread for them through their fellowship. The command would be to build fellowship, to be a body, to love one another with the eucharistic celebration as the center of this body-building process. In effect, Jesus would then be saying: "Do this again and again by remembering me at your table fellowship. But you remember me if you know my presence with you is through one another whom I am fashioning into so many members of my own body. Therefore, each time you come together remembering me, I remember you to me and to one another."

Does this explanation retain its plausibility when we proceed to the cup? It would appear to be the case. Note, first of all, that the cup was blessed and offered after supper (v. 25). In Corinth, it seems the agape meal was enclosed within the two blessings. In the pre-Pauline tradition that Paul is handing on, Jesus says: "This cup is the new covenant in my blood. Do this as often as you drink it, in remembrance of me" (v. 25). There is not a problem of unclear referents here. The "this" in the first part is an adjective modifying the cup. The cup affords the one receiving it the opportunity for participation in the new covenant. This new covenant is a new relationship to salvation made possible by the atoning death of Jesus. What is new about the origins of this covenant is described by the phrase "in my blood." What is new about the effects of this covenant in his blood for those who drink it? Paul himself puts it succinctly: "The cup of blessing, which we bless, is it not a participation (*koinonia*) in the blood of Christ? The bread that we break, is it not participation in the body of Christ? Because there is one bread we who are many are one body for we all partake of the one bread" (1 Cor 10:16–17).[14] This participation in the body of Christ is a communion with the whole Christ, the exalted Lord and the body of believers. This new order of salvation is an eschatological order which empowers those who are called into it to taste of the life to come and of the reign in which Jesus is Lord. To partake of the cup of the Lord, then, means that one comes into and under the reign of the exalted Lord. The believer cannot partake of the cup without being drawn into the reign. But believers could not be drawn into the reign and continue to act as they had prior to their incorporation into all that this reign entailed. The sacramental and the social, rather than being two sides of the one reality, stood in contradiction to one another in Corinth. Like the eating of the bread, the drinking of the cup involved something much deeper and broader than the liturgical act of consuming the blessed species. That "something more" is not created by those partaking but it must be "done" by them nonetheless. For their part, they must "do" what they were being made.

It was not being done by the Corinthians. What was being done was the absolutizing of the sacramental communion. They were eating and drinking at the agape meal with one spirit and eating the blessed bread and drinking the cup with another. By their "sacramentalism," they misjudged themselves. "To discern the body, to esteem Christ's body in its peculiarity, means that the body of Christ given for us and received in the sacrament united the recipients in the body of the congregation and makes them responsible for one another in love."[15] Bornkamm continues: "If this is correct it indicates that verse 29 is directed against the profaning of the body of Christ precisely under the mask of an increasing sacralization of the eucharistic food."[16]

After quoting the words of institution, Paul begins his own midrash with verse 26: "For as often as you eat this bread and drink this cup, you proclaim the Lord's death until he comes." His choice of words gives a further proof that Paul was anxious to root out the anti-somatic gnostic tendencies which were having such an effect on the corporate consciousness he had hoped to inculcate in the Corinthian Christians. The important words in this verse are "death" and "until." Paul was anxious to emphasize they were between two moments, one when the Lord gave himself up in death and the other the coming of the Lord in the future. These words are significant because they are contrary to a "fanatical transcending of the boundaries of time in a spiritual-eschatological enthusiasm."[17] The enthusiasts proclaimed the Lord's and their own resurrection with the Lord as something they were now experiencing. In their state of spiritual euphoria, they were inducing a triumphalistic degree of glory that Paul found false. Instead, he roots their celebrations within time and calls them back to the historical realism with which his letters are replete. "For as in Adam all die, so in Christ shall all be made alive. But each in his own order: Christ, the first fruits, then at his coming those who belong to Christ" (1 Cor 15:22–23).

These Corinthians were, of course, being drawn into the realm of the risen Lord but they were immaturely imagining themselves to be in a condition of exaltation which was simply untrue of them. In addition, they were distancing themselves from the bloody sacrifice of the cross. Concretely, they were embracing a faith that cost them little. Paul connects their theology with their individualism, domestic privatism and the drunken disregard of some for their fellows in Christ.

RELATIONAL WHOLENESS

There are several social indicators in the Pauline letters that reveal Paul's way of detecting whether groups of Christians were coming under the lordship of Christ. He would not have been satisfied that the simple confession that Jesus was their Lord was sufficient, although that would have to be part of it.[18] One of the key tests, the one we will concentrate on, was whether a relational wholeness was developing among the believers who confessed Jesus as their Lord. If he really was their Lord then individuals would be submitting to what the Lord was doing to them. But that submission would take a very definite direction or shape. Strays became a flock. Individuals became a people. Individual stones, so to speak, became part of a living temple. "I's" became "We's."

Paul's favorite expression for describing the relational wholeness he observed in Christian communities and in his experience was to call his wholeness Christ's body. If Jesus was really becoming Lord of individuals, then individuals were really changing their relationship to the other individuals who also confessed Jesus as their Lord. The change was sufficiently different that it had to be named differently. Paul did not see individual Christians simply in relationship to one another, he saw them as members of one another.

Over the years, scholars have expended considerable energy trying to discover the conceptual precedents, or some of the more likely sources, for such an idea. One whole school chooses as its candidate the Stoic philosophy which sees the state as a body with interdependent members as the place where Paul hit upon the idea. Another school is sure that the idea occurred from the corporate personality notion in the Old Testament. Still a third alleges its source to be the gnostic myth of the "redeemed-redeemer's gigantic body."[19] Though any one or all of these in combination could have been the actual source of the idea for Paul, these explanations seem to overlook a much more obvious and immediate explanation, namely, his own experience in relating to his brothers and sisters in Christ plus his own observation of Christian communities. Either or both of these made the idea of a single body which had, at the same time, endless differences within it while retaining its unity, a very apt description. It can be neither proven nor disproven that Paul was relying on the history of ideas in order to conjure up the language event which referred to the Christian communities as Christ's body. I am not sure such an explanation is necessary. One notices for example in all Paul's letters a degree of emotional (although that does not explain it) bonding with those to whom he writes. From the very first letter of Paul that we have, we find him emoting: "So well disposed were we to you, in fact, that we wanted to share with you not only God's tidings but our very lives, so dear had you become to us" (1 Thess 2:8).

An experiential discovery of the fact that the Lord was knitting together people as intimately as if they were so many members of his Son's own body took several years to mature. It is not until the letter to the Corinthians (probably between 53–55 A.D.) that Paul uses such an expression.[20] By then he sees the aptness of such a bold expression. It should be noted, too, that by then he was aware of the implications for "the body politic" if "the body Christian" were to fail in achieving the relational wholeness it was capable of. Were that to happen, the mission of the communities would grind to a halt.

Let me note in passing that this relational wholeness was not an end in itself. In Paul's mind there were broader social purposes and wider social implications in the quality of the relationships Christians were to experience. In a sense their mission was largely being accomplished insofar as the relations they had with one another became a sign to those in Corinth whom the Lord chose to attract to them. That sign pointed to an alternative way of being and living in Corinth. Individuals knitted together in a bonding so close as to be like a single body with many differences was evidence that a new kind of city was possible, something other than the fragmentation Corinth had known. If this point is true then the relational, the salvational, and the political can be seen as three different optics on the one thing God is doing. The knitting together of individuals would be their redemption and at the same time would be the beginning of the recapitulation of all systems in Christ.

It is good to remember, too, that the Church was not meant to be a single social system which would elbow its place into the world of social systems. It was rather meant to be Christ's own body which acted as both a sign to and a leaven for all social systems. It was not called to homogenize the social enterprise but to purify it, ridding it of the diversity that came from sin and *sarx*, so that the diversity that came from the spirit could also be the source of its unity.

But rather than treating these factors at the macro level, I will remain within the letter to the Corinthians which deals with the same issue of unity and diversity at a micro level. Some of the particulars of how this phenomenon of relational wholeness is achieved are worth simply pointing out.

Much can be gained from reading through the passage from 1 Corinthians 12:12–27. There are a number of references to interaction between people. There is first of all the clear indication that the self-sufficiency and individualism that Paul and the Christians knew before they became the Christ event no longer obtained. On the one hand, there is the experience of incompleteness in oneself because of a discovery of many powers only some of which one finds in oneself. The experiential side of this pluralism of charisms means that one finds a need for others and for the peculiar gifts that others are imbued with. Not the gifts alone, but the gifts plus the gifteds together begin to make a person a part of a whole. One cannot be oneself apart from the body. The need for one another is a key experience for Paul, so that when he finds a Christian community lacking in awareness of this kind of mutuality, he is concerned to point out that deficiency. "The eye cannot say to the hand, 'I have no need for you,' nor again the head to the feet, 'I have no need of you.' " (1 Cor 12:21). Relational wholeness, apparently, in the Pauline experience is not achieved by collectivizing a mass but rather by the upbuilding of one another through the uniqueness each has breathed into himself or herself through the Spirit.

In the passage we are examining here, Paul is dealing with the very tangible ways in which human beings relate or fail to relate to one another, but he is not treating these in the usual way. He talks about having such care for one another that one member cannot rejoice without all rejoicing nor can one member suffer without the rest being impacted by that member's suffering. He is concerned that persons be in touch with their unique giftedness, while accepting their incompleteness without others. In turn he reminds all to identify themselves not with a few but with all, with Christ himself and the whole body which has so many different functions needed in order for it to be itself and for all in it to be themselves. The doctrine of the body, in other words, is built up from innumerable experiences or concrete acts of interdependence and mutuality. Paul talks about very tangible, simple human actions and, at the same time, he does not think the degree of intimacy that he finds between those performing those actions can be explained by merely human emotion or effort. They are expressing and creating more than a human bonding. He saw them all as so many moments of upbuilding a reality bigger than any one of them. He saw nothing less than Christ's own presence being built up through the richness of what each one received from God. Before it was a doctrine to be assented to it had to be an experience looking for a name. The name Paul found apropos was body. They were Christ's body.

There is another reason why the doctrine of the body of Christ does not have the impact on us that it had on the first generations of Christianity. It suffers from having been flattened out or ecclesiologized. We have come to believe that we are in some way Christ's body but Paul is saying something much more profound than that. In 1 Corinthians 12:12 he is saying that just as a body is one with many members and all the members of a body, though many, are one body—this is who Christ is now.[21] This must be heard as a Christological statement for it to impact the hearer. Paul meant it to be a Christological statement.[22] What he is saying is not only that the many are one but that the one the many are is Christ. He is saying more than that individuals participate in Christ or that through baptism they are made part of an ecclesial reality. He is saying: together they are Christ. He is saying that in addition to being Lord of the universe, Christ Jesus is now an immanent reality. He is saying something more than that individuals belong to the Church or even that they belong to Christ's body; he is saying that many individuals together are so conjoined to the risen Lord that he and they are the Christ now.[23]

The point Paul makes by naming the experience of Christian communities in this way is so basic that it is more often than not softened so that it doesn't really say what, in fact, it means. One of our favorite ways of dulling the impact of calling these Christian communities Christ has already been mentioned, namely by assuming that the meaning of Church is being addressed rather than the question of the Christ as he now exists and reigns. Another way is to begin to distinguish the relationship between Christ and the members of his body in terms like ontological, moral, functional and other such distinctions that Paul would not himself have conceived of. Paul knew as well as anyone that there was not a total identification between the uncreated and the created, between the divine and the human. His letters abound with acknowledgement of that. Hence, the bride is distinguishable from the bridegroom, the field from the planter, the pot from the potter, and so on. But this must not soften the truth of the Incarnation nor the fact that the Word has been made *social* flesh. For us, unfortunately, the body of Christ has somehow or other come to be seen as a kind of appendage trailing on to the risen Lord. But for Paul the meaning of body connotes the whole of the person, the person acting, the person choosing, the living person.

How could a statement like 1 Corinthians 12:12 make sense? As if anticipating the question Paul answers in the very next verse: "For by one Spirit we are all baptized into one body—Jews or Greeks, slaves or free—and all were made to drink of one Spirit" (1 Cor 12:13). Paul brings together the four ingredients, so to speak, that are necessary in order to explain the remarkable assertion he has made in the preceding verse. These four theological factors are the Spirit, baptism, body and Eucharist.[24] Once the Holy Spirit is introduced into Christology the transcendent and immanent can be conjoined because the Spirit traverses the depths of each.[25] The Spirit can also knit the divine and human together into a single personality.[26] Here an indissoluble unity between the one and the many is ascribed to the Spirit.

Putting the same matter in a more Christological and chronological form Paul's belief had something of the following shape. When Jesus died, the same thing happened to him as happens in any human death, his body and his spirit underwent some kind of a separation. Unlike any other human death, however, Jesus came into a new relationship with his body. Looked at from his side he was raised; looked at from our side his own body became the created means through which his Spirit was dispensed to other human beings. Before his death, as is the case with any human being, his spirit touched the world through his body. Now his spirit would touch the universe through his body. Before his death the expressions of his personality were tied to the principle of limitation which is matter. Now his body is not limited by matter, as is true of "a body of death" but the whole of the material universe is "at the service of his manifestation."[27]

The change we're interested in here, however, is the one in which the anthropological and the Christological converge. There was a radically new possibility in the human order, given the death and resurrection of Jesus. Something is possible now that is more than that human beings can be "in Christ" or that Christ can be in individuals. Through baptism, Christ's own death and resurrection can now become more determining of individuals than their own births and deaths. But the opposite has equal truth in it, namely that if they are members of his body he is now these individuals.

By being baptized, furthermore, individuals are baptized into his death and are therefore brought out of a state of sinfulness which, among other things, left them in isolation from one another. Baptism brought them out of the state of pre-membership with which they had come into the world. Now endowed with a capacity to be members of one another in the body of Christ, the Lord who created them would bring about their redemption by bringing this capacity to realization.

Relational Wholeness and Social Systems

What is the relevance for other social systems of this experience of being members of one another in a bonding whose name is the body of Christ? Or—to remain with the letter to the Corinthians—what was the relationship between the ecclesial social system being generated by the lordship of Jesus in Corinth and the other social systems which together composed the economic, political and cultural life of the city? In the course of instructing the Corinthians, Paul provides some insight into this question. Though he would hardly have asked the question our way, he does have some definite attitudes which give a good indication of how he would have dealt with the question.

First of all, there must have been some in Corinth who took this body of Christ kind of membering so seriously that they were pushing to withdraw from every former kind of social system of which they had been part. I say this because Paul formally instructs them in several places to remain exactly as they had been before their conversion. "Let everyone lead a life which the Lord has assigned to him. . . . Everyone should remain in the state in which he was called. . . . In whatever state each was called there let him remain with God" (1 Cor 7:17–24). For example, "Are you bound to a wife? Do not seek to be free. Are you free from a wife? Do not seek marriage" (1 Cor 7:27).

This was not an exhortation to passivity or indifference. On the contrary, each believer was to behave in such a unique way as to have a definite impact on all the social forms of life he or she was in. It seems that Paul put great stock in the possibilities of converted persons' witness to the drastic change that Christ made in their lives. Paul does not expect that the person should or needs to leave the systems, but he expects that the systems should and would be redefined by the persons living within them now in a different way. For example, the social system of slavery. "Were you a slave when called? Never mind! . . . He who was called in the Lord as a slave is a freedman of the Lord" (1 Cor 7:21–22).

It seems that Paul would have quite a different attitude toward social systems than our modern mentalities have developed. It would be right to conclude that the systems themselves need not be our responsibility or the object of our concern. The object of our concern must rather be: What have I become, what have we been made by God in Christ? If we take that seriously, if one stays *in* but no longer sees himself or herself *of* the same condition as others then one will act quite differently. Hence, Paul exhorts people to be indifferent about the things that everyone else is anxious about and exhorts them to be concerned about things no one else thinks relevant. His Christology, in other words, becomes an all-consuming passion or determinant of all other social influences, factors and systems. The new creation is meant to redefine the old creation, not to accommodate to it.

Paul adopts this position in part because "The appointed time has grown very short . . . for the form of this world is passing away" (1 Cor 7:29–31). Paul's immanent-Christ doctrine must be complemented by the imminence-of-full-manifestation of that presence in the midst of believers and non-believers alike. When the things of this world, even the most intimate things such as marriage or the most necessary things such as buying or selling, are juxtaposed to the presence of the Christ and the expectation of the fullness of that presence, the former things must be taken very lightly. Hence, "From now on, let those who have wives live as though they had none . . . and those who buy as though they had no goods, and those who deal with the world as though they had no dealings with it" (1 Cor 7:30–31).

We have now advanced three different ingredients to answer this final question of the essay, namely, the relevance of the bonding of some believers for other social systems. One of the ingredients is Christological, the other eschatological and the third is Paul's reverence for all of creation. We must keep these three together in order to understand what Paul's approach would be to the question which we are attempting to answer.

Some of the things to remember about the Christological ingredient: if our Christology were as social as Paul's, a Christological answer to the question of social systems would not be the pious copout it may otherwise appear. One could also say that Pauline social analysis is radically Christological. It's even possible that Paul would suggest that if Christians came to understand and, in turn, live the degree of change the Lord has worked in them through baptism and his Spirit, then analyses of social systems themselves and Christ's would-be lordship over them might be superfluous. Social systems would be so affected by the Christians living in them that these differences would themselves presage the shape of things to come when he would be Lord of all.[28]

With respect to the eschatological, these things should be noted: once the value of this world and therefore of all the social systems within this world are accurately weighed on a scale the other term of which is the Christ presence within this world, then the former things suffer badly by comparison. So badly, that Paul is anxious to point out that attention to the things of this world will distract one from what is really important about this world. "I wish you to be free from concern," even with the most personal of social systems, namely marriage, in order to be concerned about the affairs of the Lord" (1 Cor 7:32). "One who is married is concerned about the affairs of the world, how he may please his wife" (1 Cor 7:33). For Paul, in other words, there were two ways of looking at social reality. One was to look at it in terms of itself and become distracted. The second was to look at it in relation to the Christ-presence within the world. If one did so, as Paul did, that would be a full agenda. Or could be.

It is also important to understand the meaning of Paul's judgment that "the form of this world is passing away" (1 Cor 7:31). Barrett's translation is germane. "The outward show of this world is passing away."[29] The Anchor Bible notes: the form which is passing away is "the shape the world is in."[30] The inner reality of the social systems and ultimately of creation itself is another story still being worked out in Paul's mind in the Corinthian letter.[31]

The third ingredient, Pauline secularity, is part of his Jewish reverence for all of created reality. It is not necessary for us to read into Paul a disdain for this world in order to share his awe at the Christ presence within it. One of the reasons why he does not have the Christian communities become enclaves but insists they remain part of the social realities and systems of their fellow citizens, can be traced to this same reverence. One must couple the universality of Christ's reign over all of creation to the Old Testament theme of the salvation of the nations, to see what lies behind Paul's order "to all the Churches" (1 Cor 7:17) that the faithful should remain in the diverse secular callings and systems in which the Lord found them.

Paul does not know and does not purport to know how the present shape of social existence will be transposed into the future shape of social existence, but he knows the difference between the two will be what we would describe as dialectical. "So is it with the resurrection of the dead. What is sown is perishable, what is raised is imperishable. It is sown in dishonor, it is raised in glory. It is sown in weakness, it is raised in power" (1 Cor 15:42–43). He knows finally that the future of social reality will not be one of annihilation but of transformation. As with the individual, so also, "we shall not all sleep, but we shall all be changed, in a moment, in the twinkling of an eye, at the last trumpet" (1 Cor 15:51–52).

One is left to wonder, finally, what the political effect would have been on Corinth and elsewhere if a diluted form of Christology had not been embraced and instead an experience of membering had been taken back to all the social realities of which Corinthian Christians were a part. What would have happened, for example, to the relations between men and women in Corinth, if a growing number of Corinthians came to so reverence one another that their treatment of one another transcended stereotypical gender roles (Gal 3:28)? One is left to wonder what would have happened if the vastly different social conditions and circumstances, as for example, between slaves and freemen, Jews and Greeks, did not impede a bonding with one another more intimate than those which had obtained between even family members.

"You are all one in Christ Jesus" (Gal 3:28) was a fact that had to be lived and it would have been lived much more powerfully if the relational wholeness that Paul experienced had been believed in after it was named. If it had been lived, named and exported then the question which this volume asks would have had a ready answer. We are left to speculate about the question because, for the most part, we continue to name and follow a Christ who looks more like the one our Corinthian forebears concocted than the one Paul preached. We take comfort in this diluted form of Christology because the ramifications of the Incarnation are still too preposterous to accept. We continue to name the reality of Christ from the experience of our individualism rather than from the experience of membering. Hence we name a Christ who does not include those who he said he was. We call Paul's venturesome descriptions eschatological vistas pointing to the future and forget they are also political vistas pointing to the present and to possibilities in the Christ mystery we have even stopped imagining.

NOTES

1. Conzelmann calls the Corinthians "proto-Gnostics." Contrary to many exegetes, he contends that Paul's letter to the Corinthians is attempt-

ing to counter Gnosticism not fully blown but *"in statu nascendi."* Hans Conzelmann, *A Commentary on the First Epistle to the Corinthians* (Philadelphia: Fortress, 1975), p. 15.

2. C. K. Barrett, *The First Epistle to the Corinthians* (New York: Harper and Row, 1968), p. 149. Also, Joseph A. Fitzmyer, *Pauline Theology* (Englewood Cliffs, New Jersey: Prentice-Hall, 1967): "Man does not merely have a *soma,* he is a *soma*" (p. 61).

3. *The New World Dictionary-Concordance to the American Bible* (Cleveland: World Publishing, 1970), p. 193.

4. E. Käsemann, "The Pauline Doctrine of the Last Supper," *Essays on New Testament Themes* (Studies in Biblical Theology n. 41; Naperville, IL: A. R. Allenson, 1964), p. 130.

5. C.F.D. Moule, "The Judgment Theme in the Sacraments," in: W. D. Davies and D. Daube, eds., *The Background of the New Testament and Its Eschatology* (Cambridge: University Press, 1956), pp. 464–483.

6. *Ibid.*, pp. 467–9. Also 1 Cor 2:15; 6:2. Both verses treat of not being judged while being empowered to judge.

7. E.g., ". . . that they may all be one; even as thou, Father, art in me and I in thee, that they also may be in us . . ." (Jn 17:21).

8. Barrett, *op. cit.,* p. 268.

9. The account of the Last Supper is a formulation of sacred law, according to Käsemann. His observation is based on the fact that the rabbinic terms *qibel* and *masar,* "which connote the unbroken legitimate succession of tradition," are the Hebrew equivalents of the Greek words for "received" (Παραλαμβανειν) and "delivered" (Παραδιδοναι). Käsemann, *op. cit.*, p. 120.

10. William F. Orr and James Arthur Walther, *I Corinthians: A New Translation* (The Anchor Bible; Garden City, NY: Doubleday, 1976), p. 270.

11. *Ibid.,* pp. 271–3.

12. *Ibid.,* p. 271.

13. *Ibid.,* p. 272.

14. Günther Bornkamm calls these verses the only authentic commentary in the whole New Testament on the words of institution. G. Bornkamm, *Early Christian Experience* (London: SCM, 1969), p. 139.

15. Bornkamm, *op. cit.,* p. 149.

16. *Ibid.,* p. 149.

17. *Ibid.,* pp. 151–2.

18. "No one can say 'Jesus is Lord' except by the Holy Spirit" (1 Cor 12:3).

19. Robert Jewett, *Paul's Anthropological Terms* (Leiden: Brill, 1971), p. 231, and 201–287 *passim.*

20. Barrett, *op. cit.,* p. 5.

21. οὕτως και ὁ χριστος.

22. All of Paul's anthropology is a Christology. Cf. Jewett, *op. cit.,* p. 10; Fitzmyer, *op. cit.,* pp. 16–17.

23. After analyzing 1 Corinthians 12:12 thoroughly, Jerome Murphy-O'Connor, O.P., observes: "The application of the name 'Christ' to the community must be considered to have formed part of Paul's habitual vocabulary" ("Eucharist and Community in First Corinthians," *Worship* 50 [1976] 375).

24. These are constitutive parts of Paul's unitary insight.

25. 1 Cor 2:10.

26. Lk 1:35.

27. X. Leon-Dufour, *Resurrection and the Message of Easter* (New York: Holt, Rinehart and Winston, 1975), p. 271.

28. A number of Pauline texts speak of the abrogation of individual differences that divide. This is both an eschatological vision and a description of the present for Paul.

29. Barrett, *op. cit.,* p. 178.

30. Orr and Walther, *op. cit.,* p. 219.

31. E.g., by the time of the letter to the Colossians, in Christ "all things were created . . . through him and for him. He is before all things, and in him all things hold together" (Col 1:16–17).

6
Symbol and System: Embodying Love

Otto H. Hentz, S.J.

We live in social systems which, in some measure, are our creations, the products of our freedom. But in some measure they are also a limitation of our freedom, a predetermined framework within which we must function. In any case, these interlocking systems, which we necessarily construct or endure for the sake of shared experience in a common history, are essential to human life. It must be, then, that Christ is Lord in some way of our social systems. The purpose of this essay is to provide a conceptual model by which we can understand the effective presence of Christ in and through our social systems. This model will be drawn from reflection on classic Church doctrine about the person of Christ as Word incarnate.

From one point of view the Incarnation is an obvious starting point. Christ is, in his very person, the decisive revelation about God and humankind. The personal reality of Christ provides the model in terms of which Christians understand the relationship between God and world, grace and history, the life of the Christian and secular life in the world. It makes sense, then, to explore the Church's doctrine about the Word incarnate in order to find the formula for a Christian vision of history and an understanding of the lordship of Christ in relation to social systems.

From another point of view, however, it is not obvious that the Church's doctrine about the Word incarnate is a helpful starting point. The problem is not that doctrine about the union of God and man in the person of Christ ("hypostatic union") seems abstract and makes intellectual demands. Any effort to think through the meaning of Christ's lordship will be demanding. We cannot understand how Christ is Lord unless we understand the fundamental, general relationship between God and the created world, and the relationship between the role of Christ who is Lord and the role of other human persons in the establishment of the kingdom of God. Rather, the problem in starting with the Church's teaching about the Incarnation is that it is precisely reflection on this teaching which has given rise to images of Christ and of human history which dissociate his effective presence from the concrete shape of our history and the specific social systems in and through which we live. As Monika Hellwig has indicated in the introductory essay of this volume, the doctrine of the Incarnation speaks of the person of Christ in terms of the becoming of God. This can lead to a misguided focus on the divinity of Christ which leaves in shadow the genuine humanity of Christ and the concrete shape of the actual life of Jesus, who became Lord in and through the course of his personal history. When we leave in shadow the genuinely human reality of Christ we obscure his actual relationship with us and the significance of our concrete history in the world.

What an irony, that the doctrine about God's becoming man be so interpreted as to set a gulf between God and the world and divorce the effective presence of Christ the Lord from social systems! The good news of Christ is that God is God with us, for us humans and for our salvation. The news is not about God alone, nor is it about God with us in some remote way. The news is that God has chosen to identify in his very being with us and our history. And it is the doctrine of the Incarnation which makes explicit the unsurpassably decisive way in which God is God with us: in self-emptying love God has become man.

The doctrine of the Incarnation, in fact, provides a helpful key to the relationship between the lordship of Christ and social systems. The key is the notion of "embodiment." By "embodiment" I mean the process of rendering oneself effectively present in and through the creation of an expression of oneself. A handshake, for example, is an embodiment in which I express and render present my good will toward another person. As we shall see, the dynamics of expressive embodiment are always subtle (a handshake, which expresses good will, might in fact embody a lie). And the process of embodiment becomes more complicated as the relationships to be expressed and achieved become more complicated (the establishment of a welfare system is, obviously, a quite complicated embodiment of public will). Nevertheless the notion of embodiment is most helpful. On the one hand, social systems are the necessary embodiments by which we express and render effectively present the relationships through which we live with one another in our common history. On the other hand, Jesus is Lord precisely as the one in whom God becomes embodied, incarnate: God is effectively present with us in an unsurpassably decisive way by coming to be in the man Jesus. The effective presence of Christ to us in our history should take shape in and through the social systems in which we live. But this effective presence of Christ to us, embodied in social systems, would be an extension of the process of God's incarnation in Christ.

To show that the lordship of Christ should be exercised through the embodiment of Christ's effective presence in social systems I will reflect first in a general way on human gestures and social systems as embodiments of the human spirit. Then I will turn to the person of Christ and consider the connection between the Word Incarnate and the incarnation of Christ's effective presence in social systems.

Gesture as Symbolic Embodiment

To appreciate the subtle dynamics of effective presence through expressive embodiment it is enough to reflect on a simple gesture like a handshake. Even such a simple gesture, which immediately involves only two individuals, is not removed from complex social systems. Whatever the specific context (politics or business, for example), a handshake is part of a larger social system of gestures, a system which reflects a certain cultural style of expressing personal relationships. Be that as it may, we do well to begin with an example which is, on its face, simple, because of the complexity and ambiguity present in the process of self-expression through expressive embodiment.

A handshake is a gesture which arises out of my desire to express my good will for another person. Unless I actually express my good will externally, unless I embody my good will in some gesture like a handshake (or ill will, in a hands-at-side refusal of a handshake), I am not effectively present to the other person as the one I choose to be for the other. Moreover, in making myself effectively present through a symbolic gesture I do more than touch another person. Through expressive embodiment I bring myself to full human life in the world; I am no longer what I might choose to be in a purely interior or merely tentative way. What I choose to be takes shape fully in my being, that is, in my physical body, and thereby in public, in the larger social body of which I am a part. And to the extent that I effectively shape what I mean to be for others in an embodiment of myself, I shape myself decisively and reinforce my commitment to be as I have chosen. In sum, when I make a gesture there is a unity in my person of the self which expresses itself and the expressive embodiment in and through which the self achieves explicit expression.

The unity of self and expressive embodiment in the life of a human person is complex. Within the unity there is a distinction between the self and its symbolic embodiment in gesture. This distinction-in-unity is evident in our experience: for one expressive embodiment of good will, like a handshake, we can substitute another, like a wave of the hand or a wink. But the basis for this distinction-in-unity of self and expressive embodiment is the limitation inherent in gestures. The human spirit lives in and through expressive embodiment, because the human person is a psycho-physical unity. But no gesture can exhaustively embody the human spirit. We know that our trust and love are effectively present for others only through their embodiment in word and gesture, but we also know that no word or gesture exhaustively captures the life of trust and love. Expressive embodiments, then, are symbols in and through which a deeper reality comes to expression.

Now because effective presence for others takes place through a symbolic embodiment which involves the unity-in-difference of self and embodiment, the gesture remains to some extent ambiguous. First of all, the degree of unity between the self and its expressive embodiment in a particular gesture is variable. Apart from the fact that the specific gesture selected might or might not be the appropriate self-expression (for example, a casual wink rather than a more formal handshake), the depth of personal involvement in the gesture can vary. The gesture might be from the heart, or somewhat casual, or mere acquiescence in a superficial formality. Indeed a gesture which is heartfelt might arise spontaneously from my self-disposition, as in an enthusiastic welcome, or from a determinate effort to renew a disposition which is not spontaneous, as in a moment of difficult reconciliation. There is a still deeper ambiguity in the gesture. The gesture might arise from very different intentions: the gesture might be magnanimous, or dutifully responsible, or manipulative and deceptive.

The second reason for the ambiguity in a gesture is the fact that human experience is historical. Particular gestures are not isolated events, but moments in a process. At various moments in a relationship, for example, a handshake might be more or less appropriate to represent a first, formal encounter, the enthusiasm of a friendship renewed, the heartfelt joy of reconciliation after painful separation, or the resolute agreement to dissociation without enmity.

No doubt, the most painful experience of the distinction between the self and its expressive embodiment is the experience of a gesture or pattern of gestures which assumes relatively independent status as a symbolic embodiment and resists change and constricts the free effectiveness of a person. An obvious example is addictive behavior. A shift in one's self-disposition requires a more or less embarrassing and painful shift in the familiar pattern of self-expression, in the embodiment through which one has lived. A new style of personal life requires a new "body." The point is that when I move from a tentative, purely interior intention to an expressive embodiment of my will, I put myself "on the line," so to speak, a line which sets limits with which both I myself and others have subsequently to deal.

Now, given that the human spirit is effectively present for others through symbolic embodiments, and given the subtle, ambiguous relationship between the self and its self-expression, we come to the heart of the matter, namely, the heart, one's choices, one's loves. For who I choose to be determines whether I will commit myself through the expression of specific intentions and what shape the expressive embodiment will take. There is risk involved. Apart from the fact that I am not the only agent involved and cannot control another's interpretation of my gesture or response to it, and apart from the fact that I act in a public world whose shape has already been determined historically and socially, a concrete gesture or strategy is subject to all the ambiguity of personal involvement, intention and appropriateness sketched above. And yet without a concrete gesture or strategy I do not succeed in rendering my will effectively present. For effective presence to others in the world I must both risk a concrete gesture and remain self-critical, discerning and flexible with respect to my gesture; I must commit myself to a concrete strategy and relativize my strategy for the sake of effective presence in the complex process of life with others.

How does the foregoing analysis of a simple gesture like a handshake serve our reflections on the complicated matter of the lordship of Christ in relation to social systems? The analysis reveals the basic structure of effective personal presence in society: (1) effective presence is a process of self-expression through symbolic embodiment; (2) the process of expressive embodiment involves the subtle and ambiguous unity-in-difference of the self which comes to expression in the symbolic embodiment and the symbolic embodiment intended as the expression of self; (3) what motivates, sustains and shapes the process of effective presence through expressive embodiment is a creative will which is self-critical, discerning and flexible. That basic structure applies to social systems.

The Family as a Social System

To analyze effective presence through social systems we can reflect on family life as a basic example of a complex social system. To be sure, the relationships involved in the life of a family may be quite immediate, and the social structures which embody a "system" of family life may be quite organic, in comparison with those in the life of a corporate institution, a university, for example, or an insurance company, or the larger political-economic systems of which corporate institutions are a part. But the fact is that at the heart of family life is a plurality of human subjects. Family life, in its own way, involves the power and politics inherent in all social relationships, in which individuals move to assert their freedom and be influential in shared human space. And, I might note in passing, the relationships between spouses and between parents and children furnish images used throughout Scripture to illustrate God's covenant with humankind.

The process by which two people become friends, court one another and marry is an historical process. Their mutual involvement is undertaken, sustained and developed in the freedom and risk of love. For personal revelation and personal acceptance of that revelation in faith is gratuitous. But in their relationship friends freely share their very lives, what they are at heart—their vision and values, their hopes and anxieties, their personal styles of being—shaping and being shaped in their consciousness and freedom by their gratuitous gift of themselves. Of course, the marriage moment is uniquely significant. They relate to one another through all the events in their story, through all the words and gestures by which they embody and make effective their relationship. But all these expressions are provisional in effect and ambiguous in meaning until their gratuitous relationship comes to the decisive moment of marriage, the moment in which their history together reaches a decisive culmination, at which point the meaning of their relationship is no longer tentative and ambiguous, but, in principle at least, decisively defined and expressed.

Now in varying degrees, at different stages of their marriage, the whole of their lives is shaped by the life which they share so that the words and gestures, the patterns and styles of activity by which they relate are expressive embodiments of the life which they create with one another. Some gestures, of course, explicitly and unambiguously embody their relationship—the celebration of their anniversary, for example; in others the expression is implicit and ambiguous—working day by day, caring for their house, and so on. Further, when spouses beget children and become parents, their creative love brings into being other persons with whom to share their life and love. And their children, in varying degrees of freedom, will be personal embodiments of the life shared by the parents.

To describe briefly the process by which the relationship of spouses is embodied in words, gestures, and patterns of activity is not to romanticize this process. Love is proved in deeds, and the patterns of activity in a marriage can embody a relationship which arises from a will which is in some measure egocentric and unloving. The patterns of activity which might embody and reinforce lack of communication and distance between spouses are familiar enough. And, of course, a lack of love between parents has its effect on children, just as love does.

The life of a family constitutes a social system: a congeries of roles, of characteristic patterns of activity, of structures of custom and ritual embody and shape family life. Expressions familiar in discussion of family styles witness to the reality of social system in the life of a family: "In our family we always," "My father never," and so on. Customary patterns of activity which embody a family style determine and reinforce the framework of family life and are the means by which children are educated to that style. For example, the religious dimension of life may express itself in quite explicit rituals like prayer before dinner, or regular church attendance; or, it may be, there simply is no expression of religious faith whatsoever. In such symbolic embodiments of religious consciousness (or lack of it) family members determine and reinforce or challenge the religious consciousness of family members. Educational and cultural concern, or the lack thereof, will be embodied in patterns of activity and rituals related to reading and schooling, like regular conversation about books, or the familiar discussion about how much TV before homework, or the lack of such conversation and discussions. Political values are expressed, developed and communicated in patterns of involvement with political parties, neighborhood clubs, unions and professional societies, civic and church organizations. Mutual personal concern is embodied in such rituals as celebration of birthdays, regular visits to relatives and patterns of leisure activity.

The customs and rituals through which family life takes shape involve all the ambiguity and limitation inherent in varying degrees in any expressive embodiment of personal life. For example, rules and rituals enforced without modification both for a youngster and a college senior may emphatically reinforce commitment to certain values or be, for that purpose, counterproductive—even if the enforcement does not arise, as it might, from an ideologically constricted, rigid spirit. Or consider the pattern of activity of a mother who joins the work force. In her work the mother may signal a sacrificial concern for the children, or greed, or the desire for individual achievement, or simply for adult conversation not available when she is at home constantly with only tots and plants. One way or another, in any case, her work away from home changes the patterns which constitute the system of family life.

The deepest source of complexity and ambiguity, of course, is the plurality of individual persons who constitute a family. For each is free and each must choose not only out of a congeries of personal needs and desires, but in relation to the desires and demands of the others. The choice is made in accord with, or against, the system of family life which embodies an established set of relationships. Moreover, the life of a family is always in process. Parents, for example, adjust the patterns of their lives together to accommodate children (the demands of babies, the tensions of adolescence). All in the family may be challenged to shape their lives together anew to deal with prolonged sickness, unemployment, the appearance of a special child. Always there is the ebb and flow of more or less spontaneous love or conflict in the establishment, maintenance and adjustment of more or less discerning and flexible systemic patterns and procedures which specifically embody the relationships which constitute family life and determine, for good or ill, the development of those relationships.

We have explored the experience of family life as a life involving expressive embodiment in a social system to illustrate the following points: (1) the importance of systems as symbolic-embodiments in and through which human life is shared and shaped, (2) the fluid unity-in-distinction between life shared and the symbolic embodiment through which it is shared, (3) the principle of creative will (loving or selfish) which shapes the process of embodiment. We have also seen the ambiguity inherent in the social systems as embodiments of social life. Social systems are ambiguous: they represent determinate options; they represent personal life only in varying degrees; they must be relativized as concrete strategies for a life that is in process; they arise out of a political process involving the interaction of a plurality of individual freedoms; and they determine the future of the freedoms which they shape for good or ill, in ways which, in religious terms, are salutary or demonic.

The Christ Who Is Lord

Now to explore the relationship between social systems and the lordship of Christ we turn to an explicitly theological reflection. The Church's historic doctrine about the person of Christ provides a key to the relationship between God and world, grace and history, the lordship of Jesus and us, with the structures and systems through which we live in our common history.

Two questions guide our reflection. The first question is about the relationship between Jesus the Lord and us. We acknowledge in faith that the Kingdom of God is God's achievement. And God was in Christ; God reconciles the world to himself through Christ, the one mediator between God and humankind. What is the relation of the unique Christ to us and the human history which we shape in freedom? How do we figure in the lordship of Christ? The second question concerns the significance of the social systems which we create and endure. How can the Lord be effectively present through social systems? What is the saving significance of social systems themselves?

In addressing these questions we will return to the notion of expressive embodiment and explore the Christic dimension of human embodiment in social systems. For, as we shall see, the Christian doctrine of the Incarnation teaches that God is present with us in a decisively effective way precisely through expressive embodiment, that is, through the creation of the man Jesus as God's own human being. And God's decisive presence through Jesus Christ is the pledge of his will to be effectively present for all humankind. We can, therefore, on the basis of faith in Jesus Christ, imagine what we are and achieve in our history—in and through our social systems—as a potential embodiment of the saving love of God, which he means to be effective in us so that he might become "all in all."

We may begin our reflection on the person of Christ with the formula of St. John: "The Word became flesh." God does not remain eternally "enclosed," so to speak, but in the Word Incarnate becomes God-in-the-world. God truly becomes by creating something new, something other, a human reality, as his very own human reality. In and through another, a created human reality. God expands and shares divine life, so that divine life effectively becomes divine life in and for the world. And the human reality in and through which God becomes is God's very own human reality, created as united with God, because in this human reality it is truly God himself who becomes one of us.[2]

The process of parenting provides a simple, albeit imperfect, analogy for God's becoming man in the Incarnation. Spouses who wish to expand and share their married life and love beget or adopt children. Their hope is that in some measure the children will embody, be an "incarnation," of their life and love. Children are something new and other in their married life. This otherness is the condition for the expansion of the parents' love beyond the parents themselves, the condition for incorporating others into their love. But to the extent that the children appropriate, embody and reflect the parents' love the parents' life and love truly become effectively present, "incarnate," in and through the children.

To clarify the doctrine of the Incarnation the early Church rejected misconceptions of the person of Christ and articulated its authentic teaching in a succession of Councils. The decisive formula is that of the Council of Chalcedon (A.D. 451): "one identical Son, our Lord Jesus Christ . . . perfect both in his divinity and in his humanity . . . two natures without any commingling or change or division or separation . . . united in one person."[4] It is an abstract and complicated formula. But careful analysis of the formula yields remarkable insights into the relationship between the lordship of Christ and human history.

What is striking about the formula is the type of union which it implies. In Christ there is a true union of the divine and the human ("two natures . . . without division or separation"). Indeed, because the human reality of Christ belongs to the second person of the Trinity, because it is the person of the Word which possesses and sustains the created human reality as its own human reality, the union is not merely accidental, but substantial ("one identical Son, our Lord Jesus Christ . . . two natures . . . united in one person"). But the union of the divine and the human in Christ is union with distinction. The divine person of the Word is not on the same "level" as the human reality of Jesus and not in competition with genuine humanity. The divine person of the Word, therefore, does not absorb or overwhelm the human reality ("perfect both in his divinity and in his humanity . . . two natures without any commingling or change"). This means that the unity of the divine and the human is not a threat to the distinction between them, and their distinction is not a threat to the unity. Rather unity and distinction work together. It is unity in and through distinction (God creates as his own the human reality of Christ, which is new and other); it is distinction in and through unity (it is precisely as God's very own that God creates the human reality of Christ).[5]

The notion of unity-in-distinction is not alien to our experience. Mature human love exemplifies a similar kind of unity. In the mutual love of two persons there is a real unity, a communion between the persons. Their communion does not destroy their distinctive individuality and freedom. Rather, it is precisely through their communion, through the life and love which they share, that two distinct persons achieve full human life and freedom. Again—and closer to our subject, the unique Christ—when God creates a human person and summons a person to union with God, it is precisely the human person in its distinctive individuality and freedom whom God sustains by his creative love; and it is precisely in union with the God of self-giving love that the human person finds the fulfillment of his freedom. And so, when the Church teaches that there is a radical union of God and man in the person of Christ, we can think of this union of God and man as the instance in which there is a uniquely perfect fulfillment of human being and a uniquely effective presence of the creative, self-giving love of God in and through this human being.

Our analysis of the Incarnation of the Word of God in terms of unity-in-difference indicates a principle and a procedure by which we can clarify the relationship between the unique Christ and human history. The principle is that the fundamental meaning of our world and our history must be defined in relation to Christ, and, in turn, the uniqueness of Christ's person and work must be defined in relation to our world and history. For Christ is true man, and, therefore, truly a part of our common history. There is only one way to understand how Christ, who is truly part of our history, is truly divine. We must acknowledge that the divine and the truly human, both in the unique Christ and in humankind generally, are not opposed or in competition. By God's creative, self-giving love, the divine and the human are what they distinctively are precisely in relation to one another.

The procedure by which we can draw out the implications of that principle will be to consider the Incarnate Word from the side of man and then from the side of God. From the perspective of Christ's humanity we can analyze the relation of the unique Christ to humankind generally. From the perspective of Christ's divinity we can analyze the becoming of God in Christ in relation to the becoming of God in our common history.

Christ is true man. Thus, the story of Christ is the story of the human being in whose life a unique relationship to God the Father culminates in the self-emptying death of the cross and resurrection as Lord. But if God becomes radically one with humankind in the man Jesus, it must be that human nature is the potentiality for radical union with God. Christ is the uniquely perfect achievement of the potentiality of human being.[6] And so, we can understand the union of God and man accomplished in the person, life, and destiny of Christ as the decisive revelation of what God wants to accomplish for all humankind in and through our common history. In biblical images, Jesus the Lord is the first born of many brethren, the cornerstone of a building, the head of a body.

When we focus on the human reality of Christ we see the uniqueness of Christ in relation to the whole of human history and the meaning of history as a whole in relation to Christ. Since humankind is summoned to union with God in Christ, the God of creative and self-giving love is at work throughout the whole of history. The whole of history is, in its most fundamental structure, a dramatic dialogue between the transcendently free God and the free human persons whom he creates out of love in order to share divine life. The significance of this drama remains ambiguous because what takes place is provisional until the process comes to a conclusive term. Christ is that decisive term, the *eschaton,* in whom the union of God and man is decisively achieved and revealed. He is unique precisely as the "marriage moment" in the "courtship" of God and humankind, when the outcome and significance of their historical relationship is no longer provisional and ambiguous but decided and manifest. But what is decisively achieved in Christ has been in process throughout the whole of history, so that Christ is the pledge of what God wills for all humankind. History as a whole, then, is meant by God to be a history for salvation.[7]

Reflection on the human reality of Christ and the Christian view of history which it implies yields a response to the first question posed earlier, the question of how we figure in the lordship of Christ. To assert the unique efficacy of Christ is not to assert that he alone is constitutive of salvation history, but that, in relation to him and in dependence on him, we too can contribute. History as a whole constitutes the salutary situation of the individual. What each person is and can be determines and is determined by the situation of everyone else in the one history of humanity. To be sure, salvation is union with God in Christ and is brought about by God through Christ. But what God achieves in the person and life of Jesus is the decisive manifestation of what he wills to achieve through his Spirit in the lives of all persons. And so, the history of salvation takes place "in moral action made possible by God's action, as a moment of a rightly understood self-redemption of man, given to mankind by God as its task."[8] Christ the Lord is effectively present in history in and through his "body," the human persons who live by his Spirit.

We turn now to reflection on the becoming of God in Christ. This reflection will provide a response to our second question, the question of the Christic import of social systems. For if we understand the becoming of God in Christ as the embodiment of God in his self-giving love, we can also understand the effective presence of Christ in us as the extension of that embodiment; and insofar as who we are is achieved and determined by the social systems in and through which we live, the effective presence of Christ in us takes effect in and through social systems, in and through our "public" body.

In what does the uniqueness of God's presence in Christ lie? The self-giving love of God is offered to humankind always and everywhere. All history can be in some way history for revelation and faith and salvation. But this fact of "always and everywhere" does not domesticate the utterly free love of God or make the reign of God a matter of course. Salvation is an essentially historical process, involving the freedom of God and the freedom of humankind. It is just this fact of the historicity of salvation that indicates the miracle of incalculable love in God's deed in Christ. The Christ-event is the "marriage moment," the moment of the decisive union of God and man. The uniqueness of Christ's person and role, then, lies in this, that in Christ the union of God and man is achieved unsurpassably and irrevocably, and therefore decisively.

Now the union of God and man which is unsurpassable and irrevocable must be a union which is "historically tangible," that is, the union must be expressly present in our world for what it is. As we noted earlier, explicit expression, as in a handshake or a marriage ceremony, renders decisively present what was, before its expressive embodiment, a matter of intention or merely provisional. Until God's union with man is embodied in history the union is not decisive; rather, unsurpassable and irrevocable union remains, in terms of actual history, a provisional possibility. On the other hand, if the union is not provisional, but decisively achieved, if the eschatological union of God and man is present for us in our shared world, it is manifest for what it is. The decisive union of God and man is achieved *in and through* the historical manifestation of this union. What distinguishes the Christ-event as an absolutely unique moment in history, then, is that Christ is the decisive manifestation, the incarnation of God in self-giving love.

It is in and through the man Jesus that God becomes incarnate. This human subjectivity, as genuinely human and free, has a history. The man Jesus develops through all the choices he makes in the course of his life. And Jesus becomes effectively present in and through expressive embodiment of himself in the words and deeds by which he relates to those about him, most decisively in the self-emptying surrender in death on the cross. He defines himself in and through the social systems which, in all their complexity and ambiguity, constitute the framework of his freedom. Insofar as God was in Christ, and insofar as Christ lived within social systems, God's effective presence took shape in and through social systems—in the end, it took decisive shape through a faith-endured death at the hands of religious and political powers, the structure of whose relationships was such as to defy the prophetic influence of Jesus. The result of this death and its culmination in the resurrection-faith of Christ's disciples was the institution of the Church, with its Scriptures and sacramental system.

A Sacramental Vision and Social Systems

With the notion of effective presence through expressive embodiment we can relate the lordship of Christ with a Christic vision of the world, and, in turn, with social systems. More precisely, it is the notion of "sacrament" which we can exploit to clarify the sense in which the formula for the person of Christ (the incarnation of God, the unity-in-difference of God and man) can be applied to the effective presence of Christ in the world generally.

Sacraments, we know, are signs, external expressions, through which God's love is effectively present. The signs themselves are not purely external instruments of God's grace: the love of God is effective for us in the world precisely by embodying itself in expressions which it creates to make itself felt.[9] As we saw earlier, when considering the simple gesture of a handshake, the principle of effective presence through expressive embodiment is, in a general way, basic in all our experience. We fully succeed in achieving what we mean to be in relation to one another when we succeed in actually expressing and embodying our purposes. In this more general sense of the term a most basic and immediate experience of the "sacramental" principle is, of course, the gestures by which we express our love for one another. By our words and gestures of love, by expressive embodiment, we make our love effectively present for one another. So too, in the proper, theological sense of the term, the grace of God is decisively available to us precisely through expressive, symbolic embodiments, sacraments. The point here is to relate and distinguish the proper and the more extended senses of the term "sacrament," in other words, to correlate the effective presence of grace in Christ, in the Church, and in the Church's sacraments, with the effective presence of grace in human gestures and social systems generally.

Now, what is decisively and unambiguously accomplished in Christ and proclaimed by the Church in word and sacrament is the revelation of God's will to become "all in all." The point of the distinction between the unique Christ and humanity in general, and between the Church with its sacraments and everyday life in the world, is not the difference, but the *unity-in-difference* of God's special effective presence in our world in Christ and the Church on the one hand, and on the other, God's effective presence throughout history where the human spirit is moved by the grace of God. And this effective presence of God, in accordance with the nature of our humanity and the incarnational structure of grace and salvation, embodies itself in the gestures and systems in and through which the human spirit is effective in the world. Although it is only in Christ, Church, and sacrament that the grace of God is effectively present and manifest in a decisive way, whenever the effective presence of God is incarnated through human beings in the world, there we have what we may call a "quasi-sacramental" embodiment of grace. Thus, insofar as humankind is moved by the Spirit, and insofar as humankind is effectively present in and through social systems, these have a quasi-sacramental character.

There is, of course, a profound difference between the incarnation of God in Christ and the incarnation of God's love in history generally. In Christ the love of God is effectively present in a decisive and unambiguous way. But in other persons the effective presence of God is profoundly tentative and ambiguous, because of human sinfulness, which embodies itself in our words and works. For all that Christian faith yields a sacramental vision and hope, it also yields a vision of sin and judgment, of the demonic, of principalities and powers to be overcome by Christ the Lord.

If God intends human history to be a history for salvation, it is also a history of sin. Consider, for example, a father who takes a second job. The father's motives may be worthy—for example, to provide funds for unforeseen hospitalization costs. But the father's choice will in some degree reflect a determination by larger social systems, systems which may be an embodiment of evil because they lead to grossly inflated and unmanageable health-care costs or unfair wage practices. The health-care and labor-market systems powerfully determine the father's choice. In turn the father's choice determines the family system, limiting, for example, the time available to him for meeting domestic responsibilities or the energy necessary to develop familial relationships, and thereby fracturing desirable patterns of family life and growth. Insofar as the pattern of familial activity instituted by the father's second job arises out of sin—the sin embodied in larger cultural systems—sin infects the family system and assumes the concrete power of that system. The crux of the matter is the power of systems which are shaped in freedom, and once established, shape the context and the possibilities of personal effectiveness.

The reality of sin profoundly distorts social systems, which, in turn, demonically enslave human freedom. Hence, we have trouble putting together grace and history, the reign of God and the powers of darkness, the lordship of Christ and the social systems through which we live.

Still, there is no clarity for a Christian to be found by dividing and separating grace and history. Precisely *in* ambiguity—*in* the complex process of a life of freedom in the world—we are called to life in relation to God, a life of faith and love. For the decisive revelation about grace and history is Christ, who himself became Lord in the complex process of life in the world. And this revelation is not about division and separation, but about judgment and reconciliation. In Christ we have in principle the formula of faith for grace and history.

First, the world and its history are really other than God. It is precisely distinct, free persons and their history which God creates and sustains in order to share divine life. The Christian must keep clear about the distinction of God and world, sacred and secular, grace and nature. Secular reality has its proper structure and dynamics. A faithful imagination must engage the diversity and complexity present in human history, discerning always in hope, and enacting in love, strategies for justice.

Second, although creaturely reality is distinct from the transcendent God, what defines the structure of creaturely reality is God's will to share divine life. It is for the sake of union that God creates human persons with their history. The Christian must keep clear that it is for union that there is a distinction between God and the world, grace and nature. Secular reality finds its fulfillment only through the grace of God in Christ. It is through the effective presence of the graced human spirit in the world that the grace of God is effectively present. However challenging it may be to discern how the secular can be made authentically human, Gnostic flight from the world defies the Christian vision of salvation as essentially incarnational, as the effective presence of Christ, who became Lord through the complex course of life and destiny in our common history.

Third, it is the utterly free love of God which accounts for the unity-in-difference of God and man, grace and the secular. If Christian faith and hope take the world and its history with utter seriousness, it is only because of the utterly gratuitous, creative and self-emptying love of God decisively revealed in the cross of Christ. What motivates, sustains and shapes God's creation of the human is self-giving love (just as it is the love of spouses which begets children with whom they may share life and love, albeit only by respecting the autonomous reality of the children and by relating to them through the complex, historical process of family life).

The Lordship of Christ, Social Systems, and the Church

Through a meditation on the person of Christ who is Lord we have derived a vision which impels us to take seriously our world and its history as the place and the process where the love of God should have effect. This sacramental vision integrates the dualities of God and world, sacred and secular, grace and history, Christ and humanity, Christian faith and everyday life. There is a tension in these dualities, but this tension has as its source the self-giving love of God who risks creating the otherness of a free humanity in the world and the ambiguity of human history. Though the integration of these dualities is radically subverted by sin, it nevertheless has been decisively revealed in Christ who is Lord that the saving love of God can be effective through self-surrendering love, which accepts in faith that the world is called to be God's very own and exercises this faith with creative hope. Just as there is a uniquely constituted unity-in-difference of the divine and the human in the person of Christ, and derivatively in the institution of the Church and its sacramental system, so in the history of humankind generally—and in social systems—there can be a unity-in-difference of grace and its embodiment.

As the embodiment of the grace of Christ in humankind and its systems is analogous to the Incarnation and the embodiment of grace in Church and sacrament, so are the dynamics of this embodiment analogous. The key is kenotic love, which empowers the spirit to discern and risk, in creative hope, concrete strategies, social systems, which allow for the fullest embodiment of Christian life.

The Church itself, the Lord's "mystical body," exemplifies in its life the challenging demands of kenotic love. Examples of these demands are not hard to find. Recent changes in liturgical style instituted by Vatican II have met with strong resistance. And the reasons for this resistance have not been superficial. The liturgical "system" that had previously been in place for so long embodied—and thereby educated to, and reinforced—a certain kind of religious self-understanding. The renewal of that religious self-understanding demands the risk of a renewed liturgy and the willingness to move beyond the long familiar style. Or, to look beyond the liturgical expression of the life of the Church, one might consider the conflicts involved in seeking to articulate and eventually embody the appropriate relationship between the Church's involvement in evangelization, on the one hand, and, on the other—is it other?—the Church's involvement in the promotion of social justice.

To be sure, the issues involved in relating faith and practice are always complicated, but especially so in our time, when there is such a difference between the stages of religious and social development in the many and diverse cultures within the reach of the Church. Only the power and politics of kenotic love will enable the Church to cope with these issues. The Church, an ecclesial "system," serves as a model of how complex and how challenging is the embodiment of the effective presence of Christ the Lord in social systems.

NOTES

1. My reflection is based on the Christology of Karl Rahner. The essays of Rahner important for this study are to be found in volumes 1, 4, and 5 of *Theological Investigations* (Baltimore: Helicon Press, 1961–1966). They are: "Current Problems in Christology," vol. 1, pp. 149–200; "On the Theology of the Incarnation," vol. 4, pp. 105–120; "The Theology of Symbol," vol. 4, pp. 221–252; "History of the World and Salvation History," vol. 5, pp. 97–114; "Christology within an Evolutionary View of the World," vol. 5, pp. 157–192. Also important are the articles "Jesus Christ" and "Salvation, IV Theology," in *Sacramentum Mundi,* ed. Karl Rahner and others

(New York: Herder and Herder, 1968–70). Perhaps the easiest access to Rahner's Christology is the chapter "Jesus Christ," in his *Foundations of Christian Faith* (New York: Seabury, 1978).

2. "On the Theology of the Incarnation," *Theological Investigations,* vol. 4, pp. 112 ff.

3. *The Church Teaches,* ed. John F. Clarkson and others (St. Louis: B. Herder, 1955), p. 172.

4. "Current Problems in Christology," *Theological Investigations,* vol. 1, pp. 180–83.

5. "On the Theology of the Incarnation," *Theological Investigations,* vol. 4, pp. 107–112.

6. "Salvation," *Sacramentum Mundi* 5, pp. 419–25.

7. *Ibid.,* p. 437.

8. "The Theology of Symbol," *Theological Investigations*, vol. 4, p. 242.

7
Earthen Vessels: Institution and Charism in the Church

Avery Dulles, S.J.

I. The Lord of the Church

The notion of lordship, as it comes down to us from the past, is heavily burdened with associations such as Hittite suzerainty treaties, Oriental despotism, Roman emperor worship, medieval feudalism, and Renaissance absolutism. Yet the term is still capable of conveying to believers the religious idea of God's gracious sovereignty. In the preaching of Jesus the lordship of God implied a combination of God's loving care, his trustworthiness, and his approaching judgment.[1] Especially in the period immediately following the resurrection, the idea of divine lordship was gradually affixed to Jesus himself, so that it became a fundamental datum of Christian faith. In the early decades of the new era, Christians came to be identified by their confession, "Jesus is Lord."[2] Written in the perspectives of the Easter event and the attendant eschatological expectation, many New Testament texts assert that Christ is Lord of all (*kyrios pantōn*, Acts 10:36; Rom 10:12), that God has put all things under his feet (Eph 1:22), and that at his name every knee shall bow (Phil 2:9).

If Christ is Lord of all, is he in any special sense Lord of the Church? According to Oscar Cullmann the Church, during the interval between Easter and the parousia, serves as "the midpoint from which Christ exercises his invisible lordship over the whole world."[3]

Rudolf Schnackenburg regards the Church as Christ's "direct sphere of operation, into which his divine blessings stream."[4] Hans Küng, more cautiously, states: "Even though it is not the Kingdom of God which is to come, it [the Church] is already under the reign of God which has begun. . . . The reign of Christ, the hidden ruler of the whole world, is already effective in the Church."[5]

Setting aside what is questionable or controversial in these formulations, one may say that the Church is the company of those who come together to believe, confess, and consciously submit to the lordship of Christ. It is also the congregation which, being gathered in Christ's name, enjoys his promise to be present (Mt 18:20) and to assist with divine power those who baptize, preach, and teach in his name (Mt 28:20). According to the Second Vatican Council the Church is the place where the Kingdom of God and of Christ is present in mystery[6] and is initially budding forth.[7] It is thus a sign and anticipation of God's definitive, eschatological reign.

To say all this is not to divinize the Church. Made up of sinful human beings, the community of baptized believers can easily become a forum for vanity, greed, idolatry, and superstition. While it is truly a sacrament of Christ's redemptive presence, the Church can also be a countersign—a place where the lordship of Christ is resisted and effectively denied. Only when it operates according to its true nature is it a place of grace and holiness, rendering Christ tangibly present.

II. Charism and Institution

As theologians we must inquire more closely: what is the point of impact at which Christ's reign asserts itself in the Church? A full answer to this question would require us to review the entire theology of grace, assessing the ecclesial dimensions of redemption and sanctification. Our immediate purpose, however, allows us to limit somewhat the scope of our investigation. Since the present volume has to do with social systems, we may inquire whether and how Christ is at work in and through the Church considered as a social system or a structured community.

Two answers spontaneously suggest themselves. First, it may be held that the lordship of Christ is correlated with those ministries (*diakoniai*) or activities (*energēmata*) which Paul also calls charisms (*charismata*) or gifts of the Holy Spirit (cf. 1 Cor 12:4). In other words, Christ may be said to reign in the Church insofar as its members are "charismatically" gifted by the Holy Spirit to perform distinct and mutually complementary functions in building up the body of Christ. Seen in this light, the Church as a charismatically structured community has Christ as its Lord.

Alternatively, Christ's lordship may be envisaged as occurring through the institutional structures of the Church; i.e., through its official teaching, its official worship, and its official decrees. This answer particularly commends itself insofar as certain structures of the Church are held to be divinely instituted, and to have a promise of grace attached to them through the will of Christ as founder.

Since it is difficult to see how else Christ's lordship could assert itself over the Church as a social system, we shall in the following pages content ourselves with examining the charismatic and institutional structures of the Church. Through which, if either, does Christ predominantly rule? How are the two related to each other?

Many of the tensions and conflicts in the Christian life are traceable to different assumptions or convictions about where the lordship of Christ is to be found. Some Christians take the view that God is always on the side of the institution, and that nothing can be regarded as authentically Christian unless or until it has received official approbation. These "law-and-order" Christians find it very disturbing that others, contemplating the institutional aspects of Christianity in purely human and sociological terms, find Christ and his Spirit present only in unexpected events of a prophetic character. Many ruptures in Christianity, such as the Protestant Reformation, have occurred, at least partly, because of disagreements about the respective roles of "spirit" and "structure."[8] Since the sixteenth century, conflicts of this kind have continued to occur within both the Catholic and the Protestant traditions. Especially in the period since Vatican Council II, the Catholic Church has witnessed many incidents in which priests, religious, and laity have felt justified in protesting against the official positions of the hierarchy, sometimes acting deliberately in a manner officially prohibited. In grappling with the interplay of the institutional and the charismatic, therefore, we shall be dealing with one of the most crucial problem-areas in ecclesiology.

The two focal concepts of this essay, charism and institution, are elusive and hard to define. The terms have in fact been variously used by acknowledged authorities. In sociological literature, the term "charism" (or "charisma") is often used according to the definition of Max Weber: "a certain quality of an individual personality by virtue of which he is set apart from ordinary men and treated as endowed with supernatural, superhuman, or at least specifically exceptional powers or qualities."[9] For Weber charism is not necessarily a special gift from God, or even a beneficent power. It could in fact be demonic. What is essential is that it signalize an individual as a leader, so that he is followed with utter personal devotion.

Weber believed that all profound religious and social changes are brought about through charismatic leaders. In particular, he maintained, religion originates through a charismatic surge, and is usually most intense in the first generation, when the charismatic founders are still alive. Institutionalization, for him, is a later development associated with loss of the original dynamism.

In the Pentecostal churches and in the Charismatic Renewal the term "charism" is sometimes used in a second sense, to signify certain unusual gifts attributed to the direct action of the Holy Spirit. These gifts are readily recognized through phenomena such as speaking in tongues, prophesying, and miraculous healing.

In Catholic theology the term "charism" is commonly employed in still a third sense. Francis Sullivan, summarizing the teaching of Vatican II on the subject, suggests the definition, "a grace-given ability and willingness for any kind of service that contributes to the renewal and upbuilding of the Church."[10] Although the charisms are in some sense special, since not all receive the same charisms, they are not reserved to an elite. According to the Council the Holy Spirit "distributes special graces among the faithful of every rank."[11] Every genuine vocation, as Sullivan observes, must be seen as a charismatic gift. The term in this sense is not reserved for exceptional or miraculous gifts (as tends to be done by Pentecostals), nor is charism to be seen only as a gift of community leadership (as by the sociologists who follow Weber). The theological usage agrees with the Pentecostal as against Weber in regarding charism as necessarily coming from the Holy Spirit, and hence as beneficial.

Modern theologians, following Paul's teaching in First Corinthians, insist that charismatic gifts are always bestowed for the upbuilding of the Church as body of Christ. The Spirit distributes charisms to each for the sake of building up the body in unity. Because the charisms are mutually complementary, resulting in a certain "division of labor," we can speak, with numerous contemporary theologians, of "charismatic structures" in the Church.[12] According to Paul, the body of Christ is structured with vital organs, limbs, and other members according to the spontaneous impulses given to individuals by the Holy Spirit. Many modern sociologists have adopted this "organic" conception of structure.[13]

Institutional structures, as contrasted with charismatic, are those which are regularly established, publicly recognized, stable, repeatable, and uniform. In the Church, institutional structures may conveniently be divided into four categories: (1) doctrines and doctrinal formulations which are normative for all the members, such as creeds, dogmas, and canonical writings (Scriptures, conciliar pronouncements, etc.); (2) forms of public worship, such as sacraments and other approved rituals; (3) structures of government, i.e., offices with the powers and duties attached to them; (4) laws and customs regulating the behavior of members.

In the present essay we shall direct our attention to those institutions which are constitutive of the Church as such, rather than those which arise through the free and voluntary activities of members—for example, religious orders and congregations, church-related schools, hospitals, relief agencies, study clubs, prayer groups, and the like. In all these religious and church-related agencies, a measure of institutionalization is inevitable. No social movement can long endure as a purely charismatic phenomenon.

To summarize the concepts of charismatic and institutional, we may conclude that they present contrasting features. Charism is spontaneous, personal, temporary, and fluid. Institution is prescribed, typical, stable, and clearly defined.

III. DIVERGENT VIEWS: PROTESTANT AND CATHOLIC

Theologians, seeking to identify the point where Christ's lordship over the Church is brought to bear, have at times emphasized the charismatic and at times the institutional. The extreme positions may be labeled "Protestant liberalism" and "Catholic authoritarianism" though, of course, not all liberals are Protestants and not all authoritarians are Catholics.

Liberalism accords primary and normative status to the charismatic alone (which thus becomes, in a certain sense, an institution). At the end of the nineteenth century the French liberal Protestant, Auguste Sabatier, held that Jesus professed a pure religion of the Spirit, opposed to all religions of authority. Sabatier promoted the ideal of a Christianity without dogmas, priesthood, and sacraments.[14] Early in the twentieth century, the Strasbourg historian and canonist Rudolph Sohm contended that originally the Christian community was made up of individuals responsive to the Holy Spirit, capable of achieving harmony and coordination by recognizing one another's gifts.[15] Toward the middle of the century, the Swiss Protestant, Emil Brunner, portrayed the true Church as a purely personal community (*Personengemeinschaft*) directed in a pneumatic way by the Holy Spirit. In such a community, Brunner held, organization and institution have no place, and yet anarchy does not arise. Ecclesiastical institutions, such as laws, sacraments, dogmas, offices, according to Brunner, can only be substitutes for an absent Spirit.[16]

Liberal Christianity has never been at home in the Catholic tradition. But it has had a certain influence on some Catholic theologians such as Hans Küng, and even more on Küng's erstwhile disciple, Gotthold Hasenhüttl, whose ecclesiology has been partly shaped by the radicalism of the Frankfurt sociologists. Hasenhüttl pleads for a Church free from all structures of domination (i.e., for a *herrschaftsfreie Kirche*), which would be a pure community of love. He rejects ecclesiastical institutions insofar as they impose any obligatory patterns or roles.[17]

The Catholic emphasis since the sixteenth century has been predominantly on the institutional, especially on the hierarchical. The late Scholastic and Neo-Scholastic authors since Trent have particularly favored this approach. Christ, they hold, founded the Church as a visible society and equipped it from the beginning with institutional means adequate for every occasion. The hierarchy, having the fullness of the apostolic ministry, is in charge of the official doctrine, worship, and discipline of the Church. As Johann Adam Möhler put it, summarizing the Enlightenment ecclesiology which he opposed, "God created the hierarchy and thus provided more than sufficiently for the needs of the Church until the end of the world."[18]

In the ecclesiology of this vintage elaborate proofs are given to show that Christ gave jurisdictional powers to the apostles, and to the bishops as their successors, and that he instituted all seven sacraments, the papal office, the sacrifice of the Mass, and whatever else is essential to the Church. In the article on "charisma" in the *Encyclopedic Dictionary of the Bible* (an English adaptation of a Dutch work of the 1950s) it is explicitly stated that while charisms were "of great importance for the infant Church . . . they did not belong to the essence of the Church, which is not primarily a merely charismatic movement but a hierarchical institution, founded on the apostles and their authority."[19]

This Neo-Scholastic point of view was represented by a number of Fathers at the Second Vatican Council. At the second session Cardinal Ernesto Ruffini made an intervention objecting that the schema *De Ecclesia* attached far too much importance to the charismatic. "For the charisms, frequently mentioned in the apostolic writings, were abundant at the beginning of the Church, but later they gradually diminished to such an extent that they almost died out. . . . Hence we cannot stably and firmly rely on charismatic laymen for the advancement of the Church and the apostolate, for charisms—contrary to the opinion of many separated brethren who freely speak of the ministry of charismatics in the Church—are today very rare and entirely singular."[20]

Neo-Scholastic institutionalism thus goes to the opposite extreme from Protestant liberalism. It holds that the charisms, far from constituting the essence of the Church, are unimportant and, at least in the modern era, marginal. The two approaches, however, agree in distinguishing between a primitive charismatic Church and a modern institutional Church.

The dominant trend in both Protestant and Catholic theology during the past few decades has been to seek an ecclesiological balance that respects both the institutional and the charismatic as necessary components. Building on the discussion of the so-called "Protestant" and "Catholic" tendencies at the Amsterdam Assembly of the World Council of Churches, the French Reformed theologian, Jean-Louis Leuba, rejected two extreme positions.[21] The first would be a "Judaizing" error that precludes creative innovation; the second, a "Marcionite" error that devalues continuity. The Bible, in Leuba's opinion, reveals two interconnected aspects of God's redemptive work. The institution, as a stable entity, represents the fidelity of God, who abides by his covenant promises. The event, as a fresh and unpredictable exercise of God's sovereign initiative, provides the transcendent dynamism which alone can give life to the institution. The "institutional" apostolate of the Twelve in the New Testament is complemented by the "charismatic" apostolate of Paul. Both ingredients are essential to Christianity.

A tendency to rehabilitate the institutional is evident in many of the studies on institutionalism that have been conducted in the Faith and Order Commission since the Lund Conference of 1952.[22]

A corresponding rehabilitation of the charismatic has been at work in Catholicism since the 1940s. Pius XII, in his Encyclical on the Mystical Body (1943), seeking a middle road between false rationalism and false mysticism, taught that the structure of the Church essentially included both hierarchic and charismatic grades, and that the two cannot fail to be in harmony since they derive from the same divine source.[23] "There can be no real opposition or conflict between the invisible mission of the Holy Spirit and the juridical commission which rulers and teachers have received from Christ."[24] As for the relative dignity of the two sets of structures, we read in one passage: "That those who exercise sacred power in this Body are its first and chief members must be maintained uncompromisingly."[25] But later the Encyclical asserts that as the human body is inferior to the soul, "so the social structure of the Christian community, though eloquent of its Divine Architect's wisdom, remains something inferior, when compared to the spiritual gifts which give it beauty and life and to their divine source."[26] Thus it cannot easily be said whether the hierarchic or the charismatic receives priority in *Mystici corporis*.

IV. Vatican Council II

At the Second Vatican Council a sharp debate took place between those who, like Cardinal Ruffini, wished to downgrade the charismatic and others who, like Cardinal Suenens,[27] wished to give it stronger recognition. The Constitution on the Church, as it finally emerged, betrays the same kind of dualism and ambivalence we have noted in *Mystici corporis.* The charismatic element in the Church is highly praised, and is in many passages set over against the institutional or hierarchical. This is notably the case in articles 4, 7, and 12, which contrast hierarchical with charismatic gifts. In article 12, those who preside in the Church are given competence to judge the authenticity of charismatic gifts. On the other hand, article 8 asserts that the "society furnished with hierarchical agencies" is an instrument of the "spiritual community . . . enriched with heavenly things (*coelestibus bonis ditata*)," even as the humanity of Christ was an instrument of his divine nature, thus implying a real distinction between the institutional and the charismatic, and the superiority of the latter over the former.

Yet it is not clear that the Council meant to make an adequate distinction between the hierarchical and the charismatic, for in some texts the hierarchical gifts of popes and bishops are themselves spoken of as charismatic, even as charisms. The Constitution on Divine Revelation states that bishops are gifted with the "sure charism of truth" (*charisma veritatis certum,* a phrase taken from Irenaeus of Lyons), and the same idea appears in different words in article 21 of the Constitution on the Church. In article 25 of that Constitution the infallibility by which the pope defines doctrine *ex cathedra* is described as a charism, though infallibility, rather surprisingly, is said to be a charism of the whole Church "individually present" in the pope.

Vatican II, like *Mystici corporis,* left unsettled two major questions which continue to be debated in the post-conciliar Church. First, is the charismatic superior or inferior to the hierarchical? Second, is the charismatic a free and unpredictable ourpouring of the Spirit, or is it, at least sometimes, a permanent gift attached to certain offices?

V. Contemporary Catholic Theological Opinion

In the Catholic theology of the post-conciliar period the theme of institution and charism continues to be energetically discussed. As leaders in this discussion one may mention Yves Congar, Hans Urs von Balthasar, Karl Rahner, and Hans Küng. It may be helpful to present here brief summaries of the contributions of these four authors, even though it will not be possible, in a few paragraphs, to do justice to the full complexity of their thought.

a. Yves Congar

Congar, whose essential positions were worked out in writings published in the 1950s, holds that in the period since Pentecost Christ exercises his lordship in a predominantly prophetic and priestly, rather than in a strictly regal, manner. The Church represents in the world Christ's prophetic and priestly kingship, communicated in the form of spiritual authority. The Church as institution is the totality of the means of grace conferred by Christ upon his Church. It consists of the threefold apostolic deposit of faith, sacraments, and ministry.[28] The institutional activity of the Church is vitalized by the Holy Spirit, who effects inwardly what the apostolic ministry, by means of word and sacrament, effects exteriorly.[29] Congar, then, identifies the structure of the Church with its visible organization, which stems from the mission of the Son. The charismatic element, to his mind, comes from the mission of the Spirit, and is subsequent. "First comes the organization," he writes, "afterwards life and movement."[30] The Holy Spirit, as a distinct person, is not bound by the institution, but retains a certain autonomy to intervene in incalculable ways.[31]

In the decade before Vatican II, Congar did much to rehabilitate the prophetic mission of the laity without jeopardizing the institutional authority of the hierarchy. But from the standpoint of contemporary ecclesiology, certain questions have to be asked about Congar's preconciliar writings. Does he assume too hastily that the sacraments were specifically instituted by Jesus in his public ministry? Does he attribute sufficient importance to the role of the Spirit in the life of Jesus and in the pre-Easter community? Is it true without qualification that institution is prior to life and structure prior to community? Or does individual and communal experience promote institutionalization? Further, does Congar treat word and sacrament too narrowly as means of grace, rather than as events of grace—events which embody and express a spiritual gift really present in the Church? Does he define "structure" too narrowly, inasmuch as he treats it as a synonym for institution, thereby excluding the concept of charismatic structures? And finally, is Congar over-inclined to restrict the notion of charism to exceptional and uncovenanted graces, thus diverging from many official Catholic statements which speak of hierarchical charisms, charisms of office?

Because questions of this character have been raised by many critics, Congar, in recent essays, has clarified and modified some of his earlier positions.[32] He acknowledges that the term "structure" can be used in a wider sense, so that in some sense the non-sacramental ministries of the laity may be said to belong to the structure, and not simply to the "life," of the Church. He likewise admits that in some sense the priorities between the community and its official ministry are mutual, so that it is not adequate to say that the hierarchical structures are prior to the community. Congar still seems to leave somewhat obscure the question whether "charism" can be used to include gifts given in view of the office held by their recipient.

b. Hans Urs von Balthasar

Hans Urs von Balthasar has treated the theme of charism and institution in many of his collected theological essays and again rather recently in his book, *Die Wahrheit ist symphonisch* (1972). After noting the exaggerated institutionalism of the late Middle Ages and the Counter Reformation, Balthasar points out the inadequacies of various anti-institutional reactions such as pietism, personalist phenomenology, and Weberian sociology.[33] He argues that the Church is a totally unique society which becomes its true self only by existing in Christ, whose form of existence it prolongs in the world.[34] More specifically, it participates in the selfless love with which Jesus went to the cross. In order that it might be perpetually receptive to the form of Christ, the Church was from its inception equipped with the institutional elements of word, sacrament, and office.[35] Office, even in its most institutional features, represents the love inherent in the Church, and therefore demands love for its proper exercise.[36] Office is a form of discipleship requiring renunciation and service.[37] Far from being opposed to charism, office is itself a special charism for coordinating other charisms and integrating them into the unity of the Church as a whole.[38] Charism is institutionalized, particularly in ordination, though the charism of the ordained may need to be re-kindled by renewed reflection on the sacramental grace.[39]

Von Balthasar has developed a profound theology of ecclesiastical office, in which the charismatic and the institutional are richly interwoven. Better than others, he shows how the Church requires institution and office in order to be a community of living discipleship. His method of argument is sometimes disconcerting, because he does not use the standard historical-critical approach to biblical texts, but argues at times from quotations taken out of context, even from symbolic meanings and metaphors. He tends to be rather defensive against democratization and sociological analysis, and one-sided in his emphasis on receptivity, obedience, and submission. He fails to insist that initiative, personal responsibility, candor, and creativity are inseparable from true discipleship.

c. Karl Rahner

Karl Rahner, in a series of essays going back to the middle 1940s, has elaborated his theology of charism and institution in the light of his vision of the Church as sacrament—i.e., as the visible sign of God's invisible grace effectively at work in the world. The Church as sign achieves its fullest tangibility when it acts publicly—that is to say, as institution—in its ministry of word and sacrament.[40] The institutional forms of the Church express and mediate the life of grace. Grace, moreover, equips and impels its recipients to fulfill tasks within the ongoing life of the pilgrim community, and is therefore inseparable from charism.[41] Just as all grace has a charismatic aspect, so too, according to Rahner, office itself is charismatic. Entrusted with spiritual responsibilities of great magnitude, those appointed to office must have the corresponding gifts. God, in willing the Church, wills also to provide for the ecclesiastical ministry a special assistance that belongs to the charismatic order.[42] In addition to the charisms of office there are free, spontaneous charisms, expressing each individual's immediate relationship to God. The charismatic element, Rahner maintains, is "the true pith and essence of the Church," the point where the lordship of Christ is most directly and potently exercised.[43]

Rahner succeeds better than most others in overcoming the dualism between institution and charism while still recognizing the distinction. Like von Balthasar, he sees the institution itself as charismatic. But he emphasizes more than von Balthasar does the limitations of the institution when unaccompanied by a transitory charismatic assistance, requiring personal cooperation. The external structures of the Church, in his system, are seen as subordinate to the self-actualization of the transcendental subject, achieved by grace. Some complain that Rahner's ecclesiology is too much tied to his idealistic anthropology, and that it owes more to Kant and Fichte than to the biblical tradition.[44]

d. Hans Küng

Hans Küng, our fourth and final witness, looks upon the Church as the congregation of believers convoked by the risen Christ, who becomes Lord of the Church in sending the Holy Spirit.[45] Created in the Holy Spirit, the Church was charismatic from its beginnings. Ministries in apostolic times, according to Küng, were charismatically structured, inasmuch as the Holy Spirit called different individuals to different functions.[46] When the apostolic leaders began to die off, and the parousia was "delayed," a certain "decline into institutional ministry" was inevitable. This began very early in the Palestinian communities, under the influence of Judaism, and somewhat later in the Pauline Hellenistic communities.[47] Office and organization, for Küng, are purely human responses to changing needs, and are not be be attributed to "divine institution." Only the charismatic, Küng appears to say, has divine authority.

Küng's critical approach to office and institution may be considered a positive gain insofar as he shows, more clearly than many other scholars, how difficult it is to claim direct dominical institution for the modern structures of any Christian community. On the other hand, his emphasis on the charismatic features of the apostolic Church is exaggerated and exegetically vulnerable. He underestimates the institutional aspects of the early community, including the apostolic ministry of Paul and the Twelve. In his work thus far, Küng has given only scant attention to sacraments as effective signs of grace.[48]

VI. A Proposed Synthesis

In the light of the official teaching of the Church, especially in the Second Vatican Council, and the work of contemporary theologians, such as the four just mentioned, it may now be possible to propose some theses on Christ's lordship over the Church, as exercised through institution and charism. These theses will express the views of the present author.

a. Unity in Distinctness

1. *The institutional and the charismatic are irreducibly distinct aspects of the Church in its pilgrim condition.*

Both institution and charism pertain to the life of the Church. Such is the clear teaching of *Mystici corporis* and *Lumen gentium,* and of most contemporary theologians. Each of these structures is essentially linked to service and is subordinate to the life of grace or union with God, which it expresses and seeks to promote. For this reason, they pertain to the wayfaring Church. In the heavenly Church, to which Christians look forward, neither of these sets of structures will survive as such, but what is foreshadowed in them will be possessed in plenitude. The faithful will be visibly united in the one Body of Christ, animated by the one Spirit. In the words of von Balthasar, "What never falls away is the nuptial encounter between God and the creature, for whose sake the framework of the structures is now set up and will later be dismantled. This encounter, therefore, must be the real core of the Church."[49]

The institutional element in the Church is the public, the regular, the officially approved. It may conveniently be divided, according to Congar's schematization, into the functions of teaching, sanctification, and pastoral rule—functions correlated with Christ's three offices of prophet, priest, and king. On the other hand, the three functions cannot be adequately distinguished. In the Church teaching is pastoral, priesthood is royal, and government is priestly.[50] Some institutional features of the Church—such as the Bible, with its wealth of symbolic stories and images—do not seem to fit conveniently into this triple division.

The institutional includes, but is wider than, that which is held to be of "divine institution"—a concept which is itself capable of many different interpretations.[51] It is increasingly recognized that the institution, while possessing a certain relative stability, is constantly being modified. Institutionalization is a process always occurring in the Church, not without the assistance and guidance of the Spirit. Insofar as it emanates from the Holy Spirit, the process itself mediates Christ's lordship.

The notion of the charismatic has been under revision during the present century. In the early decades the term was primarily used for extraordinary gifts conferred outside the normal functioning of the Church. The charismatic in this sense could easily be marginalized. But since the middle of the century the charismatic has been extended to all gifts of grace, insofar as these equip and dispose their recipients for special service in the Church. In this sense charism is applied not only to "free" graces, imparted according to the good pleasure of the Holy Spirit, but also to spiritual gifts proportioned to a person's office, state of life, and social responsibilities—for example, as bishop, confessor, king, mother, teacher. It is characteristic of the Holy Spirit to be a source of creativity, energy, enthusiasm, and freedom.

Having established the distinctness of the two aspects, we must now emphasize their inseparability.

b. Sacramentality

2. *The dialectical tension between institution and charism must be understood in the framework of the Church as sacrament.*

Christ himself is the fundamental sacrament, for his visible human existence embodies, symbolically manifests, and communicates God's powerful redemptive love. The Church, analogously, is a sacrament or symbolic reality which prolongs in time and space the event of God's merciful approach in Jesus. As Rahner puts it: "In accordance with the incarnational principle of sacred history, the Church is a quasi-sacramental unity of Spirit and historical visible embodiment."[52]

A sacrament, in the Catholic theological tradition, has two aspects: it is a sign of present grace and a symbolic cause or transmitter of grace.[53] The Church as a whole is a sign of Christ and his grace. The institutional features of the Church—such as its apostolic ministry, its baptism, its eucharistic worship, its rites of absolution, as well as its Scriptures and credal formulations—externally signify what the Church represents and effects in the world.

The institutional in the Church, therefore, is never merely institutional. It is essentially linked to the presence and promise of grace. It is misleading to assert that ecclesiastical institutions are a substitute for the absent Spirit. They may be, should be, and normally are to some extent, symbolic manifestations of the present Spirit, for the risen Lord has promised to be present with his disciples to the end of the age (Mt 28:20).

The charismatic aspect of the Church's life is no less essential than the institutional, for the grace of Christ, symbolized and transmitted by the institution, is variously appropriated by different individuals, each of whom is brought by grace itself into immediate union with God. The institutions, being external and uniform, cannot supply for, or adequately signify, the intimacy of the divine call which comes to each in a distinctive way.

Grace, insofar as it is received by individual spiritual persons, always has a charismatic aspect, for it equips its recipients to fulfill particular tasks within the pilgrim community.[54] Since each receives grace in a unique manner, grace equips and inclines the members to bring their own special gifts to the body.

The Church, then, would not be truly Church without both the institutional features, whereby it manifests its own abiding essence, and the charismatic features, whereby God efficaciously transforms the interiority of concrete persons. The relation between institution and charism is a particular instance of the general relation between sacramental signs and the spiritual realities to which they point.

c. *Necessity of Institution*

3. *The Church never has been, and never can be, without institutional elements.*

As we have seen, some liberal theologians have postulated a primitive Golden Age in which each individual in the Church spontaneously followed the leading of the Spirit without institutional mediation. Certain exegetes, influenced by this hypothesis, tend to dismiss as unauthentic every allusion to fixed forms of belief, worship, and government in the apostolic Church. But more careful scrutiny of the sources indicates that institutionalization is as old as the Church itself.[55] Even in the pre-Easter period Jesus taught his disciples patterns of prayer, speech, and conduct that identified them as his disciples. Paul, in letters of unquestioned authenticity, appeals to an apostolic norm of belief and worship (1 Cor 11:23; 15:1,11). Undoubtedly the institutions of the Church were in the beginning rudimentary, but in this respect the primitive period ought not to be emulated. For the abiding identity of the Church further institutionalization was found to be necessary, so that the Church progressively furnished itself with creeds, New Testament Scriptures, liturgical ceremonies, and an episcopal form of government. We are not arguing here that the institutional forms adopted in the patristic, or any other, period must endure forever, but that institutionalization answers a real need and ought not to be dismissed as a kind of fall from an original state of charismatic innocence. Even Hans Küng, when he speaks of a "decline into institutional ministry," gives the impression of longing to repristinate an idealized charismatic springtime.

Our thesis is opposed not only to the liberals who postulate a purely charismatic Church at the beginning, but also to certain radical theologians, such as Hasenhüttl, who foresee a gradual withering away of the institutional as the Church approaches the glory of the end-time. Hasenhüttl's position, which revives in modern form something of the Joachite theology, is apparently indebted to the Marxian idea of the "withering away" of the State in the classless society of the future. He takes an excessively negative view of office and institution, as though they were synonyms for domination and oppression. By recourse to the sacramental concept of the Church, as sketched above, one can better perceive the positive and essential role of the institutional. Without Scriptures, creeds, sacraments, and pastoral office the Church could not sufficiently define itself against all that is alien to Christ; it could not visibly represent the permanent and universal scope of God's redemptive grace, nor could it bring its own members into a concrete and historically experienced relationship of obedience to their Lord. The Church realizes itself most fully in its public worship, where the institutional elements of word, sacrament, and apostolic ministry converge in powerful symbolic events.[56] Scripture and liturgy, through their impact on the Christian imagination, are an unceasing source of vitality within the Church.

d. Necessity of the Charismatic

4. *The Church never has been, and never can be, without charismatic elements.*

The indispensability of the charismatic has already been established in our second thesis. Since charisms, in the widest sense, are simply concretizations of the life of grace, a Church without charisms could only be a Church without grace. Such a Church would be a false sign; it would betoken the presence of what is absent; it would be a pseudo-sacrament, and for this reason it would not be truly Church.

The thesis as it stands is directed against some who postulate a period when the Church existed without yet being animated by the Spirit and against others who affirm that charisms died out soon after the apostolic age. Congar himself, at least in his earlier writings, apparently held that in the order of time the institution precedes the interior gifts of grace. We have quoted his formula: "First comes the organization, and afterwards life and movement."[57] Is this not to infer too much from a few biblical texts, such as the scene of Pentecost as described in the Acts? Vatican II, in its Decree on Missionary Activity, asserts that "the Holy Spirit was already at work before Christ was glorified"[58]—an opinion which it supports with patristic and other authorities. In following Jesus and in confessing him as Lord and Christ, even in the public life, the apostles were inspired by grace (Mt 16:17; cf. Jn 6:44; 1 Cor 12:3). The charisms and the institutions would seem to have grown concurrently, and to have done so most strikingly in the period after Pentecost.

Our thesis is directed, second, against the neo-Scholastic view (which in its way curiously resembles that of Sohm and Weber) that the charismatic element was proper to the apostolic age, when other signs of credibility were lacking, but that charisms in no way pertain to the essence of the post-apostolic Church. Cardinal L.J. Suenens, speaking to the Council six days after Cardinal Ruffini, correctly challenged the opinion "that charisms are nothing more than a peripheral and unessential phenomenon in the life of the Church."[59] He recalled that according to St. Paul the Church must be seen "as a living web of gifts, of charisms, of ministries," and that "each and every Christian, whether lettered or unlettered, has his charism in his daily life."[60] The Constitution on the Church, while it did not say that charisms pertain to the very constitution of the Church, asserted that "they are exceedingly suitable and useful for the needs of the Church."[61] Pius XII had gone even further in *Mystici corporis,* which condemns the view that the structure (*structuram*) of the Church consists solely of hierarchical elements and not of charismatic elements as well, and which asserts that charismatically endowed individuals will never be lacking to the Church.[62]

It is rather commonly supposed that charisms were more abundant in the early Church than at any later period. Rahner does well to challenge this opinion: "It is not clear what grounds there are for saying that the early Church was, in fact, more charismatic. . . . It goes without saying that as the Church grew, its 'machinery' grew too. . . . But this is no proof that in the early Church the wind of the Spirit blew with more vigor than later."[63] These words may have appeared somewhat audacious when Rahner first published them in 1957,[64] but in the light of the Charismatic Renewal their truth seems almost self-evident today.

e. Dependence of Charism on Institution

5. *The charismatic in the Church lives off the institutional.*

Charisms are sometimes divided into non-institutional and official.[65] The first of these categories refers to charisms not given to office-holders, or not given with a view to the performance of official duties. But these charisms do not normally arise apart from institutional influences. As James Gustafson wrote in response to Harvey Cox, "The faith that is made visible in the modern saints' activities in cities did not come to them out of the blue; its soil was tended by parents against whose inadequacies we fulminate, by ministers whose piety we ridicule, by Sunday-school lessons whose emptiness we excoriate, by worship of God, whose name we now believe should be left unspoken."[66] Even such outstandingly charismatic phenomena as prophecy and glossolalia are often induced by the reading of Scripture, by the recitation of traditional prayers, and by ceremonies such as the laying on of hands. This is true today, and it was true in Christianity from the beginning, if we may allow our judgment to be guided by passages such as Acts 8:17 and Acts 19:5–6.

Further, it is unacceptable to imagine that charisms are always given in an uncovenanted and unpredictable way, without regard to a person's status and official responsibilities. The theological tradition therefore speaks of graces or charisms of office, such as the Fourth Gospel ascribes to Caiaphas (Jn 11:51). Office in the Church is a profoundly spiritual thing, never fully definable in juridical categories. In ordination, as von Balthasar remarks, charism is institutionalized. Hierarchical charisms are inseparable from priestly ordination.[67]

In a text of major importance for the Catholic theological tradition, Irenaeus of Lyons spoke of the "firm charism of truth" (*charisma veritatis certum*) bestowed upon presbyters ordained in the apostolic churches.[68] Although the Greek text of this passage has not survived, the Latin translator apparently used the term "charisma" to designate "the sacramental ordination of the presbyter-bishop, who by that act became one of the prophetic order," equipped to teach revelation with fidelity.[69] Vatican II extended this notion by implying that all bishops (and only bishops?) "have received through the apostolic succession the sure gift of truth (*charisma veritatis cer-*

tum)."[70] Vatican I had already applied to the pope the idea of such a charism. It asserted that God conferred upon Peter and his successors "the charism of unfailing truth and faith *(veritatis et fidei numquam deficientis charisma)*."[71] The access to revelation in such a case is not formally identified with the office, but is attached to the office, for God has promised so to assist the pastors that the faith of the Church will never be corrupted by erroneous official teaching. The charism of office, which depends for its actual exercise on a transitory divine help, is not the same thing as the juridical power of office, which can at any time be validly exercised according to the discretion of the incumbent.

f. Dependence of Institution on Charism

6. *The institutional in the Church lives off the charismatic.*

This thesis states the converse of the preceding; it asserts the dependence of institution on charism. In general terms, the institutional in the Church owes its existence to charismatically endowed persons, including especially Christ himself and the leaders of the foundational period. Institutional features, such as doctrine, sacrament, and office, all seek to preserve and transmit insights that were originally charismatic. The Bible, as an institutionally approved and canonical body of literature, owes its existence to the charism of inspiration and is an unceasing source of consolation and guidance for the Church and its pastors (cf. Rom 15:4; 2 Tim 3:16–17). At councils the bishops invoke the assistance of the Holy Spirit, and the acclamations with which their decisions have been greeted are often interpreted as signs of the working of that Spirit. The Fathers and Doctors of the Church, whose writings enjoy a certain official status, were spiritually gifted preachers and teachers, outstanding for holiness as well as for learning.

The pastoral office itself presupposes gifts of the charismatic order. Candidates for office must not only exhibit a sufficiency of natural talent and training but must show positive signs of an interior vocation from the Holy Spirit—a vocation that belongs to the charismatic order. One must be spiritually attuned to the office to which one aspires.[72] The vocation, in turn, must be discerned by the community and its leaders—a process which itself requires spiritual endowments.

Finally, in this context, we must note that the proper exercise of office in the Church demands a continuing openness to the Spirit. The sacrament of ordination—as the traditional doctrine of the "priestly character" suggests—effects a profound spiritual transformation, assuring a regime of charismatic graces. These graces do not operate automatically, but demand a continual "rekindling" of that which was bestowed at ordination (cf. 2 Tim 1:6).

Hierarchical office does not remove the pastor from the community but is, as von Balthasar points out, a radicalization of the discipleship demanded of all Christians.[73] It demands total and manifest renunciation for the sake of the Lord and of the flock. For this reason von Balthasar can say—and the phrase is one he repeats often—hierarchy is crystallized love.[74] To speak of office in the Church without acknowledging its spiritual and charismatic dimensions would be to invite serious misunderstandings.

g. Role of Pastoral Office

7. *The pastoral office, charismatically exercised, fosters other charisms in the Church while correcting their deviations.*

The special charism of the pastoral office is not to replace or diminish other charisms but to bring them to their fullest efficacy. This involves several distinct functions. First, the pastoral office must authenticate genuine charisms and distinguish them from false charisms. According to Vatican II, "Judgment as to the genuineness and proper use belongs to those who preside over the Church, and to whose special competence it belongs, not indeed to extinguish the Spirit, but to test all things and hold fast to that which is good (cf. 1 Thess 5:12; 19–21)."[75] As the last three verses of this biblical citation indicate, the task of discernment does not rest on the hierarchy alone but also on the community.

Second, hierarchical leaders have the function of stimulating and encouraging the charisms. This task they perform especially by their ministry of word and sacrament. Members of the community must be helped to acknowledge one another's gifts and to use their own gifts with full effectiveness.

Third, the pastors must direct the charisms according to the norm of apostolic faith and thus bring them into subjection to the law of the cross. Office may and normally does seek to commend itself by love and gentleness, but in the event that these attitudes fail to meet with the necessary response, the responsible office-holders may properly exercise severity and mete out punishment.[76]

Finally, office, as a kind of general charism, has the responsibility of coordinating all the particular charisms so that they may better achieve the goal of building up the total body of Christ. The pastoral office prevents the prior unity of the Church from being fragmented by the free responses of the enthusiasts, and reminds the spiritually gifted of their duty to obey the one Lord of the Church.[77] The characteristic temptation of the free charismatic is to follow the momentary impulses arising out of transitory local situations, without sufficient regard for established order and for universal, long-term needs. The pastoral office therefore integrates the possibly distorted self-sufficiency of the particular charisms into the greater unity of ecclesial love.[78]

h. Sources of Renewal

8. *The confluence of charism and institution is important for the appropriate renewal and reform of the Church.*

In the course of history it often happens that existing institutions, although well adapted to earlier times, become obsolete and dysfunctional. Innovation, if it is not to be a betrayal of the original inspiration, demands an intense experience of the grace of the foundational period. The resources of Scripture and Tradition, both of which belong to the institutional aspect, can effectively stimulate the Christian imagination to arrive at creative solutions. The assistance of the Holy Spirit, mediated through institutional channels such as these, can supply the force and discretion needed for appropriate initiatives.

The task of Church reform, charismatic though it be, has often been most ably conducted by holders of ecclesiastical office, as the names of Gregory VII and John XXIII serve to remind us. The founders of great movements of reform, such as Francis of Assisi, Ignatius of Loyola, and Teresa of Avila, have been loyal servants of the institution. Generally speaking, the more deeply a prophet or reformer is immersed in the heritage, the more successfully will he or she be able to transform and renew it with fidelity to its authentic spirit.

Without minimizing the charismatic gifts of official leaders, we may acknowledge that, in a sinful world, those who hold office will commonly be tempted to employ their power in a dominative and manipulative way.[79] They can easily tend to sacrifice other values to the demands of law and order and to misconceive of loyalty as if it meant merely passive conformity. In this they are abetted by certain segments of the laity who use submisson to pastors as an excuse for failing to exercise responsible initiatives in response to the needs of the hour.

The tension between adherence to the accepted patterns and adaptation to emerging situations has been felt in the Church since the first generation. The Church at Antioch, with Paul and Barnabas as spokesmen, departed from what the authorities in Jerusalem regarded as essential by divine institution. History was on the side of the innovators, but they had to battle fiercely for their views, appealing, in some instances, to charismatic phenomena (e.g., Acts 15:7–12).

As the controversy between Peter and Paul at Antioch reminds us (cf. Gal 2:11–14), it may be necessary in exceptional situations for charismatically gifted leaders to take responsibility for resisting the official leadership. What is disobedience to a particular pastor, who fails to perceive the bidding of the Spirit, may be obedience to the Lord of the Church. It may be a reenactment, on a lesser scale, of the kind of dissent that brought Jesus into conflict with the civil and religious authorities of his day.

We may conclude, then, that the charismatic, by offsetting the vocational hazards of the official, helps to prevent the institution from becoming rigid, mechanical, routinized, and domineering.[80] Office-holders who try to quench the Spirit (cf. 1 Thess 5:19) are subject to correction. Criticism, however, can have no place in the Church unless it proceeds from faith, from love, and from recognition of the rights of office, and unless it aims to build up the body of Christ in unity.[81] As von Balthasar rightly observes, those who criticize from the margins of the Church make it impossible for authority to respond in an atmosphere of trust and love.[82]

i. Harmony of the Two Elements

9. *The harmony between the institutional and the charismatic cannot be assured by the institutional alone, without the charismatic.*

Ideally the institutional and the charismatic, since they proceed from the same Lord and are intended for the same goal (the edification of the Church in love), should be responsive to each other. Correction from either side, where needed, should be humbly accepted by the other in a spirit of gratitude and conciliation. But as Church history abundantly attests, clashes occur in which each side is convinced that it cannot yield without compromising on a matter of principle. Such clashes, always painful, sometimes lead to the brink of schism, and beyond. Are there rules for resolving these conflicts?

It is often said that the last word lies with the office-holders, since it is their function to discern between true and false charisms—a point made more than once in the Constitution on the Church.[83] The presumption does lie with the hierarchy, but the presumption cannot be absolutized. Rahner wisely remarks: "Provision has to be made that bureaucratic routine, turning means into ends in themselves, rule for the sake of rule and not for the sake of service, the dead wood of tradition, proud and anxious barricades thrown up against new tasks and requirements, and other such dangers, do not extinguish the Spirit."[84] Thus there is no ultimate juridical solution to collisions between spiritually gifted reformers and conscientious defenders of the accepted order. The Church is not a totalitarian system in which disagreement can be ended by simple fiat. Rather, it is an open society in which all parties are subject to correction. All must recognize their limitations and treat the others with patience, respect, and charity.[85]

In a pilgrim Church time is needed to sift the good grain from the chaff, the weeds from the cockle (cf. Mt 13:24–30, 36–43). If a true consensus is to be achieved, it must be the work of the Spirit, who dwells not in the hierarchy alone but in all the faithful, as we are taught by Vatican II.[86] In this sense, charism has the last word. To quote Rahner again: "The harmony between the two 'structures' of the Church, the institutional and the charismatic, can only be guaranteed by the one Lord of both, and by him alone, that is to say, charismatically."[87]

j. The Lordship of Christ

10. *The lordship of Christ in the Church as a social system is exercised, always provisionally, through the interplay of the institutional and the charismatic.*

The manner of Christ's lordship in the Church inevitably reflects the nature of the pilgrim Church itself. In establishing it as a structured community having both official and charismatic dimensions, Christ implicitly commits himself to work in and through these structures. To describe the Church, as some do, as Christ's "direct sphere of operation" could be misleading if taken to imply that Christ bypasses the social structures. Christ rules the Church indirectly in the sense that he communicates his intentions and graces through a concatenation of human agencies, no one of which, taken alone, adequately represents him.

To speak accurately, we should here note that the Church possesses a multiplicity of institutions and a multiplicity of charisms. There is interaction among the institutions, as seen in the collegiality of pastors, in the liturgical setting of the preaching and teaching ministries, and in the biblical sources of Christian doctrine. Even the highest teaching authorities in the Church remain permanently subject to the word of God in Scripture, as Vatican II declared in its Constitution on Divine Revelation (no. 10).

In like manner, the charisms interact. In the Church as body of Christ, no one's gift may be despised. The inspired prophet, the devout layperson, the learned theologian, and the experienced pastor—each has a proper and distinctive charism, and is bound to respect the charisms of the others. Authentic progress is achieved through the interplay of all. Their mutual tensions, though sometimes conflictive, bring about a richer harmony than could be achieved by reducing the choir to a single voice.

To grasp the full measure of the lordship of Christ we must take account of the tensions among institutions, and tensions among charisms, and the tensions between the institutional and the charismatic. To identify Christ's lordship with the charismatic alone would be, at root, uncatholic, for it would overlook the sacramental quality of institutions in the Church as "sacrament of Christ." To identify Christ's lordship exclusively with the institutional would be equally one-sided. The institutional is capable of becoming opaque and of impeding the communion that should obtain between the members of the Church and their divine Lord.

If the nature of the Church as a sacrament is any clue to the way in which it embodies the lordship of Christ, we may surmise that Christ is most fully its Lord when the charismatic and institutional elements converge and mutually reinforce each other.

k. Secular Parallels

11. *The tension between institution and charism in the Church, insofar as it is anthropologically grounded, has parallels in other social organizations.*

In the vast realms of human and cosmic history, the Church is a unique reality because its total existence is consciously ordered to Jesus Christ as the supreme revelation of truth and meaning. To believe in him, to bear witness to him, to offer worship to God through him is the specific task of the Church and of no other human community. The Church as "system" has Christ as its Lord insofar as he equips it for its divinely assigned task by furnishing it with appropriate institutional and charismatic structures.

Alongside of the Church, many other communities exist, and they too comprise persons in a complex network of relationships. In any large or enduring community one finds both the individual component of personal uniqueness and the societal component of institutional structure. The institutions are not autonomous. Stemming from personal initiative, they aim to promote personal growth. But the institutions are indispensable. In the words of Lewis Mudge, "What sociological analysis has taught us . . . is that no idea, no human possibility, can survive in our society without a definite social expression, and this has to be an institutional expression."[88] Institutional factors such as law and office, ceremony and indoctrination are by no means peculiar to the Church. In almost all human associations, the desired ratio between social conformity and individual freedom becomes a matter of dispute. Conflicts arise between conservative partisans of law and order and liberal partisans of progress and reform.

Thus the polar interplay between the institutional and the charismatic, which we have analyzed in an ecclesiological framework, has counterparts in secular societies. Some sociologists, describing the general characteristics of social existence, speak of a dialectical process having the three "moments" of externalization, objectification, and internalization.[89] Others speak of an alternation between "dwelling in" the tradition as handed down and "breaking out" in order to revitalize and enrich the tradition.[90] Whatever the categories, the dynamics they describe are basically similar to those we have studied under the rubrics of institution and charism.

How does the lordship of Christ assert itself in these other societies? To what extent are their institutions means by which God establishes his kingdom "of truth and life, of holiness and grace, of justice, love, and peace?"[91] Does the charismatic take on a specifically different form in societies that are not considered to have Christ as their "head" and the Holy Spirit as their "soul"? To what extent are social prophets and humanitarian reformers agents of the Holy Spirit and adversaries of the demonic? By what criteria are we to recognize Christ's presence and activity in the secular movements of our time? To seek answers to questions such as these would take us beyond the scope of the present chapter. Without anticipating what other contributors to this volume will say, we may surmise that if Christ is at work in these other social systems—that is, if he is truly Lord of all—his influence is to be sought in the critical moments of the social process. The foregoing study of the institutional and the charismatic in the Church may therefore be of service in discerning how the grace of Christ is mediated through secular social systems.

Depending on how Christ is judged to be present in the secular, we may regard Christ's lordship in the Church as a paradigm for his lordship over other systems or simply as a special case to be compared with other cases. In any event, we must heed the admonition of the Second Vatican Council to be alert for the ways God may be addressing the Church through the world that surrounds it. The Church can neither insulate itself from secular developments nor uncritically accept them. It must labor "to decipher authentic signs of God's presence and purpose" in current events.[92] It has the duty of "scrutinizing the signs of the times and of interpreting them in the light of the Gospel."[93] This process of discernment requires close collaboration between pastors, representing the institutional Church, and gifted laity, representing the charismatic.[94] Thus the response of the Church to the forces of secular history offers a fruitful field of application for the general principles we have endeavored to elucidate.

NOTES

1. On the concept of God as Lord see, most recently, E. Schillebeeckx, *Jesus: An Experiment in Christology* (New York: Seabury, 1979), pp. 141–54, with references to other important works.

2. On the origins of the credal pattern, "Jesus is Lord," see Schillebeeckx, *Jesus,* pp. 405–10; V. H. Neufeld, *The Earliest Christian Confessions* (Grand Rapids: Eerdmans, 1963), p. 67; O. Cullmann, *Christology of the New Testament* (Philadelphia: Westminster, 1959), p. 216.

3. O. Cullmann, *Christology of the New Testament,* p. 229.

4. R. Schnackenburg, *God's Rule and Kingdom* (New York: Herder and Herder, 1963), p. 313.

5. H. Küng, *The Church* (New York: Sheed & Ward, 1968), p. 95.

6. *Lumen gentium,* art. 3; E.T. in W. A. Abbott, ed., *The Documents of Vatican II* (New York: America Press, 1966), p. 16. This edition will be used in future references to Vatican II in the present essay.

7. *Lumen gentium,* art. 5; p. 18.

8. Jaroslav Pelikan has traced Luther's own development from the "spirit vs. structure" position of his early polemical works to a more balanced position of "spirit in structure." Much of Luther's later writing is directed against what he regarded as the unbridled enthusiasm of the left-wing Reformers, who, as he put it, had "swallowed the Holy Spirit, feathers and all." See J. Pelikan, *Spirit vs. Structure* (New York: Harper & Row, 1968); also his *Obedient Rebels* (New York: Harper & Row, 1964).

9. M. Weber, *On Charisma and Institution Building,* ed. S. N. Eisenstadt (Chicago: Univ. of Chicago Press, 1968), p. 48.

10. F. A. Sullivan, "The Ecclesiological Context of the Charismatic Renewal" in K. McDonnell, ed., *The Holy Spirit and Power* (Garden City: Doubleday, 1975), p. 125. Somewhat similar definitions of charism are given in H. Küng, *The Church,* p. 188, and in R. Laurentin, "Charisms: Terminological Precision" in C. Duquoc and C. Floristan, eds. *Charisms in the Church (Concilium* vol. 109; New York: Seabury, 1978), p. 8.

11. *Lumen gentium,* art. 12, p. 30.

12. K. Rahner, *The Dynamic Element in the Church* (Quaestiones Disputatae 12) (New York: Herder and Herder, 1964), pp. 50–52; H. Küng, *The Church,* pp. 179–91; L. Sartori, "The Structure of Juridical and Charismatic Power in the Christian Community" in *Charisms in the Church* (*op. cit.*), pp. 56–66.

13. E. Durkheim is summarized as holding that a social structure means "the mesh of mutual positions and interrelations in terms of which the interdependence of the component parts may be described; the 'function' of any part is the way it operates so as to maintain the total system 'in good health.' " So E. R. Leach, "Social Structure," *International Encyclopedia of the Social Sciences,* vol. 14 (New York: Macmillan, 1968), p. 482.

14. A. Sabatier, *Religions of Authority and the Religion of the Spirit* (New York: McClure, Philipps, 1904).

15. R. Sohm, *Kirchenrecht* (Munich and Leipzig: Duncker & Humblot, 2 vols., 1923), esp. vol. 1, p. 26.

16. E. Brunner, *The Misunderstanding of the Church* (London: Lutterworth, 1952).

17. G. Hasenhüttl, "Church and Institution" in G. Baum and A. Greeley, eds. *The Church as Institution (Cocilium* vol. 91; New York: Herder and Herder, 1974), pp. 11–21.

18. J. A. Möhler in *Theol. Quartalschrift* 5 (1823), p. 497; quoted by Y. Congar, *L'Eglise de S. Augustin à l'époque moderne* (Paris: Cerf, 1970), p. 383.

19. Art. "Charisma" in L. F. Hartman, ed. *Encyclopedic Dictionary of the Bible* (New York: McGraw-Hill, 1963), col. 351.

20. Speech of E. Ruffini on Oct. 16, 1963 in *Acta synodalia Concilii Vaticani II,* vol. 2, Pars 2 (Vatican City, 1972), pp. 629–30.

21. J.-L. Leuba, *L'Institution et l'evenement.* E.T.: *New Testament Pattern. An Exegetical Inquiry into the "Catholic" and "Protestant" Dualism* (London: Lutterworth, 1953).

22. N. Ehrenström and W. G. Muelder, eds., *Institutionalism and Church Unity.* New York: Association Press, 1963.

23. *AAS* 35 (1943) p. 200. E.T.: *The Mystical Body of Christ* (New York: America Press, 3rd ed. 1957), no. 21.

24. *AAS* 35 (1943), p. 224; E.T., no. 79.

25. *AAS* 35 (1943), p. 200; E.T., no. 21.

26. *AAS* 35 (1943), p. 223; E.T., no. 77.

27. L.-J. Suenens, "The Charismatic Dimension of the Church," in H. Küng and others, eds., *Council Speeches of Vatican II* (Glen Rock: Paulist Press, 1964), pp. 29–34.

28. Y. Congar and others, "La Seigneurie du Christ sur l'Eglise et sur le monde," *Istina* 6 (1959) 131–66; cf. Y. Congar, *Lay People in the Church* (Westminster, Md.: Newman, 1957), pp. 55–73, 88–92.

29. Congar, *Lay People*, pp. 103–104; Congar, *The Mystery of the Church* (Baltimore: Helicon, 1960), p. 186.

30. Congar, *The Mystery of the Church,* p. 170.

31. Ibid., p. 176. While recognizing that office-holders may be charismatically gifted, Congar seems to identify the charismatic, at least predominantly, with extraordinary and unforeseeable graces.

32. See especially Congar's *Ministères et communion ecclésiale* (Paris: Cerf, 1971), pp. 15–19, 35–39, 43–48; also Congar's "Renewal of the Spirit and Reform of the Institution," in A. Müller and N. Greinacher, eds., *Ongoing Reform of the Church* (*Concilium* vol. 73; New York: Herder and Herder, 1972), pp. 39–49.

33. H. U. von Balthasar, *Church and World* (New York: Herder and Herder, 1967), pp. 46, 100–102.

34. Ibid., pp. 23–36, 113–15.

35. Ibid., p. 109.

36. Ibid. pp. 131, 148.

37. Ibid., pp. 28, 79.

38. *Sponsa Verbi* (*Skizzen zur Theologie,* vol. 2; Einsiedeln: Johannes Verlag, 1960), p. 326; *Pneuma und Institution* (*Skizzen zur Theologie,* vol. 4; Einsiedeln: Johannes Verlag, 1974), p. 150.

39. *Sponsa Verbi,* p. 330.

40. K. Rahner, "The Church and the Sacraments" in his *Inquiries* (New York: Herder and Herder, 1964), p. 204.

41. "Observations on the Factor of the Charismatic in the Church," *Theological Investigations,* vol. 12 (New York: Seabury, 1974), p. 83.

42. *The Dynamic Element in the Church,* p. 44.

43. "Observations on the Factor of the Charismatic," pp. 85–86.

44. For some critical appraisals of Rahner's anthropology and ecclesiology see, for instance, P. Eicher, *Die anthropologische Wende* (Freiburg, Switzerland: Universitätsverlag, 1970); idem, *Offenbarung; Prinzip neuzeitlicher Theologie* (Munich: Kösel, 1977), pp. 347–421; M. Kehl, *Kirche als Institution* (Frankfurt a. M.: Knecht, 1976), pp. 171–238; also the literature cited in these works.

45. H. Küng, *The Church,* p. 166.

46. Ibid., p. 190.

47. H. Küng, *On Being a Christian* (Garden City: Doubleday, 1976), pp. 490–92.

48. For an expository and critical survey of Küng's views on the Church as institution see M. Kehl, *Kirche als Institution,* pp. 123–71.

49. Von Balthasar, *Church and World,* p. 128.

50. Congar speaks of a "perichōrēsis" of the three functions of Christ and of the Church; "La Seigneurie . . .," p. 145; *The Mystery of the Church,* p. 151.

51. Cf. A. Dulles, "*Ius divinum* as an Ecumenical Problem," *Theological Studies* 38 (1977) 681–708.

52. K. Rahner, *Theology of Pastoral Action* (New York: Herder and Herder, 1968), pp. 70–71.

53. Cf. K. Rahner, *The Church and the Sacraments,* pp. 216–22.

54. Cf. K. Rahner, "Observations on the Factor of the Charismatic," pp. 83–84; cited above, note 41.

55. Cf. B. Gerhardsson, *The Origins of the Gospel Traditions* (Philadelphia: Fortress, 1979).

56. Cf. Vatican II, *Sacrosanctum Concilium,* art. 7, p. 141; *Lumen gentium,* art. 26, p. 50; also Rahner as cited in note 40 above.

57. Cf. above, note 30.

58. Vatican II, *Ad gentes,* art. 4, p. 587.

59. "The Charismatic Dimension of the Church," p. 29.

60. Ibid, p. 31.

61. *Lumen gentium,* art. 12, p. 30

62. Cf. note 23 above.

63. *The Dynamic Element,* p. 57.

64. "Das Charismatische in der Kirche," *Stimmen der Zeit* 160 (1957) 170.

65. E.g., by K. Rahner, *The Dynamic Element,* pp. 42–48; also in his article, "Charism," *Encyclopedia of Theology: The Concise "Sacramentum Mundi"* (New York: Seabury, 1975), pp. 184–86.

66. J. M. Gustafson, "A Look at the Secular City," in D. Callahan, ed., *The Secular City Debate* (New York: Macmillan, 1966), p. 14.

67. Von Balthasar, *Sponsa Verbi,* p. 324.

68. *Adversus haereses* 4.26.2.

69. Such, at least, is the interpretation recently offered by J. D. Quinn, " 'Charisma Veritatis Certum': Irenaeus: *Adversus haereses* 4.26.2," *Theological Studies* 39 (1978) 520–25.

70. *Dei Verbum,* art. 8, p. 116.

71. Vatican I, *Pastor aeternus,* Chap. 4; DS 3071.

72. Cf. Rahner, *The Dynamic Element,* pp. 98–100, with footnote 13.

73. *Church and World,* p. 79.

74. *Church and World,* p. 27; cf. p. 37; also *Sponsa Verbi,* pp. 331, 335.

75. *Lumen gentium,* art. 12, p. 30; cf. art. 7, p. 21.

76. Cf. von Balthasar, *Die Wahrheit ist symphonisch* (Einsiedeln: Johannes Verlag, 1972), p. 127.

77. Cf. von Balthasar, *Pneuma und Institution,* p. 151.

78. Cf. von Balthasar, *Die Wahrheit ist symphonisch,* p. 88.

79. Cf. K. Rahner, *The Dynamic Element,* pp. 52–53; *Freiheit und Manipulation in Gesellschaft und Kirche* (Munich: Kösel, 1970), pp. 37–43; H. Küng, *On Being a Christian,* pp. 486–87.

80. For a penetrating analysis of these hazards, see T. F. O'Dea, "Five Dilemmas in the Institutionalization of Religion" in his *Sociology and the Study of Religion* (New York: Basic Books, 1970), pp. 240–55.

81. Cf. von Balthasar, *Pneuma und Institution,* pp. 154, 196; *Die Wahrheit ist symphonisch,* pp. 116–120.

82. *Die Wahrheit ist symphonisch,* p. 128.

83. Cf. note 75 above.

84. *The Dynamic Element,* p. 52.

85. Cf. K. Rahner, *The Dynamic Element,* pp. 74–78; "Observations on the Factor of the Charismatic," pp. 88–89. Rahner's portrayal of the Church as an "open system" has some affinities with the idea of the Church as an "open system" proposed by P. Granfield in *Ecclesial Cybernetics* (New York: Macmillan, 1973), pp. 5–8.

86. *Lumen gentium,* art. 12, p. 29; art. 25, p. 49.

87. *The Dynamic Element,* p. 52.

88. Lewis Mudge, in his response to R. N. Johnson, "Styles of Ecumenism in the United States," *Unity Trends* 1/12 (May 1, 1968) p. 11.

89. P. L. Berger and T. Luckmann, *The Social Construction of Reality* (Garden City: Anchor Books, 1967), esp. p. 61.

90. M. Polanyi, *Personal Knowledge* (New York: Harper Torchbooks, 1964), pp. 195–202.

91. Vatican II, *Gaudium et spes,* art. 9, p. 237.

92. *Gaudium et spes,* art. 11, p. 209.

93. *Gaudium et spes,* art. 4, pp. 201–202.

94. Vatican II, *Presbyterorum ordinis,* art. 9, p. 553.

Part III
Lord of the World

8
The Emperor's New Clothes: Christ and Constantine

Francine Cardman

With the advent of a Christian emperor in 312, the relationship between Christ and culture,[1] Church and society, Christology and the social and political realities of the day, took on a decidedly new cast. The change was manifest in both experience and perception, conscious articulation and unconscious expression. It was felt by ordinary folk, no longer moved by fear of persecution, threat or hope of martyrdom. Among the educated, many of the new Christian elite rhapsodized the new age, analyzing it with a curious combination of uncritical theology and moralistic history, celebrating the emperor who had brought about the change of fortunes that so quickly came to look like God's plan for Christianity and for the world. Almost overnight old certainties were stood on their head. The rhetorician Lactantius, already a Christian, demonstrated that emperors who persecuted met suitably horrible deaths; the Christian bishop Eusebius became court biographer to the emperor and the first Christian church historian.[2] Through it all moved Constantine, his wardrobe changing with the times and also changing them—Constantine the soldier, the Christian, the emperor, "bishop" and benefactor, and, finally, neophyte.

Constantine's victory at the Milvian Bridge on October 28, 312, marked the beginning of a decisive transition in Christian history and Christian hope. Yet the change had been in the making long before. Regarded as aloof, haters of humanity, atheists who threatened the very fabric of society by their abstention from civic and imperial cult, Christians were popular scapegoats for the misfortunes of the empire. Nero found them a handy means of diverting attention from his own responsibility for the great fire in Rome in 64.[3] In a vivid complaint the Christian apologist Tertullian (c. 198) decried the extension of this scapegoating philosophy to cover natural disasters as well as those of human making:

> If the Tiber rises as high as the city walls, if the Nile does not send its waters up over the fields, if the heavens give no rain, if there is an earthquake, if there is a famine or pestilence, straightaway the cry is, "Away with the Christians to the lion!"[4]

His sardonic reply—"What! Shall you give such multitudes to a single beast?"—only underlines the irony of the situation. Yet even Justin, later to be known as "the Martyr," could argue (c. 150) that Christians performed the most useful social function possible by praying for the emperor.[5] An anonymous apologist, writing to an unidentified pagan (quite possibly the emperor Hadrian) sometime around 129, could make the bold claim that "What the soul is in the body, that Christians are in the world."[6] And even Tertullian, cognizant as he was of the mistreatment and death of Christians at the hands of Roman officials, could cite Christian conduct and example as a force for morality and public order. Although Christians were, he declared, "those on whom the end of the ages has come," they nevertheless "prayed for the delay of the end," finding it in their own interest as well as that of their pagan neighbors to hold off that terrible day.[7] Jesus, the crucified and risen Lord whom the early Christians prayed to "come quickly"—*Maranatha!*—and bring history to its end, was becoming, by the start of the third century, the Lord of history, whose will was made known in the ongoing and increasingly intertwined histories of the Roman empire and the Christian Church. That Constantine should have found this "God of the Christians" mighty in battle on his behalf should come as no surprise, then, even as it is seen to alter the face of Western history.

By examining three stages or moments in the career of Constantine as Christian and as emperor, I hope to show some of the complexities, conflicts and compromises in the interaction of Church and empire as loci for the manifestation of Christ's lordship in human history. Although the fourth century situation may at first seem far different from our own, its very complexity is a warning against any easy identifications of God's purposes in the world. Then, as now, the lordship of Christ could not be known apart from the social structures that mediate human experience; but neither could it be known in its totality through them. And, as the case of Constantine shows, sometimes that lordship is obscured and compromised, even when it seems to shine forth most brightly. The first critical moment to be examined is the "conversion" of Constantine on the eve of the battle of the Milvian Bridge. From Constantine's subsequent victory under the Christian God there emerged a plan for the unification of Church and empire. The role of Constantine in the shaping of Christological dogma at the Council of Nicaea is the second moment considered, along with some of the consequences for liturgy, Christology, and what could be termed "political theology." Finally, Constantine's church building program in the Holy Land is taken as an example of the continued Christianization of the empire and the concomitant imperialization of Christianity under Constantine.

From Soldier to Christian Victor

Son of Constantius Chlorus, the soldier-emperor who had been Augustus of the West for little more than a year, Constantine was acclaimed emperor by the troops after his father's death in 306. Although recognized only in the second-ranking office of Caesar by the Eastern (and senior) emperor Galerius, Constantine nevertheless pressed his claim to the title of Augustus. A soldier himself, Constantine worshiped his father's god, Apollo or Sol Invictus, the Unconquered Sun. On campaign in Gaul around 310, he had visited a temple of Apollo and been blessed with a vision of the god. A pagan orator recorded the apparition:

> . . . O Constantine, you saw, I believe, your protector Apollo, in company with Victory, offering you laurel crowns each of which bears the presage of thirty years. . . . You really saw the god and

> recognized yourself in the appearance of one to whom the prophecies of poets have declared that the rule of the whole world should belong.[8]

With the aid of Apollo, Constantine seemed destined to be the hero predicted by Virgil's Fourth Eclogue, the one to usher in a new age of peace and prosperity.[9]

Within a few years of that experience, Constantine was camped outside Rome, preparing to do battle with the usurper Maxentius. Pagan and Christian alike considered Constantine's unlikely victory the next day at the Milvian Bridge to be the result of divine aid. Within six years of the event, the rhetorician Lactantius related how Constantine had come to have the help of the Christian God:

> Constantine was directed in a dream to mark the heavenly sign of God on the shields of his soldiers and thus to join battle. He did as he was ordered and with the cross-shaped letter X, with its top bent over, he marked Christ on the shields.[10]

This is the origin of the famed "Chi-Rho" symbol that came to be the mark of the Christian emperor and the special divine protection of his realm.

Writing considerably later than Lactantius, and indeed after the death of Constantine, Eusebius presented a longer and seemingly embroidered account of the event. Whether the embroidery is Eusebius's or Constantine's, from whom he claims to have gotten the story, is impossible to tell. After remarking on Constantine's uncertainty about the efficacy of the traditional gods, Eusebius related Constantine's resolution to the dilemma of ascertaining which god could provide him with victory.

> Accordingly, he besought his father's god in prayer, beseeching and imploring him to tell him who he was and to stretch out his right hand to him in his present difficulties. And while he was thus praying with fervent entreaty, a most incredible sign appeared to him from heaven. . . . He said that about noon, when the day was already beginning to decline, he saw with his own eyes the trophy of a cross of light in the heavens, above the

> sun, and an inscription, CONQUER BY THIS, attached to it. At this sight he himself was struck with amazement, and his whole army also, which followed him on an expedition and witnessed the miracle.
>
> . . . night overtook him; then in his sleep the Christ of God appeared to him with the sign which he had seen in the heavens, and commanded him to make a likeness of that sign . . . and to use it as a safeguard in all engagements with his enemies.[11]

The transition from Apollo to Christ was made smoothly and effectively.

The nature of Constantine's "conversion," the interpretation of the events at the Milvian Bridge and Constantine's subsequent attitude to Christianity, are the subjects of endless debates among scholars.[12] Ranging from the cynical to the credulous, scholarly opinions judge Constantine to be anything from a brilliant statesman and political opportunist to a sincere and unselfish Christian believer. Henry Chadwick offers what seems to be the most judicious observation on the nature of Constantine's actions before the Milvian Bridge: "At the crisis of his career . . . Constantine invoked the mighty aid of the Christian God and was not disappointed."[13] At the very least, his father's god, clothed now as the God of the Christians, had proved a potent means to victory. Although worshiped by only a small fraction of the empire's population,[14] this God was a powerful ally. Through Christ, and perhaps also through the small but growing Christian Church, Constantine perceived the way of victory and ultimately of unified rule. Monarchy and Christian monotheism were to go hand in hand.[15]

Soon after Constantine and the Eastern co-emperor Licinius had affirmed the freedom of all religions and decreed the restitution to Christians of property lost or destroyed in the persecutions—the so-called "Edict of Milan"[16]—Constantine began the subtle shift from simply allowing Christians the freedom to follow their religion, to actively favoring the religion of the Christians. Restoration of Church property soon led to the granting of tax exemptions to Christian clergy on the same basis as pagan priests, and this practice quickly gave way to the provision of cash grants to the Christian clergy. But the imperial generosity soon ran afoul of ecclesiastical realities. In the wake of the last great persecution—ended by Galerius's Edict of Toleration in 311 and followed by the declaration of Constantine and Licinius in 313—the Church in North Africa had split into factions in a bitter dispute over the proper conduct of Christians under persecution. Confronted by the schismatic Donatist church, Constantine was bewildered: to whom should his imperial largesse go? Who *was* the Church in North Africa? From 316 until 321 Constantine toiled fruitlessly to resolve the controversy, finally abandoning the project in despair. His failure with the Donatists galled him, however, for it concerned more than the mere disposition of money; the very integrity of the empire was at stake.

For Constantine had, at some time impossible to specify, begun to regard Christianity as the glue to hold his empire together. The God who had granted him victory and who continued to provide for him, could not fail to be displeased with the fractious state of affairs in the Church. Schism was as intolerable to the emperor as it was to God. Should it arise, it must be speedily eradicated,

> lest the Highest Divinity may be aroused not only against the human race, but against me, myself—to whose care, by his decree, he entrusted the governance of all things below.[17]

The one God was the God of unity, both in the Church and in the empire.

And the Church was to be the vehicle for the unification of Constantine's empire. From it, the source of concord, *homonoia* would flow throughout the lands. Constantine's plan for the Church was, as Massey Shepherd aptly puts it, "the sanctification of the temporal order through the Christian renovation of the empire."[18] To this end Constantine lavished gifts on the Christians, building churches, decorating them grandly, furnishing them with newly copied volumes of the Scriptures and precious vessels of every sort.

The Church welcomed this embarrassment of riches with open arms, considering it, apparently, confirmation of God's favor. Clothed in imperial magnificence, the Church increased in numbers and influence. With the emperor as its most influential (although unbaptized) "member," it was perhaps inevitable that the Church should turn, sooner or later, to theological discussions, disputes, and ultimately definitions that would clarify its faith in Jesus Christ, the Son of God, who was its Savior and Lord. The internal logic of doctrinal development was as significant in focusing the fourth century consideration of Christology as were the emperor's generous attentions to the Church. But it is doubtful that the road to the First Ecumenical Council of Nicaea would have followed quite the same route without Constantine.

> The Church, thanks to Constantine, had attained new wealth and public prominence. To express it there was only one obvious language of magnificence, the language of the imperial cult and court. But in that fact was implicit the danger of a friend becoming a master.[19]

In the meantime, however, the mighty deeds of God continued to be made manifest, even after the death and resurrection of the Savior, in the beneficent and providential rule of the pagan soldier who had become emperor of the West and, in some as yet unclarified sense, a Christian ruler. With the sign of Christ on his soldiers' shields and on his own helmet, Constantine had made the transition from pagan soldier to Christian victor.

The Christian Emperor and the Christian's Lord

After the victory that had made him emperor, Constantine regarded the Christian Church with favor. He seems to have considered himself a Christian, although his public professions remained ambiguous for some years, and his personal profession of faith in baptism was not to take place until shortly before his death in 336. Despite his difficulties with the Donatists, Constantine's apparent sense of himself as a Christian emperor whose well-being depended on God and the unity of the Church increased in the years prior to the Council of Nicaea in 325. Constantine's involvement in the council and the events surrounding it grew out of his perception of the mutual dependence of Church and empire. The role he assumed at that time would evoke transmutations of both Christian and imperial self-consciousness. It began with a theological dispute that had been gathering momentum in the eastern empire since its outbreak in 318; the dispute soon disrupted his peace and, he ruefully reports, his sleep.[20] Alexander, bishop of Alexandria, and Arius, one of his presbyters, had become embroiled in a conflict over the origin and nature of the Son of God. Arguing brilliantly, though ultimately unpersuasively, Arius claimed that the Son was the perfect creature, created out of nothing, having a beginning. "Before he was begotten," Arius reasoned, "he was not."[21] For his part, Alexander defended the "traditional" faith of the Church, which rejected this rarefied understanding of the Son's creatureliness, but the controversy soon spread beyond Alexandria and throughout the East. Once again the unity and concord of the Church were threatened, and with it, the empire. Constantine's investment in the Church had grown in every way since the Milvian bridge, and so a projected trip to the Holy Land, set for 324, was postponed so that the emperor could orchestrate a speedy resolution to the conflict.

Constantine's intervention in the theological dispute followed closely on the heels of his victory over Licinius in that same year. As a result of that triumph, Constantine had assumed authority as sole emperor of a united empire. The unity of rule and empire would gain strong legitimation if it were seen to reflect the unity (*monarchia* had been the key term of a third century Christological debate) of God and the Son, his image. If the emperor imitated the sovereignty and providence of God, the model and original of such divine imitation was, for Christians, the Son. That the ecclesiastical controversy in which he found himself embroiled should have concerned Christology was not Constantine's doing. Yet it served his interests as the one Emperor of East and West to support a strong Christological position. Perhaps it suited his rudimentary knowledge of the faith as well.

For nearly a century before Nicaea, the Church had been dealing with doctrinal or disciplinary disputes by means of regional synods. Despite the fact that in one notable instance the decisions of the gathered bishops could only be enforced several years afterwards, with the aid of the Emperor Aurelian's troops, the synodal process was, on the whole, developing well. Left on its own, it might have reached sufficient maturity in another generation or two to be able to withstand outside pressure.[22] But it is one of the small ironies of history that at this critical juncture Constantine should have stepped in and decisively affected the process of development from regional synod to ecumenical council. Universally binding dogmatic definition became a possibility and a reality for the Church only when the Christian emperor had provided the machinery for deliberation and enforcement.

At Nicaea, the assembled bishops—numbered, by custom, 318 for the members of Abraham's household, though in reality closer to 200—condemned the teachings of Arius. The Son was declared divine, clearly God and not one of the creatures, consubstantial (*homoousios*) with the Father, begotten and not made. Appended to the creed of Nicaea was a list of Arian opinions; anyone holding such opinions was declared anathema. All but two bishops signed the council's decrees, despite widespread disagreement about the interpretation and even the suitability of the key word *homoousios.* After a brief lull, the dispute would revive, growing in intensity and divisiveness over the subsequent fifty years. But for the time being, Constantine was well-pleased with his efforts to reconcile his "fellow servants" of God, the bishops.[23]

Once Constantine had become "fellow servant" to the bishops, a revolution in imperial and Christian imagery began. The revolution is attested to by Eusebius's account of the Council of Nicaea, by the evolution of the imperial self-image, by the changing image of Christ, and by the development of the liturgy in the period after Nicaea.

Thirteen years after the council, in the midst of renewed ecclesiastical controversy, Eusebius wrote lyrically of the emperor's achievement at Nicaea:

> Constantine is the first prince of any age who bound together such a garland as this with the bond of peace, and presented it as a thank offering for the victories he had obtained over every foe, thus exhibiting in our own times a similitude of the apostolic company.[24]

There is no need to doubt whose role Constantine played in the apostolic company described by Eusebius. The similarity between the

Christian emperor and the Lord of the Christians is even more striking in the report Eusebius offers of the opening of the Council:

> At last he himself [Constantine] proceeded through the midst of the assembly, like some heavenly messenger of God, clothed in raiment which glittered as it were with rays of light.[25]

The banquet that closed the council also served to celebrate the emperor's *vicennalia*—the twentieth anniversary of his accession to power. Eusebius's unabashed description of the feast says worlds about the new social and political position of the Church as well as about the new theological interpretation of empire that was emerging:

> One might have thought that a picture of Christ's kingdom was thus shadowed forth, a dream rather than a reality.[26]

Empire, emperor and Church were all bound together in Eusebius's view. The lordship of Christ is exercised in history through the governance of the emperor, the *Autokrator Augustos.*[27] According to Eusebius, the Christian emperor is the *eikon,* the image, of the ruler of the world. At the same time, he is also imitator of Christ the Logos.[28] The emperor thus exercises the dual function of sharing in the priesthood of Christ, by offering himself as ruler to God, and sharing in the saving work of Christ, by serving as the instrument of his victory in the world.[29] Eusebius's retrospective theological evaluation of the role played by Constantine at Nicaea is evidence of the increasingly complex interaction of Christology and political theology in the fourth century. Constantine's architectural efforts in Rome, Jerusalem and Constantinople give further witness to the growing identification of the purposes and destiny of Church and empire: "The churches built during this period in the three centers stood as symbols of the triumph of the Christian Church on earth."[30] A new conception of the kingdom of God on earth entered Christianity with Constantine. Not only had the Christianization of the empire begun, but the imperialization of Christianity as well.

If the lines of demarcation between Church and empire, Christ and the emperor grew blurred in political theory and theology, so the distinctions between Apollo, Christ and the Christian emperor become more difficult to discern in both Christian and imperial iconography. Constantine's pagan vision of Apollo had already suggested the association of emperor and sun god. And indeed, Constantine's coinage first bears the image of Sol about 310.[31] The new coin was clear and deliberate repudiation of the Western Augustus, Maximian, to whose position Constantine aspired, and his god, Hercules. Politics and religion were already intertwined, for "the cult of the sun god also contained a claim to universal monarchy."[32] Soon after the defeat of Maxentius in 312, coins began to appear depicting Constantine with the Chi-Rho symbol on his helmet,[33] evidence of some sort of Christian conviction on his part. Yet in 313 it was still possible to represent Constantine in profile, accompanied by Sol Invictus, and Sol remains on Constantine's coinage at least until 321.[34]

Although the sun god is banished from Constantine's coinage after this date, his influence nevertheless perdures in the numismatic portraits of the emperor. After some early false starts, the imperial portrait of Constantine settled on a style immediately distinguishable from that of his predecessors. The new imperial portraiture resulted from the blending of two portrait types. The basic model or type was that of the "young ruler," the prototype of whom is Augustus. Evelyn Harrison describes the type:

> The young ruler is shown as young, not only because he may actually have been young when he came to power and idealization will not let him grow old, but because he is a son. He holds power by virtue of his royal or divine father.[35]

Portraiture of this first type was particularly well-suited to Constantine's beliefs and biography; its Christological implications are obvious. The second is characterized by Harrison as the "Apollo type." In it, the subject's features are sharp, the nose aquiline, and, most characteristically, the eyes are uplifted, as if in prayer (as Eusebius and other Christians may have interpreted it) or under the influence of divine inspiration (as many pagan Romans would have understood it). The prototype of this portrait style is Apollo as inspired musician. The Apollo type contrasts sharply with its alternative, the Herakles type: "Herakles stands for human *arete* and the immortality achieved by a man's own work and virtue; Apollo stands for reliances on prophecy and divine inspiration."[36] What could have been more suitable to the Christian emperor than this latter style? And what more useful in bringing together Christian and pagan, Christ and Sol? "Christianity has little or no use for a Herakles type. The Apollo type is the one that is serviceable both for Christ as the Son of God and for the emperor as the ruler who ascertains and performs the will of God."[37] The emperor's portrait suggested both Apollo and Christ and, in doing so, furthered the unification of Church and empire.

Later in the fourth century, and due at least in part to the merging interests and identities of empire and Church begun with Constantine, Christian iconography also underwent a transition. The representation of Jesus as the Good Shepherd began to give way to the image of Christ the *Pantokrator,* the governor of all creation.[38] Consonant with the dogmatic definition of Christ's divinity at Nicaea, and paralleling and interacting with the development of the imperial image, the portrayal of Christ increasingly took on the trappings of imperial court and rank. The throne, purple cushions, halo and *proskynesis* associated with the emperor's court were all assumed into the heavenly audience hall in which Christ sat surrounded by apostles, angels and saints. In the developing "iconographic repertoire," Christ and the emperor were virtually interchangeable. R. A. Markus described the situation graphically:

> Christ becomes the heavenly emperor, his throne the replica of the emperor's; the nimbus around the emperor's arrival at a city and his reception provide the prototype for Christ's entry into Jerusalem.[39]

Under the influence of the imperial style, and in response to the Christological decisions of Nicaea, the Christian liturgy underwent significant developments during and after the Arian controversy. Already apparent in the scale and magnificence of the churches built under Constantine, the imperial style continued to dominate the externals of the liturgy. The bishop became an ecclesiastical version of an imperial official: he had the privilege of being accompanied in procession by incense and lights, being greeted at the church door by a choir, and being waited upon at throne and altar with covered hands.[40] Although he looked like an imperial functionary, his role in the liturgy placed the bishop in obvious parallel to both Christ and the emperor. Seated on his throne in the basilical church—a structure quite likely modeled after the imperial basilica or audience hall—the bishop could evoke images of the heavenly as well as the earthly throne rooms.[41]

Not surprisingly, the theological overtones of the liturgy changed as well. Josef Jungmann has shown that it was in the wake of the Arian controversy that liturgical prayer came to be addressed directly to Christ.[42] Increased emphasis on Christ's divinity and a growing separation of Christ from ordinary humanity was one result of this change. In the struggle to avoid every kind of subordinationism, Christ was exalted to new heights. His priesthood came to be regarded less as a mediation in and through his humanity than as the act of a divine agent transforming the gifts and effecting the eucharistic sacrifice. As the epithets normally applied to the emperor were transferred to Christ, the liturgy took on an increasing sense of mystery and awfulness.[43] Cultic dread had become a significant liturgical factor by about the middle of the fourth century. Especially in the East, where the Arian troubles were greatest, the awe-inspiring eucharistic mystery came to be seen as an encounter between the king and his servants. Johannes Quasten sums up this development succinctly:

> The Eucharist, at the beginning a simple *cena dominica* in the private homes of the Christians, takes more and more the forms of a court ceremonial, of the reception of a king. . . . Not a private home, but the king's hall, the basilica, is now the place where the royal ceremonial is celebrated.[44]

A new kind of liturgical and personal piety, centered on the incarnate life and death of Jesus and on his eucharistic presence, would be a later consequence of these fourth century liturgical developments.[45] Again it is Constantine who, wittingly or not, gave impetus and direction to these future developments.

Clothed so as to recall both Apollo and Christ, Constantine began the transition from Christian emperor to "bishop," from benefactor of the Church to the earthly representative of its Lord.

From Benefactor to Bishop

Constantine's program of church building throughout the empire promoted the emperor while aiding the Church. His ecclesiastical and imperial agendas were mutually reinforcing as he carried out his plan for the Christian renovation of the empire. Nowhere did his efforts come together more strikingly than in his "Holy Land plan," and nowhere can the interaction of liturgy, Christology and imperial theology be seen more clearly.

At the urging of his mother Helena, and perhaps in expiation for the execution of his son Crispus and his wife Fausta, Constantine ordered the erection of churches at the site of Christ's passion and resurrection (the Church of the Holy Sepulchre) in Jerusalem, the place of his birth (the Church of the Nativity) in Bethlehem, and the mountain from which he ascended (the Eleona Church), the Mount of Olives.[46] Prompted by the scandalized reports of his mother-in-law Eutropia, who had been distressed to find the celebration of pagan rites beside the sacred oak of Mamre where the Lord and two angels had appeared to Abraham (cf. Gen 18) the pious emperor built yet another church. Unlike the churches commemorating places associated with the Incarnation, the Church at Mamre was dedicated to the Holy Trinity, thus interpreting Abraham's heavenly visitors in the light of Christ while also recalling God's promise that Abraham would be the father of a numerous people.

The monumental style of Constantine's churches, wherever he built them, had the effect of emphasizing the historical as over against the eschatological situation of the Church. As Massey Shepherd observes, this new emphasis tended to stress the importance of the temporal, which was now seen not merely as transitory but as a "true image and copy of the eternal glory of the communion of the saints." Those churches that were also *martyria,* monuments to victorious saints and martyrs, increased the stress on "historical testimony over against eschatological hope."[47]

That he had perceived at least some of the implications that this church-building program had for his imperial designs is evident in Constantine's arrangements for his own burial. Already, in the time after Nicaea, Constantine had had occasion to refer to himself as a "bishop," instructing a group of bishops as to his status: "You are bishops whose jurisdiction is within the Church: I also am a bishop, ordained by God to oversee whatever is external to the Church." Eusebius's comment on the situation is revealing: "Truly his measures corresponded with his words; for he watched over his subjects with an episcopal care. . . ."[48] Certainly his words and his measures corresponded when it came to the provision of his final resting place: in the Church of the Holy Apostles in Constantinople, surrounded on either side by the cenotaphs of the apostles.

The activities of the "Thirteenth Apostle" left their mark on the Holy Land in a physical sense while also affecting the further development of liturgy, both there and in the West. The Church of the Holy Sepulchre and the Jerusalem liturgy are but the most striking examples of Constantinian influence in this sphere. Again Eusebius's perspective provides a starting point:

> After these things [Nicaea] the pious emperor addressed himself to another work truly worthy of record, in the province of Palestine. . . . He judged it incumbent on him to render the blessed locality of our Savior's resurrection an object of attraction and veneration to all.[49]

Once the site had been located with the aid of Makarios, bishop of Jerusalem, and the rubble of centuries and the remains of deliberate desecration removed, the cave of the Savior's tomb was exposed to sight, as was the hill of Golgotha. Constantine instructed Makarios and his retainers in Palestine to construct the most magnificent monument possible around this holy place.

> Accordingly, on the very spot which witnessed the Savior's sufferings, a new Jerusalem was constructed, over against the one so celebrated of old. . . . It was opposite this city that the emperor began to rear a monument to the Savior's victory over death, with rich and lavish magnificence. And it may be that

> this was that second and new Jerusalem spoken of in the predictions of the prophets.[50]

It is noteworthy that the builder and maker of this new city is not God but Constantine.

Both Constantine's activities and Eusebius's evaluation of them bear out Shepherd's argument about the historicizing of Christian hope. The catechetical lectures of Cyril of Jerusalem, preached most likely between 348 and 350, show that Eusebius's assessment was no aberration. Repeatedly in his instructions to the catechumens—delivered in front of the Anastasis, the small building surrounding the Lord's tomb—Cyril makes references to the holy places of the faith: the tomb, of course, but also the rock of Calvary, the Mount of Olives, the cave of Bethlehem. In short, the sacred geography of Palestine, preserved in Christian memory and later memorialized by Constantine's building program, offered the historical testimony that could enhance or even in some sense validate present-day Christian faith. The concluding chapters of the fourteenth catechetical lecture illustrate Cyril's style while also demonstrating the shift in perspective that had begun with Constantine:

> Many witnesses there are of the Savior's resurrection—the night and the light of the full moon; . . . the rock of the sepulchre which received him; . . . even the stone which was rolled away itself bears witness to the resurrection, lying there to this day. . . . And this house of the holy Church, which out of the loving affection to Christ of the Emperor Constantine of blessed memory was both built and beautified as thou seest.[51]

Just as the lordship of Christ was translated into historical terms with the emergence of a Christian *imperium,* so too was the liturgy historicized as a result of imperial beneficence. If an increased sense of awe and mystery enveloped the liturgy as a result of the Arian controversy, a countervailing trend developed as well, anchoring that mystery in the particular, linking the divine with the concretely historical, and so, perhaps, making its new power available for the temporal purposes of empire. By emphasizing the particular events of the Lord's life in connection with their commemoration in particular places, the fourth century liturgy in Jerusalem began to move from the celebration of the Mystery to the celebration of the mysteries as events to be relived and appropriated for oneself. In a land filled with holy places, it is little wonder that the Eucharist should come to be seen as the relic *par excellence,* the actual and awful presence of the king in our midst. The subsequent allegorization of the anamnesis, in which images from the liturgy were mixed with moments from the life of Christ,[52] could have no more striking expression than the depiction of the grotto of the Nativity on a reliquary lid from the sixth century.[53] There a massive cube with a niche in the center represents an early form of a block altar with its space for a relic, and—astonishingly—the Christ child is depicted as lying on top of the altar rather than in the crib. Allusions to the eucharistic sacrifice seem obvious, and perhaps there is the barest beginning here of the cult of Eucharist as relic that would so permeate the high Middle Ages.

The Emperor's New Clothes

The historicized sense of liturgy, brought about in part by Constantine's displays of munificence in the Holy Land, was consonant with the emperor's own religious sensibilities. Constantine was, as Massey Shepherd observes, a man who could appreciate the import of theophany far more than the expectation of parousia. It was this appreciation of theophany, Shepherd suggests, that motivated Constantine to erect the church at Mamre.[54] In God's appearance and promise to Abraham, Constantine apparently found a paradigm for his own role in the historical unfolding of God's purposes. For the immediate and historical dimensions of theophany contribute to the legitimation of *imperium* in a way that future-oriented expectations of God's kingdom cannot do. Similarly, the heightened sense of eucharistic mystery that developed in the decades after Constantine's reign might also be understood, at least in part, as a consequence of the emperor's regard for divine manifestations and interventions.

With the aid of that same God who was present in the Eucharist, Constantine had overcome his foes, no longer merely a Roman general but a Christian victor. As in some sense "Christian" emperor, Constantine drew ever nearer to the Christians' God, so that in time popular imagination could move easily between images of the emperor and images of Christ. As the imperial benefactor and protector of the Church, Constantine also regarded himself as an equal and partner with its bishops, a sort of vicar of Christ to those outside it.[55]

Any assessment of Constantine, the Church and culture in the fourth century must take into account the change and effects of the emperor's self-conception from the time of the Milvian Bridge until his death in the city that bore his name. Whether Constantine's reign imaged Christ's lordship, and whether his joining of Church and empire shadowed forth God's kingdom or not remains, finally, a matter for individual historical and theological judgment. The many layers of meaning in the making of a Christian emperor and of the empire and Church that were stamped with his mark reveal, however, the intricacies of historical analysis and the ambiguities of theological evaluation. For whatever image Constantine had projected in life—messenger of Apollo, Christ-like emperor or latter-day Abraham—his last earthly appearance was in the white garment of a newly baptized Christian. Thus arrayed in his new clothes, the emperor began his journey home.

NOTES

1. For the classic statement of this problematic, see H. Richard Niebuhr, *Christ and Culture* (New York: Harper, 1951).

2. Lactantius, *On the Death of Persecutors;* E.T. Fathers of the Church (Washington, D.C.; Catholic University of America, volume 54, 1965); Eusebius, *Ecclesiastical History, The Life of Constantine, Oration in Praise of Constantine;* E.T. Nicene and Post-Nicene Fathers, second series, volume 1.

3. Tacitus, *Annals* XV.44; E.T. in J. Stevenson, ed., *A New Eusebius* #3 (London: SPCK, 1965), 2–3.

4. Tertullian, *Apology* 40.2; E.T. Ante-Nicene Fathers, volume 3 (Grand Rapids, MI: Eerdmans, 1963), p. 46.

5. Justin, *First Apology* 12, 17, 28; E.T. in C. Richardson, *Early Christian Fathers* (New York: Macmillan, 1970), p. 253; Origen, *Contra Celsum* VIII, 73–74; E.T. H. Chadwick (Cambridge: The University Press, 1965), p. 509.

6. *Letter to Diognetus* 6.1; E.T.C. Richardson, p. 218.

7. Tertullian, *On the Dress of Women* 2.9; *Apol.* 39.

8. *Panegyrici Latini* 6(7). 21-3-6, quoted in J. Stevenson, *A New Eusebius,* #258, 298.

9. Hermann Doerries, *Constantine the Great,* transl. Roland Bainton (New York: Harper and Row, 1972), 24.

10. Lactantius, *Death* 44; quoted in Stevenson, #259, 298.

11. Eusebius, *The Life of Constantine,* I.28.

12. E.g., Doerries; A.H.M. Jones, *Constantine and the Conversion of Europe* (New York: Collier Books, 1962); Norman Baynes, *Constantine the Great and the Christian Church* (New York: Haskell House Publishers, Ltd., 1975 reprint); Ramsey MacMullen, *Constantine* (New York: Harper and Row, 1971).

13. Henry Chadwick, *The Early Church,* The Pelican History of the Church, 1 (Baltimore, MD: Penguin Books, 1967), 122.

14. A. A. Vasiliev, *History of the Byzantine Empire* (Madison, WI: University of Wisconsin Press, 1952), I, 47.

15. Aloys Grillmeier, *Christ in Christian Tradition,* vol. 1, transl. John Bowden (2d rev. ed.; London: Mowbrays, 1975), 251. For an analysis of Eusebius's thought on the unity of Christian society as a reflection of the kingdom and polity of heaven, see F. Edward Cranz, "Kingdom and Polity in Eusebius of Caesarea," *Harvard Theological Review* 45, 1 (Jan. 1952), 47–66.

16. There is no "Edict of Milan" as such; the decisions made by Constantine and Licinius at their meeting in Milan are known to history only through a letter from Licinius to a provincial official.

17. As quoted in MacMullen, 114.

18. Massey Shepherd, "Liturgical Expressions of the Constantinian Triumph," *Dumbarton Oaks Papers* 21 (1967), 75.

19. MacMullen, 120.

20. Letter of Constantine to Bishop Alexander and the Presbyter Arius, in Eusebius, *Life of Constantine* II.72 (E.T. p. 518): "restore to me, then, my quiet days and my untroubled nights."

21. Athanasius, *On the Synods* 15, quotes various of the philosophical, theological and scriptural arguments used by the Arians.

22. MacMullen, 237.

23. Letter of Constantine to the Catholic Church of Alexandria, in Socrates, *Ecclesiastical History,* I.9.

24. Eusebius, *Life* III.7 (E.T. p. 521).

25. Eusebius, *Life* III.10 (E.T. p. 522).

26. Eusebius, *Life* III.15 (E.T. p. 524).

27. Norman Baynes and H. St. L.B. Moss, eds., *Byzantium* (New York: Oxford, 1961), 269.

28. Eusebius, *Praise* 1. For the precedents in Hellenistic kingship philosophy for considering the emperor as imitator, see N. H. Baynes, "Eusebius and the Christian Empire," *Byzantine Studies and Other Essays* (London, 1955), 168–72.

29. Grillmeier, 254.
30. Vasiliev, I, 54.
31. MacMullen, 61; Doerries, 24.
32. Doerries, 32.
33. Andrew Alfoldi, *The Conversion of Constantine and Pagan Rome,* transl. Harold Mattingly (Oxford: Clarendon Press, 1948, 1969), 17, 27.
34. Alfoldi, 54–55; MacMullen, 112 and plate III.
35. Evelyn Harrison, "The Constantinian Portrait" *Dumbarton Oaks Papers* 21 (1967), 95.
36. Harrison, 96.
37. Harrison, 96.
38. Theodore Klauser, *A Short History of the Western Liturgy*, transl. John Halliburton (London: Oxford University Press, 1969), 36.
39. R. A. Markus, *Christianity in the Roman World* (London: Thames and Hudson, 1974), 101.
40. Klauser, 34; Shepherd, 62; cf. MacMullen, 236.
41. The origins of the basilical church are much debated among scholars. Richard Krautheimer, *Early Christian Art and Architecture* (Baltimore, MD: Penguin Books, 1965), 17–22 argues that the imperial audience hall is the model for the Christian structures built during and after the time of Constantine. Cyril Mango, on the other hand, claims in *Byzantine Architecture* (New York: Abrams, 1975), that Christians were building basilical churches previous to Constantine's interest and influence.
42. Josef Jungmann, *The Place of Christ in Liturgical Prayer,* transl. A. Peeler (Staten Island, NY: Alba House, 1965), especially ch. 11.
43. Jungmann, *The Mass,* transl. Julian Fernandes, ed. Mary Ellen Evana (Collegeville, Minn.: The Liturgical Press, 1976), 51–53.
44. Johannes Quasten, "The Liturgical Mysticism of Theodore of Mopsuestia," *Theological Studies* 15 (1954), 438–39.
45. Klauser, 31.
46. John Wilkinson, *Egeria's Travels* (London: SPCK, 1971) translates Egeria's account of her journey, and discusses the sites and churches as well as the Jerusalem liturgy and lectionary.
47. Shepherd, 72, 74.
48. Eusebius, *Life* IV.24 (E. T. p. 546).
49. Eusebius, *Life* III.25 (E. T. pp. 526–527).
50. Eusebius, *Life* III.33 (E. T. p. 528).
51. Cyril of Jerusalem, *Cathechetical Lectures* XIV.22; *Nicene and Post-Nicene Fathers.* Second Series, volume 7, p. 100.
52. Jungmann, *Mass,* 53.
53. Kurt Weitzmann, "Loca Sanctorum and the Representational Arts of Palestine," *Dumbarton Oaks Papers* 28 (1974), 38–39.
54. Shepherd, 78.
55. Eusebius, *Life* IV.24.

9
The Earth Is the Lord's: Thoughts on the Economic Order

Philip Land, S.J.

Anticipating modern thought as he often did, Aquinas saw that, as modified by culture, raw humanity takes on a second nature.[1] If drives of "first nature" shape behavior, so do those of culturally imposed nature. A whole body of recent writing centers on the mutual influence which obtains between these drives and, on the other hand, consciousness and the knowing process. What occupies us in this essay is the cultural development of the human reality as operative precisely in economic structures.[2]

The question before us is two-fold: first, do the mindsets and structures of the American economic system embody, and in what degree, the lordship of Christ; secondly, to the extent to which they do not, what sort of economic order would represent such an embodiment?

This essay's response, after some preliminary remarks about the lordship of Christ, is given in four parts. *Part One,* assuming the essays of Walsh and McDermott, briefly describes the *Way* of Jesus as embodiment of his Father's kingdom. The succeeding three parts analyze three forms or phases of kingdom embodiment through three forms or phases of human mediation: embodiment through practical reason working with imagination to fashion principles of social action *(Part Two);* embodiment through our critical faculty as it reflects on our economic system in light of Jesus' Way and of these social principles *(Part Three);* some features of a more adequate embodiment of the kingdom in economic life, as proposed by a

Christian imagination working from biblical sources and in the light of practical reason *(Part Four).*

The Lordship of Christ and Structures

Though other essays have explored various facets of the lordship of Christ in this world, let me say briefly how I here understand it. Given the necessity of social structures for the fullness of the human, the kingdom, insofar as it has for partial scope humanization, must be embodied in the social order. The expectations of Israel were of the God who would reveal himself as Lord in an absolute future precisely by establishing a kingdom of *Shalom* within Israel's history. The synoptics reveal Jesus as responding to these expectations by revealing a kingdom, constituted in his resurrection, which is not just private but also political. Through and beyond personal transformation, the new creation is brought into human institutions and makes a difference for the political order.

The Lord himself declares that feeding the hungry and clothing the naked are signs of his reign. This kind of love of neighbor is our concrete way of loving God, and it urges us to create structures that minister to needs. An economy that serves people is life-giving, and often I can best give a cup of cold water by extending a waterpipe to a village deprived of running water. Such creative works "are the flowering of his own mysterious design," the "kingdom already present in mystery."[3] Effected by the Lord through our human providence, such creative transformations are the work of "that forward looking imagination" of which Paul VI speaks in his *Octogesima Adveniens.*[4] Once liberated by the Lord, imagination is empowered to shape, to "externalize," to humanize the very structures which have shaped us and our mindsets. Through this operation imagination frees structures from subjection to the powers and principalities, transforming them into structures of the kingdom. However imperfect and transient, such embodiments of the lordship of Christ will remain at least in the fruits of our charity, when the Lord comes to establish his definitive kingdom. "On this earth that kingdom is already present in mystery. When the Lord returns, it will be brought into full flower."[5]

I. Jesus Paradigmatic for Economic Life

We may distinguish at least two ways in which Jesus exercises his lordship: the lordship of his Spirit in shaping the Christian imagination, and the lordship precisely of his *Way* in enabling us to understand living humanly and humanizing structures. The first of these, developed in Brian McDermott's essay, is implicit in the treatment I shall here give to the second. I choose the *Way* of the Lord in particular because it highlights the role of Jesus as challenging the mindsets of his society and the structures of power of his day, and equally as offering an alternative. My sketch is illustrative and in a methodological vein. It is limited for the most part to the gospel of Luke, though I will draw upon a few other symbols developed by the early Christian community.[6]

My reading of Luke, following numerous commentators, is highly selective. I focus on Jesus as he stands in the public eye, hence (in this sense) the "political Jesus." I thus set aside (obviously without dismissing) Jesus' preaching of the Father, the commandments, the judgment, the life beyond this earth. Nothing of Jesus' exhortation to prayer and interiority appears here or his call to the imitation of his virtues. Indeed, it is partly in protest against that primary focus that I write, for it filtered out with moralizing spectacles the Jesus who, on the written record—in the evangelist's understanding of him—lived a very public life at grips with social issues, and so was, I believe it accurate to say, involved in politics.[7]

Luke's presentation of this "political Jesus" may be briefly presented under eight statements:

1. *Jesus Announces the Kingdom in Liberation Language.* Echoing his mother's *Magnificat* and Zechariah's canticle, Jesus early in his Nazarene ministry (4:16–21) announces that Isaiah's prophecy of one who would "preach the good news to the poor, proclaim release to captives and recovery of sight to the blind and liberty for the oppressed" is in that moment being fulfilled in the hearing of his listeners. He concludes by identifying himself with the Lord of the Jubilee, an event of Israel's ancient social order in which land was to be restored and debt remitted.

Shortly after that Jesus confirms this reading of his ministry when John the Baptist sends emissaries to ask if he, Jesus, is the Messiah. Jesus' answer is, "Tell John that the blind see, the lame walk, lepers are healed, the deaf hear, the dead are raised to life, and the poor have the good news preached to them" (7: 22–23).

2. *Jesus Denounces Love of Riches.* Further delineation of his kingdom takes a double form: Jesus denounces and announces. He denounces certain evils of social life and he announces a counter-culture.

Chapter 16 of Luke starts with the warning that we cannot serve God and money (v 13). At this declaration "the Pharisees who were lovers of money scoffed at him" (v 14). This prompts Jesus to propose the parable of Lazarus and the rich banqueter (vv 19–31), and to warn that it is easier for a camel to pass through the eye of a needle than for a rich man to enter the kingdom of heaven. On another occasion, against the solicitude of the acquisitive and the avaricious, Jesus offers his parable of the man who built ever larger barns only to have death mock his security system (12:16–21). In contrast to this search to secure our future uniquely in stocks, bonds and real estate, Jesus bids us consider the lilies of the field which grow without toiling or spinning yet are clothed in glory (12:27) and the birds which also do not sow or reap yet "God feeds them" (12:24).

3. *Jesus Denounces Love of Power.* A number of Lucan commentators are agreed that the three temptations of Jesus (4:1–13) were all temptations to rely for establishment of his messiahship on earthly power: turning stones into bread as sign of the messianic banquet; accepting the offer of all the kingdoms of earth if he would kneel to power; descending from the pinnacle of the temple in a display of power that would win over the crowd to unquestioning acceptance of his leadership.[8]

To the disciples arguing which of them was the greatest Jesus responds "he who is least among you" (9:48). Explicit denunciation of abuse of power is frequent, and it brings from priests and Pharisees repeated threats to his life. Let us look at a few instances.

As a sample, there are the woes announced against the Pharisees for their abuses of power. "Full of extortion" (9:39), "tithers of mint and rue . . . but neglecting justice and love of God" (v 42), lovers of the best seats in the synagogue and of salutations in the marketplace (v 43). The lawyers likewise are condemned (12:45–48 and

20:45). Angered, the scribes and Pharisees were "lying in wait for him" (v 53). We shall see later other instances of denunciation of abuse of power, coupled with the growing determination of priest, Pharisee and scribe—the three most important classes of society—to put Jesus to death.

4. *Jesus Denounces Love of Honor.* When invited to a banquet (we are taught in still another parable) we must not seek the first place but the lowest "for everyone who exalts himself shall be humbled . . ." (14:11). The theme of the exalted being humbled and the humble exalted is repeated in still another parable, that of the Pharisee in temple prayer justifying himself whereas the tax collector dared not lift his eyes to heaven (18:9–14). And Jesus warns the people to beware of the scribes who affect long robes and love salutations and the best seats in the synagogue (20:45).

5. *Jesus Announces His Counter-culture.* Counter to the ruling classes' society of privilege, based on power—power of the temple, power of the book of which they pretended to be exclusive interpreters, power of wealth—Jesus proclaims a society of service. Against abuses of the poor and the weak, a society of justice. Against love of wealth, poverty. Against love of honors, humility. Against contempt for little people, love of all one's fellow men and women. Virtually all the texts which we have used to show Jesus condemning abuses show him also proclaiming their opposites.

The proclaimed kingdom of love and justice is epitomized in the Sermon on the Mount, especially but not exclusively in the beatitudes. The world opened up there is totally foreign to the society enjoyed by priests, Pharisees and scribes. In fact, it excludes these leaders of the people, for they are not poor, hungry, rejected (6:20–22). Indeed the very condition of blessedness excludes them, for the blessedness of the poor does not consist in their poverty but in the fact that, unlike the rich, they do not rely on their own resources but on God. It is this that helps us understand the frightful implications of the woes for the rich and powerful.

The sermon adds other details of Jesus' counter-culture. People of his kingdom will love their enemies (v 27), pray for those who abuse them (v 28), offer the other cheek, yield their cloak to one who has stolen their coat (v 29), and give to beggars without anticipating return (v 31). They will forgive. They will love. And when they offer a dinner they will invite, not those who can repay the favor, but "the poor, the maimed, the lame, the blind . . ." (14:12–14).

Jesus' society will be one of service. "Let the greatest among you be as the youngest and the leader as one who serves . . . I am among you as one who serves" (22:26–27). Symbolizing his being among them as one who serves, Jesus at the Last Supper laid aside his garments, girded himself with a towel, and knelt to wash the feet of his disciples (Jn 13:4–5).

6. *Jesus Associated with the Marginalized.* The word typifying the people Jesus chose mainly to associate with is "marginalized." They did not count. They could not hope for deliverance from the power structures which, far from helping, bound them. In the entourage of Jesus we find women, counting for little in that male-dominated society. He deliberately confronts this abuse by talking—to the amazement of his disciples—with the woman at the well (Jn 4:27). Children, unpossessed of the rights of adults, were unimportant in the Israel of Jesus' day, and yet they were named as paradigm of the kingdom (9:46–48). Tax collectors, prostitutes are with Jesus. And symbolic of these dismissed people is Zachaeus, who is so short that he had to climb a tree to see Jesus, and who is invited to break bread with the Lord as symbol of the messianic banquet (19:1–10).

7. *Jesus and His Companions Set a Distinctive Style.* Sent out on the road the disciples are bidden to take nothing for the journey, no staff or bag or bread or money, and are not to have two tunics (9:2–3). "The foxes have holes and the birds nests, but the Son of Man has nowhere to lay his head" (10:57). Presumably this condition of Jesus' own travel must have been shared by his disciples. At any rate it is consonant with the severity of the above mentioned travelling injunctions. In some mitigation of the rigors of this stark regime Jesus (in a second statement) is portrayed as allowing the disciples to live in homes that welcome them and there to eat and drink what is provided, giving as justification that the laborer is worthy of his hire (10:7).

For those opting to follow his Way there are fearful consequences. They will have to take up the cross (15:27). That is, as Jesus dares denounce injustice and for that must face death, so their acceptance of this same mission of justice will bring the same cross to them. And because the way of Jesus will put them in conflict with their society, and with their families as endorsing that society (the exploited accepting the ideology of their exploiters), they must hate father and mother, brothers and sisters (15:26). Such a challenge is not to be taken lightly. Accordingly Jesus bids his disciples in the following two verses shun the example of a ruler who would not, before warring, calculate the strength of the enemy, or a builder of a tower who would fail to estimate the total cost of the venture.

8. *Jesus' Standard Finally Clashes with That of the Priests.* Three items more need to be woven into our story of the Way. The first is Jesus' entry into the temple, and his cleansing it of buying and selling. Several commentators view the event as a final showdown in the struggle of two religious viewpoints, that of the priests—the objectivized version of religion which they had imposed—and the religion of the "deviationist" Jesus. Typifying much of the priests' religion was the decadent situation of the temple: a "den of iniquity," of exploitation, of harsh taxation, of control through the temple's treasured Scriptures as interpreted by the custodians of it, of people chained to the Sabbath. That religion Jesus replaces symbolically by taking possession of the temple, asserting his right to purify it and make it a house of prayer. Quite as radically he declares that the Sabbath is made for women and men. That episode is concluded with the chief priests and the scribes and the principal men of the people seeking to destroy him (19:47).

In the second of the final incidents Jesus once again, in parable form, challenges the abuse of power. The story has the owner of a vineyard calling for a reckoning from the vine tenders (20:9–20). He sends emissaries to demand the account, all of whom are successively put to death by the vine tenders. The owner then decides to send his own son in the belief that him at least they will respect. They on the contrary seize this as an opportunity to take over the vineyard by killing the heir. Jesus concludes his story by assuring his listeners that the owner will destroy those vine tenders and turn the vineyard over to other hands. The chief priests and scribes present understand well enough that they are the unworthy vinekeepers about to be dismissed. "When they heard this they cried 'God forbid'." As usual they turn to the only solution imaginable to them. "They tried to lay hands on him . . ." (20:19).

In the final episode the initiative has passed wholly from Jesus to his enemies. An integral Christology ought to integrate with Jesus' active engagement for the kingdom his passive role, in which kenosis characterizes the work of achieving lordship. In Luke's account the chief priests and scribes are the protagonists from the garden to the hauling of the prisoner before Pilate, then to Herod, and back to Pilate where "the chief priests stood by vehemently accusing him" (23:10).

They accuse Jesus, in Luke's account, of perverting the nation, forbidding tribute to Caesar and making himself king. In Mark blasphemy is the accusation. None of the first three charges have validity. And the blasphemy consisted in rejecting the priests' religion and proclaiming a program that would terminate their power.[9] If the priests brought the charges, Rome was the executioner. The type of death Rome decreed signifies that this Jesus who could not be called an insurrectionist like the Zealots, was just as much of a threat to Rome as the Zealots by the program he preached.

Space allowing, other extremely relevant symbols developed by the early Christian community for understanding the kingdom could be treated.[10] But we must pass on to our next theme which is the mediation of lordship through social principles.

II. MEDIATION OF LORDSHIP THROUGH PRACTICAL REASON AND IMAGINATION

Here we are engaged with two questions. The first is methodological. How do we get from ultimate principles and images to more specific norms of ordered social economic life? The second shifts from method to its application and asks what might be these more specific norms. Linked to the first is the role of imagination in bringing us to practical norms of moral life and to specific decisions in life situations.

A. The Methodological Question

There are those who believe that concrete, specific moral norms can be derived directly from the Scriptures. "It's all in the gospels," they say. Moreover, since the Word of God is absolute, that is, universal and unchangeable, so are the conclusions.[11] Few Catholic moralists agree with either proposition today.[12]

Another school has also believed that from primary principles it could derive a code of specific moral norms for social life. This is the Catholic school (though there are Protestant adherents) of natural law. According to this school the will of God for social life is mediated through an order inserted in human nature through creation. These tendencies are natural laws. Since they are reflections of the divine ideas they participate in the universality and unchangeableness of the divine ideas. And so do the secondary precepts derived from them.[13] The most eminent spokesperson for this school was the Jesuit Gustav Gundlach of the Gregorian University, Rome.[14] That norms stated by the official teaching Church as absolutes sometimes have been ideological derivations is shown by David Hollenbach.[15]

This conception of natural law has, since Vatican II, been virtually abandoned in Catholic circles.[16] A splintering has resulted. The theologians I personally follow reject on the one hand, abstract, deductive, ahistorical, and unbiblical speculation and, on the other, purely inductive, individualistic situational ethics. This school, with varying approaches, accepts the "natural" as a beginning point around which the human person "reasons" practically (action-oriented reason or practical reason) in terms of his/her humanness, personhood, experience, and situation, in order to arrive, first, at proximate norms of moral action and, secondly, at specific decisions. From these norms results a rightness of social order which, while not absolute, is nevertheless objective, because the human can never not be human.[17] Humans must always conduct themselves humanly.

Among recent authoritative elaborations of this position are those of Josef Fuchs, S.J., of the Gregorian University.[18] Only two points of his extensive treatment are needed here. First, there is far more variability in human nature than was imagined by the earlier natural law tradition.[19] Secondly, the search for the objectively right norm takes place within the framework of human nature only if viewed as unfolding under the guidance of what is most essential to humanness—reason.

This operation is that of *recta ratio* or right reason. It is not at all an innate discernment of moral norms somehow inscribed in nature as if it could be read off as natural reality. No, the nature appealed to as affording objective moral norms is formally nature as possessing and exercising a reasoning power that seeks the right. Thus conscience does not simply apply precepts to concrete cases. *Recta ratio* or practical reason operates in the light of ultimate wisdom, faith and love under the direction of the total person as evaluative, observing, understanding. On occasion it may be quite intuitive. This understanding the reasoning person applies to the total reality of his/her existence in order to assess the worth, value, significance of alternatives available for action.

The norms thus arrived at possess "rightness" only insofar as in final analysis they conform to authentic humanness in its fullest sense and to Christian faith and love. Only so do they possess objectivity.

It has always struck me that this modern understanding of how to get practical norms of moral action and then decide within their framework was anticipated centuries ago by Thomas Aquinas. This is not the place to attempt to establish that fact. But let me make a few observations. At the beginning of this essay I cited Aquinas' assertion that "second nature" is quite as vital a force as given nature. This second nature will produce more variability than given nature. Hence Aquinas is little interested in universal norms and much more in those which he calls *ius gentium,* or law of nations. This is mainly what he means by natural law.

Here is a typical expression of his: "Habit has the force of nature."[20] From this he elsewhere argues: "That which belongs to the natural law is modified according to the different states and conditions of people."[21] My other remark is that Aquinas gave surprisingly little space in his process of arriving at the guidance of moral action to natural law even in the sense of *ius gentium.* What he does focus on is what he calls the virtue of prudence. This is the capacity of the human person to work out moral solutions. He devotes a single question to natural law but has over fifty, each with several articles, on prudence. It is there that he argues that the person arriving at moral decision is an artist and that the ultimate practical judgment—the *HOC bonum faciendum* (*this* good must be done)—is exclusively the work of the individual making it. No one else can make it for us.

This expression of Aquinas, that moral-making is the work of an artist, links us to the modern approach to imagination as principal instrument of the humanization of life. In a recent article William Dych maintains in the same vein that "to live a human life which is free and responsible and creative making, then, we all have to do something similar to what the artist does with his material and in-form the 'materials' of life with shape, form, meaning, sense and direction."[22]

This is also because, argues Dych, life is not like a jigsaw puzzle in which the finished product is already laid out for us on the cover of the box, with the only thing required of us being to fit the pieces together according to the model. "Suppose there is no picture on the box, no antecedent blueprint, that the pieces can be put together in any number of right ways . . . imagination in this case has no choice but to be free and creative. . . ."

Citing William Lynch's statement that "images think" Dych argues that "images contain the real, objective concreteness and particularity of the objective world" whereas concepts abstract from this. Images catch "the conscious and affective relationship with concrete realities." This task of imagination in naming reality and guiding the humanization of life makes it central to life.

Paradigm of this function of imagination is Jesus as "the image through which the Word entered into history." Theology today responds by diminishing its reflections on the ontological structure of Jesus in favor of a "deeper sense of the importance of the narrative and story within theology. . . ." It will be apparent that the first part of my chapter is fully in accord with this approach to Jesus.

Dych concludes that "To see God in the glass which is Jesus and to see Jesus in all of his brothers and sisters (allusion is to the Last Judgment based on giving a cup of water in the Lord's name) is to have an imagination which is integrally human, and in being a truly human imagination it is also a Christian imagination."[23]

We shall be much concerned with that Christian imagination in the two following parts. Meanwhile let me repeat my conviction that this sense of imagination is close to, if not identical with, the concept of practical reason with which we began this essay.

B. More Specific Norms of Economic Life

The mediatorship of the kingdom through practical reason and imagination has produced a body of social principles which demonstrate "rightness," coherence, a certain organicity, and the power to receive acceptance. "They make sense." The first set of principles are statements about human society, the second about the organization of that society. These also are generally accepted in the tradition. Still a third class of principles of economic organization has more questionability either because they belong to a matrix of considerable opaqueness or because opinion has not solidified on them. The first two categories are too well known to require here anything but the briefest statement.

1. *Social Principles of Societal Living.* The nature of the human being is a *social one.* Affectively stated in terms of heart, love, concern and sacrifice this translates as *solidarity.*[24] Such solidarity urges on us the creation of *community.* Motivational force for social living is *social love,* an idea to which John Paul II returns twice in his first encyclical. But always with reference to the human, for "the foundation, cause and end of all social institutions" is the individual human person.[25]

This social living must be reduced to more concrete norms. Here recent Catholic statements have called upon the biblical image of *stewardship* with which are associated *service* and *sacrifice.*

2. *Principles of Social Organization.* But social living and a social economy require organization. Toward this goal the Catholic tradition has named several norms. First is that of the *common good,* to which individual good must be subordinated even while the common good ultimately serves the humanization of the individual person. Who does what for the common good? Who gains what from it? *Social justice* is the organizational principle which first calls on everyone and every component of society including the State to serve the common good, and then asks for a distribution of the commons in such a way that the good of all will be promoted with love, justice and equity. It is only within the framework of social justice that commutative and distributive justice can assure that one receives one's due.

The actors in economic life are persons at work with materials of nature and with tools, both of which are addressed by the notion of *private property* (in productive goods) which is upheld in the tradition. Partly for the pragmatic reason of offering incentive to produce, and partly as providing the possibility of human beings impressing their image upon matter and so possessing the fruits of their labor, this ideal calls obviously for wide distribution of property. Much more should be said about property rights, but space does not permit.

In some sense all economic actors are *workers* and the Christian tradition often couples intellectual with manual work. What it seeks is the humanization of all work. Work is the exercise of co-creativity with God. The tradition also seeks defense of the rights of workers.

A third actor in economic life is *government*, whose intervention in various forms of stimulation, regulation, supplementation, planning, is recognized. The relationship of these three actors—property-owners (largely business enterprises), workers and government are held together by *subsidiarity*. According to this principle the values of individual initiative and small community self-help should be honored. Hence the operations of the higher levels of society should serve, not displace, those of the lower and of individuals.

Some of the above precepts can be formulated differently. Thus, for many the notion of self-reliance replaces the norm of permitting the smaller groupings of society and individuals to do what they can for themselves. Another naming of the same is "Small is beautiful."

There is also room for insertion of *new* norms as the problems of economic organization are perceived differently. One example is the principle of *participation*. Originally framed to give propertyless workers some control over the capital (plants and equipment) which controlled their lives, it now is viewed more widely as a fundamental thrust of human nature. For example, John XXIII's *Pacem in Terris* saw it as a "sign of the times."[26] It also appears coupled with still another "new" principle. This is that an economy ought to be geared to meeting *needs*. Though that idea is found implicitly in the earlier tradition its explicit formulation is due to the fact that in the developing nations the needs of the masses are not being met even while the elites living in the modernizing sectors do very well.

It will escape no one that the mere statement of the preceding principles gives no guidance as to how to combine them. Some accordingly will ask what they are worth. The answer can only be that such is the human condition. Values and goods and goals do not necessarily travel in the same direction. They have to be combined. Some of this and some of that. What must guide us here, according to Aquinas, is the virtue of political prudence, understood in the sense already given it.

The two sets of norms arrived at from practical reason and imagination suffice for the purpose they will be put to (alongside the Way of Jesus) in the two parts that follow. Were this a treatise on Catholic social teaching much more would have to be said about such other subsidiary organizational principles of economy as private profit, competition, markets, and still others.

III. Second Mediation, through the Critical Faculty

Catholic theologians generally consider this function of the critical faculty an important one in the Church.[27] The Synod of 1971 in its *Justice in the World* calls for an education which will "awaken a critical sense, which will lead us to reflect on the society in which we live and on its values."[28] In fact this mediation of the kingdom is nothing short of what Jesus himself did when he criticized and denounced the structures of power in his society.

The critique of this part of our essay focuses on our American economic system in the light of the Gospel symbols of part one and the social principles of part two. From these two sources emerge the following benchmarks of evaluation. Does our economic system 1) liberate from famine, poverty, disease, oppression—does it advance the dignity and rights of the person; 2) does it humanly value material acquisition; 3) correctly understand and rightly use power; 4) honor people for the right things; 5) cherish the values of work; 6) serve needs in stewardship and solidarity; 7) with self-giving; 8) and with love and friendship?

How does the American system stand up in response to those questions? Conceivably the answer might be either that it fully embodies all our symbols of biblical revelation and practical reason or that it fails to do so utterly. In between would be various degrees of partial embodiment—the chaff growing along with the wheat. A fully adequate evaluation would require considerable space to set out facts, analysis, expert opinion, interpretation. Even with that, a significant element of purely subjective "exteriorization" would be operative. Experience, temperament, reading of past and contemporary history, general philosophical attitudes, would all combine to make one's reading of the "objective" situation ideological in some degree.

With the preceding two caveats and with the understanding that the main thrust of this third part is methodological I enter the following substantially negative judgment. If readers disagree they will at least recognize that the questions do originate in the two sources given and are relevant.[29] In fact, in my opinion most could be amply documented from much secular writing as well as from official Catholic teaching of the last several decades. For brevity's sake I will use that tradition, and because it is admirably summed up in John Paul II's first encyclical letter, *Redeemer of Humankind,* I shall quote extensively from that.

But first I must briefly describe the system which is here under criticism. How can I do so without writing a textbook? Let me attempt to sketch out the main features of the system, in its domestic and then in its international aspects. The general reader as well as the economist will not miss that the description anticipates, to a large extent, the more formal critique which shall follow.

The American Economic System

A more adequate sketch might run in terms of three factors: first, the productive process; secondly, the real (and not theoretical) directing force of the system; thirdly, the impact of power.

1. *The productive process:* In an overall or macro-view, there is exchange of goods and services against money. If all that is earned in wages and profits is not spent against wage-goods (consumption goods) and producers' goods (plants, equipment and inventories), the system breaks down. Consumption goods remain stacked in warehouses or machine tools can't be sold. In either case businessmen will revise downwardly their expectations for the next period with consequent unemployment.

There are three circuits involved in the production process and at each we can test the impact of Berger and Luckmann's noetic scheme.[30] We can also test for justice. We can ask, further, where and how the kingdom of the Lord is present.

The first circuit is that in which businessmen hire workers and buy raw materials to start up production, paying out money for these. To grow, the business will pour as much money as possible into increasing work force, materials and equipment. The system can be jammed at this hiring stage either by workers (e.g., refusing to work) or by employers (e.g., hoarding cash instead of putting it into employment). Outside forces can jam the works, as illustrated by OPEC's quadrupling the cost of energy-input.

The second circuit or phase is the conversion of the labor thus hired and the machines and materials so assembled into finished goods. This phase is carried out within the factory. Efficiency is demanded to turn out quality products in the desired quantity. Inefficiency is possible on the side of management and its technicians and engineers as well as on the side of labor. Each year millions of tires and hundreds of thousands of cars are called back because of bad engineering.

At the third stage the finished goods or services are sold. It was the assumption of neo-classical economics that such selling was done in markets of perfect competition, with consumers in the driver's seat "dictating" what they wanted produced, and with sellers forced to respond with prices that covered all costs of production, leaving no surplus.

The reality, as we shall see, is quite otherwise. But for understanding the system we need to add that breakdown can occur here too—fickleness of consumers, imports that compete, taxes that discourage buying, suspicion that the products are poor quality and badly serviced.

It is obvious that a break in any of the three circuits spells trouble. It is also obvious that millions of human actors are involved, with their motivations, their power.

2. *The real directing force of the system:* Textbooks start off by posing the problem of economics in terms of using scarce productive means to satisfy freely determined demands. You decide what you want. Firms respond. Choice controls the system. And since the pub-

lic decides, the enterpriser cannot be blamed if the goods produced are trivial in value, noxious, dangerous to health and fail to meet basic needs. The business community thus escapes responsibility for socially objectionable production. If an irrational public demands stupid and dangerous goods the business world can only in duty comply.

That textbook model quite possibly portrayed the reality and behavior of the economy in Adam Smith's day when firms were small and many, and so responded to changing costs of production and changing demand (over which they had no control). It was the thesis of Bentham and his followers that satisfaction and even well-being were thus maximized. And so was profit—the goal of producers—maximized. If one could not produce what was demanded or produce it at costs comparable with those of one's competitors, one got out of business. Those who could meet demand and costs prospered—but only because capable of meeting conditions dictated by the market. Competition, in a word, was seen as the directing force.[31]

If a few corporations hold 70% of assets in manufacturing (there is nearly the same concentration in banking, finance, transportation, utilities), it cannot be said without stretching the imagination that competition directs this dominating sector of the economy. This is not to say there is total absence of competition. General Motors does compete against Ford, Toyota and Volkswagen, and there is competition between automobiles and airplanes. But *planning* rather than competition directs here. It governs pricing policy, expansion, tax approach, financing, merging, product diversification, technological advancement, advertising policy and indeed control of the social environment through the educational system and through delivering the message of free enterprise.

3. *The impact of power:* It is a matter of everyone's observation that the neo-classical model of many small producers, powerless to influence either side of the market, supply or demand, does not faintly correspond to present-day reality. In many of the most important industries it is a few—indeed a very few, no more than four—that control two-thirds or more of production. This is true, for example, of steel, aluminum, locomotive, automotive, aircraft, tire, telephone, engine and turbines. And the list could be lengthened.

And the concentration of manufacturing assets grows. Two

hundred giants control two-thirds of these. Still another way of looking at the concentration is to ask what percentage of the public owns these assets. The answer is that in 1962 80 percent of corporate stocks were owned by the top 1.6 percent of the population. That was approximately one and a half million people. Of that fraction of the rich 75,000 owned 40%.[32]

Obviously, this is enormous power, and it spreads also, though in lesser degree, over much of the one-third of manufacturing not owned by the top two hundred firms. It is equally visible in agriculture.

Power is also in determining and fixing prices. And in controlling the buying public through skillful brand name advertising. Power, too, in selling alongside particular goods the generalized American way of free enterprise and the golden dream of two cars in the garage for everyone. Power over state and national legislatures.

Businesses exercise their power as much by gaining government purchases as by gaining and holding the consumer public's favor. The corporate world's power to receive accommodating treatment in foreign investment will be taken up shortly. Then there is the joint power of the industrial-military complex—and, it must be admitted, the power of business also over the Church and education.

There is still another facet of the power of bigness and concentration. This is the fact that the modern enterprise typically involves intense use of technology. Here, control of production costs becomes less important than control of the social and political environment in which the technology is to be developed and its services marketed.

Business and concentration, as coupling assets and technology, present still another phenomenon of new concern. This is the spirit of hyperexpansion. Most representative of this is Herman Kahn and his Hudson associates.[33] These reject *Limits To Growth,* chiding its authors for losing their nerve. The future is ours, they boldly proclaim, if we have the courage to extend over nature and cosmos the mastery in our hands. Planets can be colonized. A superior breed of men and women can be cloned. Cybernation can enormously increase efficiency. Let the industrial world turn over control to the innovative technocrat, the bold industrial planner, the scientific establishment.

Out of all the productive processes and ideological baggage attendant on them that might be discussed, I shall mention only two of more immediate importance for our study. The first is the unending shift of normal activities out of households and communities into the industrial economy. Households cook less of their food (witness the sudden growth of eating breakfast out), mend less of their clothes, do fewer small house repairs. All this and much more—taking care of children and the elderly, growing vegetables, canning foods, sick-care—were not so long ago the personalized contribution of household and community. It was not paid work. Often it was done as a matter of exchange of services, or even as a gift. With industrial growth all this becomes commercialized. It now has a money tag on it. It is monetized. Writers like Ivan Illich call for the demonetization and decolonization of much of this with its restoration to home and community before it's too late.

This is part and parcel of the mystique of GNP or growth of the Gross National Product. The bigger GNP is, the better off we are—so it is claimed. GNP becomes the lodestone of the economy—indeed of the American people. We become wedded to the notion that GNP is what it is all about. The ultimate absurdity of this will escape no one. We could double GNP without increasing by an iota the total of goods and services of the nation. For the national product is simply the total of goods and services produced, multiplied by their price tags. If then we were to monetize all activities GNP would shoot up staggeringly. One set of neighbors might cook meals for other neighbors, charging restaurant prices for the service. Reciprocating, the others would at a price now mow lawns for the first set. Children could charge one another for pushing a swing, teaching how to operate a skate board. Apart from the entertaining absurdity of this, there is the more sinister implication that GNP and national well-being grow no matter what is produced; more beer and bowling and less health care could conceivably add up to a higher GNP.

Structures of International Economic Domination

Space permits only a brief description of the economic structures that bind the American economic system to that of the Third

World. There is, of course, more than one interpretation of the origins and character of the acknowledged relationship of growing inequality and dependency which obtains among nations. It is an observable fact that the rich North, with its technical, industrial, scientific, financial, political and military power, is able to control three-quarters of the world's resources and to make the decisions that determine the destinies of a vast part of humanity.[34]

Three structures in particular are conveyors of this dependency and inequality: trade, financing and investment. On each we must say a word.

1. *International trade:*[35] Classical and neo-classical trade theory makes the following claim. With rising prosperity in the rich, industrial world, demand grows for the raw materials and minerals of the South. Prices of these rise, thus benefiting the poor lands. Also as industrialism develops, labor supply grows tighter and more expensive. This moves entrepreneurs to shift investment to lands where labor is cheaper, thus launching the industrial development of the latter.

It would be contrary to fact to say that there is no spread of benefits at all. But there is not the benefit claimed. The reason is that classical trade theory supposed a high degree of equality between traders. It is the high concentration of power in the hands of the North that attenuates the spread of benefits. Think only of the fact that a large part of international trade today is buying and selling between parent body and filial units of a multinational corporation. More generally the rich have power to stockpile raw materials in prevision of a shortage. Powerful investors from the North, often aided and abetted by their governments, have been able to wrest favored treatment that in effect made them divest the Third World of raw materials, petroleum and minerals.

In addition, there is the power of the industrial nations to exclude the exports of the developing nations whether these be raw materials, foods, manufactured goods. It is estimated that the North spends some $20 billion a year to protect its farmers from the South's agricultural products. The U.S. and its industrial partners especially keep out semi-processed and processed materials and foods (cocoa beans come in free of duty to be processed by us; ground cocoa meets a high tariff barrier). Of a total bill of $200 billion paid by the North for foods and goods originating in raw materials produced in the South, the latter receives only $30 billion.

2. *Financial structures:*[36] If the South is to develop and industrialize it must be able to acquire the technology of the North. It can do this either through its earnings from export or by borrowing on future growth prospects. Indebtedness of the developing world since 1972 (especially due to quadrupled prices of oil, food, industrial equipment) is huge, with grave burdens of interest and amortization.

Present structure of financing is through short-term debt to be repaid in relatively short periods. But such short-term lending, whether owed to banks and other private lenders or to the International Monetary Fund, presumes that the debt situation is a normal one and not the abnormal situation created by OPEC pricing and the industrial world's inflation.

3. *Foreign investment—the multinationals:*[37] Multinational corporations are very large oligopolies with hundreds of millions of dollars of sales each. They are mainly based in the North with affiliates spread over the South. According to a 1975 *Fortune* survey the top 500 U.S. plus an additional 300 foreign large corporations have well over 30 million employees and generate $350 billion a year of products outside their own companies.

These do a large part of the world's trading, and, as observed above, much of trade turns out to be within the multinational corporation itself, with the parent company buying from its satellites in the Third World and selling to them—a relationship that permits it to price at will and to shift profits to wherever taxes are least.

The South is convinced it pays an exploitative price for the multinationals' contribution to technology, know-how and management. They also point out that there is a reverse flow of capital since the parent company puts only 25 cents into every dollar of Third World investment, the rest coming from the filial unit in the Third World.

Probably the greatest challenge to the multinationals is on the score of what they produce. For they are the producers of luxury goods and nonessentials (though admittedly tractors and sewing machines are needed). But anyone driving in from an airport to Buenos Aires or Rio sees the same billboard on view as in a drive into Rome, London or Los Angeles. With these products aggressively advertised and sold (for example, Nestle's bottle-baby formula), the multinationals become the protagonists of the American way of life as the model of development.

The Social Teaching of Pope John Paul II

The preceding description of our economic system in its domestic and international workings may be viewed by some readers as highly partisan. I would submit that, in its broad features, it corresponds to economic reality. I would also acknowledge that, in a kind of hermeneutical circle, it has been informed by the moral evaluations contained in the social teaching of the Catholic Church over the past century. Pope John Paul II's first encyclical letter, *Redeemer of Humankind,* admirably sums up the relevant part of that teaching, and for that reason I can let it stand for the whole.[38]

The encyclical represents an appeal for the fullest development of the human person under the Lord's redemption, and the humanization of society to that end. John Paul gets down to specifics in Part III, entitled "Redemption of Humankind and Its Situation in the Modern World."

"For the Church," the pope begins, "all ways lead to the human." That is followed by a largely negative assessment of the processes of industrialization. "People today seem ever to be under threat from what they produce." This productive activity results in an "alienation" in two senses: one is dispossessed of the product of one's work; the product turns against or is turned against the producer.

The pope then devotes several columns to detailing specific ways in which the industrial system is alienating, an alienation which "seems to make up the main chapter of the drama of present-day human existence in its broadest and universal dimension".[39]

Inserting John Paul's evaluations into our eight categories of questions the following results:

1. Does the system liberate—does it promote dignity? That it liberates impressively from famine, ignorance and disease will hardly be disputed.[40] But we must ask who bears the cost of this liberation.

Like his predecessor, Paul VI, in his *Development of Peoples,* and the 1971 Synod in its *Justice in the World,* John Paul concludes that much of the prosperity of the industrial North is achieved at the expense of the developing South. He denounces "the propensity to dominate . . . to exploit for the sole purpose of dominating others or of favoring this or that [read capitalist, Communist] imperialism."

This domination takes specific forms, bringing "into question the financial, monetary, productive and trade mechanisms which, resting on various political pressures (alliances of business with governments and with the military), support the world economy." John Paul likens the resulting disparity to the relation between the rich banqueter of the Gospel and the poor Lazarus. He condemns accumulation by "the rich, highly developed societies," and a situation in which "the consumer civilization" enjoys "a certain surplus of goods" while "the remaining societies—at least broad sectors of them—are suffering from hunger . . ."

In the name of solidarity John Paul calls for "indispensable transformations of the structures of economic life. . . ."

2. Our second question asks: what attitude does our society take toward acquisition? Our symbols of Bible and reason combined to say that material things must be subordinated to the spirit. They condemn all greed and avarice, all possessing at the expense of others. John Paul's conviction that the rich nations possess at the expense of the poor has already been noted. Using the language of *The Development of Peoples* he condemns having for the sake of having. "It is a matter . . . not so much of having more but of being more."

Another name for acquisitiveness is consumerism. One is familiar with the sharp criticisms made by John Kenneth Galbraith in *The Affluent Society* and by Vance Packard in *The Image Makers.* Affluence according to them is promoted as the right of all Americans and as an ideal. It is also believed by the business world to be necessary to keep the system running. Back in the mid-fifties Victor Lebow argued that our enormous productive economy demands that we make consumption our way of life, that we convert the buying of goods into rituals and seek spiritual satisfaction in consumption.

To promote a quick turnover of consumer goods psychological obsolescence was frankly promoted. Again in the mid-fifties, industrial designer Brooks Steven once wrote that an economy based on planned obsolescence is not organized waste but a sound contribution to the American economy. *Redeemer of Humankind* condemns this consumer society, first for the resulting disparity between rich and poor, secondly because it destroys the human person. It terms this "a certain abuse of freedom . . . an abuse linked precisely with a consumer attitude uncontrolled by ethical considerations . . ."

3. Our third question is: does the U.S. economic system correctly understand and rightly use power? That economic power is enormously concentrated in the American system is clear from what has been said above. We have already quoted *Redeemer of Humankind* on the alienation resulting from our industrial processes. The paragraphs above only spell out those processes. John Paul concentrates on the power of "manipulation . . . through the whole of the organization of community life, through the productive system, and through pressure from the means of social communication" (themselves largely controlled by the productive system). The result is that the human person becomes the "slave of things . . . of economic systems . . . of production. . . ."

Five of our eight questions remain to be addressed but space does not permit this. Nor is it really needed; for, first, they are mainly explicitations of the first three; secondly, if answers to the first—and fundamental—three reveal so little embodiment of the lordship of Christ and so much of the reign of the principalities and powers, answers to the remaining five questions could not possibly demonstrate enough rightness to outweigh the wrongness evidenced. In fact, answering the remaining five would only serve to reinforce the substantially negative record of the first three.

In concluding this third part, let me repeat the caution that I have not detailed what is right and beneficial in the system which, overall, I find wanting by standards of the Gospel. Doubtless many of the insights and benefits developed within our present economic system need to be affirmed even as we render a general negative evaluation, and search for an alternative which better respects human dignity.[41] I should also acknowledge that subjecting only the American capitalist system to kingdom critique may give the impression that I believe the kingdom is embodied in Communist alternatives. That I do not believe. But neither is that the subject of my inquiry.

IV. Third Mediation, by Creative Imagination

In the introduction to part three we saw that Metz, among others, limits the function of the Church in the social order to the negative role of political criticism. Rahner and Schillebeeckx with many others assign it a further role of seeking to draw from its resources values that ought positively to be present in the political order.[42] There is no question here of drawing up a blueprint for society—that surely is beyond the Church's competence.

What I propose to do—in however sketchy a form—in this last part is to propose a set of values for economic life. In effect part four is parts one plus two minus three. It tries to take part two into the future. It works from the symbols of the Scriptures and of reason in an exercise of social imagination. It is a response to the invitation of *Octogesima Adveniens* to seek the new with the eyes of "forward-looking imagination." It is that Christian imagination of which Dych speaks, in action within the economy.

I know what I shall say will sound to many exceedingly, even absurdly, utopian. Yet I believe my reflections, as they are those of an economist, conclude to cold sober realities that are the only alternative to an all too inhuman productive system. E. F. Schumacher, whose writings have nourished my reflections, believed that it might not be necessary to change radically more than 10 per cent of the system to get the economy returned healthily to people-orientation. I should be content if the following benchmarks served at least the purpose of helping to check the swift march into madness.

Start with the *way* of Jesus, the platform he announced, of service; of not placing one's hope in riches; of not abusing power; of accepting as neighbor those in need; of loving and yielding and self-sacrifice; of the "smallness" of the people who were his friends and disciples; and the smallness of the mustard seed destined to become the Kingdom. Add to those symbols such other biblical images as the work of creation, the Kingdom of God in his love and faithfulness, the covenant God as Lord of justice, the jubilee year, *Shalom* as the city or ordered community living in peace, love, friendship and justice with abundance promised.

Take these symbols and surely they yield us a set of values that must be embodied in our economic society. There we must be able to discover, at a first level, life and a system that serves life: freedom and the fruits of freedom; friendship and love, both expressed in mutuality and community; and peace with reconciliation and justice.

Now apply these symbols to the specifically economic sphere of people at work making a living. In this perspective our biblical symbols—but including also those of reason and human imagination—give the following values for the economic activity imbedded in social and political life.

1. *The economy is for people.* People counted with Jesus. Little people counted with him—the humble, the lowly. And they counted with him not in some abstract way (as often for managers of secular and ecclesial society) but as worth knowing and listening to. Nothing short of this is the humanism John Paul II calls for in his first encyclical. It translates John XXIII's "the origin, cause and end of society is the human person."

2. *Economics is for being, not having.* Enough has been said above on this theme. Suffice it to recall that Jesus' kind of people were not those compulsively bent on having.

3. *The economic system ought to be needs-based.* Above we extensively reviewed economic structures as geared to satisfying, not needs, but the wants of those who have the buying power to vote their wants in an impersonal market. God created the resources of the world to serve the needs of all his children. So this newly voiced worldwide aspiration to meet needs—a sign of our times—has biblical validation.

This sharply contrasts with our present economy, which produces to make a profit. Not that profit-making must be rejected, but it cannot be allowed to operate as the directing force of society with its program of creating wants artificially and of planned obsolescence.

4. *The economy therefore is an act of stewardship.* If the resources of the world belong to God and are his gifts to us (creation, jubilee and the promises of the Lord of the covenant) then we in human solidarity must exercise over these gifts a loving providence. That translates into the formula of "sharing, caring and sparing." Stewardship is generally related to the use of "time, treasure and tal-

ents." But central to this ought to be work, for it is an exercise of the mandate given by the Creator to shape and transform this earth, to make it ours.[43] That work, we saw above, can be alienating both in the sense that it robs the worker of the fruit of his labor and robs workers of their human dignity.

Robbing the worker of dignity takes several familiar forms. One of the most acute is that industrialism prides itself on being labor-saving. Human skills are built into machines and processes. A society of machines is prized over one of people working with their hands. Work, in a word, is viewed as undesirable.[44]

This process of machine replacement of workers must be halted and even reversed. There must be an end to the steady erosion of people being able to do for themselves in households and communities.

We must take a great deal of economic activity out of the hands of its industrial colonializers and restore it to households and communities. This means de-monetizing (a downward re-dimensioning of the god of Mammon, a destructuring of some production), a return to people of what governments have wrongfully, if often inadvertently, taken into their domain.

Small is Beautiful epitomizes this return to the human dimension. It may only be translation into today's metaphor of the kingdom of justice which Jesus announces.

5. *The economy must be a participatory society.* If the economy ought to be people-oriented, including in that orientation belief in common people—Jesus' people—then it follows that people, workers at all levels, consumers, ought to have more say about what is produced and how it is produced. *Quadragesimo Anno* proposed certain principles toward a model of a participatory society. This is a difficult concept to realize in practice. But it will never be even attempted in a society which does not believe in people, but holds that it is for the elites (the power-holders) to decide.

6. *There must be fair-sharing.* Symbols operative here are those of community, equality of persons and social justice.[45]

7. *The system must permit self-reliance.* Once again if people and their dignity are to count, ability to rely on themselves is equally at stake. Since the heart of this truth is embraced by the idea of par-

ticipation we need not say much more here. However, it must be observed that in our highly and growingly more interdependent world self-reliance must not be reduced to autarchy.

8. *And it must be sustainable.* One would pose here the problem of limits of growth, whether these be due to dwindling supplies of minerals, fossil fuels, certain raw materials or rising costs of exploration and extraction. To that should be added the strain on the ecosystem from industrial pollution. I would insert still a third component of a sustainable society, the *social* limits to growth.[46]

9. *It must be productive.* If I have expressed considerable reservations about our industrial system I do not thereby reject its goal of productivity. I ask only in the name of common humanity that it be a *human productivity* in the several ways above indicated. Productive effort is called for also by the biblical symbols of creation of good husbandry in the use of one's talents. And economic rationality is only another exercise of practical reason. I believe that a human order of private possession of the means of production as well as private gain or profit and competition can all be fitted into the human enterprise of making a living together.

Supportive of this productive effort will be all the social principles described in part two—common good, social justice, socialization, subsidiarity.

Social justice is much more than a cold statement of rights and obligations. It is a symbiosis of justice and love—of doing justice out of love and measured by love. Human love confronting needs responds, not just with generous unreflecting impulse; it responds also with the head and with the creativity which answers the call of the creator Lord.

"Subsidiarity" builds out of the Latin word for help. It ought in biblical language to be measured by stewardship. Intelligent stewardship will organize the doing of business around people and their needs, according to individuals and smaller associations all the freedom possible to do for themselves. At the same time it will call upon local, state and national governments to play their supporting roles along the lines earlier indicated.

The nine principles just described seem to me essentials for an organization of the economy if it is to be truly human and therefore truly Christian; or, stated alternatively, if it is to be truly Christian and therefore truly human. As such, these principles, as objective representations of human reality and Christian anthropology, offer an embodiment of the lordship of Christ in economic structures.[47]

NOTES

1. *In II Ethic.*, 3 (Pirotta, 265).

2. How structures result from and in turn influence human conduct are described by Peter Berger and Thomas Luckmann in their well known *The Social Construction of Reality: A Treatise on the Sociology of Knowledge* (Garden City: Doubleday, 1967), pp. 53–61. Here the authors trace the socializing process of coming to know and describe its impact on individuals and society. There are three dialogically related moments: i) *externalization,* the process by which persons or groups impose order on their environment, and then impress that order—that image—on their world; ii) *objectivization,* in which the product of externalization is experienced by the receiving society as an autonomous reality confronting it as an external and coercive fact; iii) *internalization* of the structured and objectified reality by others, in succeeding generations, through the formation of socially induced mindsets (attitudes, values, mentalities), which have a powerful and often determining influence on how we work, what we produce, what and how we consume, etc.

3. *Gaudium et Spes* 34 and 39 (Gremillion 270, 274). Unless otherwise noted, recent Church social teaching will be cited as in Joseph Gremillion, *The Gospel of Peace and Justice: Catholic Social Teaching Since Pope John* (Maryknoll: Orbis, 1976).

4. n. 37 (Gremillion 502).

5. *Gaudium et Spes* 39 (Gremillion 274).

6. The works on Luke which I have given most attention to are the following: Richard Cassidy, *Jesus, Politics and Society: A Study of Luke's Gospel* (Maryknoll: Orbis, 1978); John Howard Yoder, *The Politics of Jesus* (Grand Rapids: Eerdmans, 1972); Norman Perrin, *Rediscovering The Teaching of Jesus* (New York: Harper & Row, 1976); H. Conzelman, *The Theology of St. Luke* (New York: Harper's, 1960); J. M. Creed, *The Gospel According to St. Luke* (London: Macmillan, 1930). Also helpful generally for the Christology which I am following were Jon Sobrino, *Christology at the Crossroads* (Maryknoll: Orbis, 1978); Karl Rahner, *Foundations of Christian Faith* (New York: Seabury, 1978); Walter Kasper, *Jesus the Christ* (New York: Paulist, 1976).

7. See, among many others, Cassidy, *op. cit.,* 32–34, 61–63; Yoder, *op. cit.,* 23–25. Yoder, p. 60, quotes Etienne Trocmé, "The question of the political dimension of Jesus' ministry . . . though it remains the object of lively

debate, has been public property for a good two score years, and is rarely ignored. . . ."

8. Especially interesting on this is Yoder; *op. cit.,* pp. 31–33.

9. Sobrino, *op. cit.,* "cross of Jesus as historical consequence of his life," pp. 202–4.

10. From the Old Testament most immediately relevant would be: creation, God's kingdom, covenant, liberation from Egyptian bondage, the exile, the Suffering Servant. From the New Testament: Mary's *Magnificat,* other parables than those here used, the resurrection, the Eucharist, the early Christian community, Paul's maintaining himself by work, the injunctions of St. James. But this is only a beginning.

Marie Augusta Neal deals particularly with symbols of relinquishment in *A Socio-Theology of Letting Go,* (New York: Paulist, 1977).

11. James M. Gustafson, *Can Ethics Be Christian?* (Chicago: University of Chicago, 1975), pp. 148–50. This volume is extremely helpful on part two, especially Chapter 6, "Religious Beliefs and the Determination of Conduct," which develops three historical approaches, and shows how Protestant theologians who cannot accept immediate derivation from either Scripture or natural law have developed an alternative to the latter in terms of "middle axioms," "inprincipled" and the like. Gustafson draws eclectically from all three for his own model. Very useful in this context, especially for the relation between biblical and non-biblical sources is: Bruce C. Birch and Larry L. Rasmussen, *Bible and Ethics in the Christian Life* (Minneapolis: Augsburg, 1976).

12. J. Fuchs treats this in "The Absoluteness of Moral Terms," in *Gregorianum* 52 (1971) 418–22.

13. In an article written with George Klubertanz, S.J. I have put together a succinct explanation of this in "Practical Reason, Social Fact, and the Vocational Order" in *The Modern Schoolman,* 28 (1951) 240–43. See also Filippo Land, S.I., "Sull'Esistenza d'una Dottrina Sociale Christiana" in *La Civilta Cattolica* 113 (1962) IV, 430–38 and 546–555.

14. "Katholische Soziallehre" in *Staatslexicon* (6th ed.; Freiburg: Görres-Gesellschaft, vol. 4, 909–30. Also his commentary on the 1942 Christmas message of Pius XII: "Ordo Internus Statuum" in *Periodica De Re Morali, Canonica, Liturgica,* 32 (1943) 79–96 and 216–224.

15. "Modern Catholic Social Teaching on Justice" in *The Faith That Does Justice* (ed. John C. Haughey, Woodstock Studies 2, New York: Paulist 1977) pp. 215f. See also the same author's *Claims in Conflict: Retrieving and Renewing the Catholic Human Rights Tradition* (Woodstock Studies 4, New York: Paulist, 1979), especially Chapter 2.

16. Gremillion, *op. cit.,* p. 9. Gremillion here shows that the Pontifical Commission on Justice and Peace approved the change.

17. Fuchs (*art. cit.,* p. 416, footnote 23) recognizes an element of absoluteness. For behavior corresponding objectively to the concrete human

Christian reality is absolutely required. For thus is achieved the objectively right which is the absolute and universal will of God.

18. *Op. cit.,* pp. 415–58. The article of David Hollenbach cited in footnote 15 is a more available exposition of this school of thought.

19. Fuchs with Rahner notes that nature is not fully stated unless we consider the composite structure of the way people act out their humanity, the fact that mutability belongs to the immutable essence of the human, and that personality is the universally concrete expression of human nature.

20. *Contra Gentiles* I, 11.

21. *In IV Sent.* 26, 1 and 3. Stanley Hauerwas in *Character and the Christian Life: A Study in Theological Ethics* (San Antonio: Trinity University, 1975) has relevant things to say on these themes in Ch. 2, "Aristotle and Thomas Aquinas on the Ethics of Character."

22. "Seeing Into God" in *The Month,* 12 (August 1979), No. 8, 62–68.

23. Hollenbach in a second article in *The Faith That Does Justice* (see footnote 15), "A Prophetic Church and the Catholic Sacramental Imagination," gives an excellent treatment of imagination in theology. He discusses (pp. 249–260) still another exercise of the kingdom in society, that is, the sacraments, a point insisted on also in the 1971 Synod's *Justice in the World* (58; Gremillion 525).

24. This solidarity should not be confused with German *Solidarismus,* which motivated Nazism.

25. *Mater et Magistra* 219 (Gremillion 190).

26. N. 40 (Gremillion 209).

27. Though Johannes Metz appears to restrict the Church's role to negative norms, he has penetrating things to say in general in *Theology of the World* (New York: Herder and Herder, 1969) on the role of the Church and Christians in the World.

28. N. 51 (Gremillion 524).

29. Nor may one argue that these norms insofar as drawn from Christian sources are not relevant for secular society, for, to repeat with Dych (above, p. 221, "a truly human imagination is also Christian imagination."

30. From various presentations of economic circuits I have adopted that of Robert Heilbroner in *Beyond Boom and Crash* (New York: Norton, 1978) Ch. 2.

31. John Kenneth Galbraith, *Economics and the Public Purpose* (New York: Houghton, Mifflin, 1973), Ch. 2, "The Market System".

32. See *Poverty in American Democracy,* produced by Campaign for Human Development, U.S. Catholic Conference (Frederick J. Perella Jr., coordinator; Washington D.C., 1974), Ch. 6, "Some Indicators of the Distribution of Wealth and Power in the United States."

33. *The Next 200 Years* (New York: William Morrow, 1976).

34. Space does not permit more analysis of the processes of domination and dependency than appears in the following paragraphs. For an example

of a widely-held (Marxist) Third World view see *Dependence and Underdevelopment: Latin America's Political Economy,* written by André Gunder Frank with James Cockcroft and Dale L. Johnson, (New York: Doubleday, 1970).

35. I have reviewed these issues in "Stewardship and the NIEO" in *The Earth Is the Lord's* (ed. Mary Evelyn Jegen and Bruno Manno); New York: Paulist, 1978) pp. 100–11.

36. I have surveyed these issues in "Trade and Debt Problems of the Developing Nations," in *Growth With Equity: Strategies for Meeting Human Needs* (eds. Charles Wilber and M. E. Jegen; New York: Paulist, 1979), pp. 175–208.

37. A good introduction is Ronald Muller and Richard Barnet, *Global Reach: Power of the Multinational Corporations* (New York: Simon and Schuster, 1975). For a shorter reflection see William Ryan "Multinational Corporations and the NIEO" in *Center of Concern* Reprint Packets, No. 1. "Global Justice and Development Issues."

38. The encyclical may be found in *Origins* 8 (March 22, 1979). The first of the following citations is from n. 15, the others from n. 16. I have modified the translation slightly (e.g., "the human" for "man").

39. *Redemptor Hominis* three times in the section noted observes that we must acknowledge the good that is in the system. Nevertheless the overall thrust of the pope's exposition is decidely negative.

40. Michael Harrington in *The Other America* (New York: Macmillan, 1962) shows, however, that even prosperous America has a large number of people living in poverty and millions hovering near the poverty line. And even as we conquer diseases, our society produces new ones, in particular psychological and mental breakdown.

41. One of the most perceptive writers on the control that technology exercises over human beings is E. F. Schumacher; cf. his *Good Work* (New York: Harper and Row, 1979), especially Ch. 1, "The End of an Era," and Ch. 2, "Toward a Human Scale Technology." Schumacher enumerates other evils of the present system than those which we have here mentioned. Its complexity makes immense claims on time and attention, depriving us ever more of real leisure (p. 25). Its authoritarian character increases as vastness of operation grows (p. 29). It is culturally exploitative (p. 30). It believes that economic development is a mechanical process, that is, inalterable, as if the system could never be altered by intrusion of values (p. 31). It disrupts organic process (p. 35), and breeds violence against nature (p. 36).

This is an appropriate place to acknowledge that subjecting only the American capitalist system to kingdom critique may give the impression that I believe the kingdom is embodied in Communist alternatives. That I do not believe. But neither is that the subject of my inquiry.

42. See Hollenbach in *The Faith That Does Justice,* pp. 239–49.

43. The centrality of work is accented in Schumacher's *Good Work* (see note 41).

44. Schumacher, *op. cit.,* p. 28.

45. A justice that cannot be confined to people within one nation but must become a global justice.

46. Fred Hirsch, *Social Limits to Growth* (Cambridge, MA: Harvard University, 1976).

47. It would represent an absurd and naive lack of political sense were I not to acknowledge that one further mediatorship of the kingdom will be necessary. This is the political processes through which the "carriers" of kingdom values will insert them into economic structures. Who these carriers are to be and what are the processes are vast questions we cannot enter into. Equally, against entrenched power the "liberating" processes may not be characterized by the harmony and equilibrium favored in traditional Catholic social thought. The kingdom in social structures may have to be mediated by conflict, confrontation and—as recently in Latin America—even on occasion by violence.

10
Touching in Power: Our Health System

Thomas E. Clarke, S.J.

The last time I had a physical checkup the doctor looked at my throat and sent me to get a chest X-ray; felt my pulse and had his nurse take my blood pressure; listened to my story and, with his stethoscope, picked up the sounds of my heartbeat and breathing. He looked and listened and touched, as doctors and nurses and other healers have been doing for a long time. His primary professional tools were his eyes, ears and hands. What signaled that he was a practitioner of modern medicine was his employment of three extensions of these human senses, mediating his perception of me, his patient. He ministered to me within a technological health system.

This commonplace experience of medical care offers a symbolic starting place for the present reflection on the American health system. The focus of my essay will be twofold: i) the technological dimensions of that system viewed as extensions of the human senses of seeing, hearing, touching; ii) the exercise of healing power by Jesus as Lord, once again with attention to the role of the senses. The question I am dealing with is whether and how the latter can influence the former for good, whether and how the lordship of Christ can be exercised in our handling of medical technology. Directly, this reflection aims at no particular patterns or policies, strategies or tactics, regarding the present crisis in American health. Its appeal is more to the heart and imagination than to the rational mind; its intent is ultimately pastoral. And it may offer one way of reflecting theologically and pastorally on the many structures and systems which so significantly affect our lives today.

I. ASPECTS OF THE HEALTH SYSTEM

The more striking features of the current situation in American medicine and health care are too well known to need detailed analysis here.[1] The fact that Congress will most likely, within the next decade, enact into law some comprehensive health plan is indicative of a state of serious crisis. The skyrocketing cost of medical care; the shortage of general practitioners of medicine in a profession dominated by specialization; the damaging impact on many urban hospitals of the move to the suburbs, with the consequent consumer demand for new and fully modern facilities; the resultant wasteful competitiveness among hospitals both old and new as they struggle to attract both physicians and patients, especially through the utilization of sophisticated and expensive technologies; the new pressures placed upon doctors and other professionals as well as on medical institutions by liability laws and their judicial interpretation; the unavailability and inaccessibility of adequate health services for large populations of urban and rural poor, for the aged, and for other groups; the damage sometimes done to patients by the very drugs, techniques, and organization of care designed to promote their health; the generally low state of knowledge regarding health and sickness on the part of many people, together with their recourse to doctors and hospitals in ways which abdicate their own responsibility for their health; the influence of various mythologies touching sickness and death, the power of the physician, the role of the hospital, and other symbolic elements affecting human health; the tendency toward the medicalization of society, that is, easy recourse to a medical model for dealing with evils and pains (alcoholism, anxiety, meaninglessness) whose remedies had earlier been sought elsewhere; the tensions and polarizations present among the various partners to the health care relationship (doctors and other professionals, hospital administrators, nonprofessional workers, patients and their families, third party participants, pharmaceutical firms and other commercial interests, government and local civic communities, religious groups); the still largely unsuccessful efforts of scientists and technologists to conquer the new "diseases of civilization"; the negative impact on the health of Americans of habits touching food and drink, exercise, narcotics, habits commonly fostered by media subservient to the economic interests of a consumer society; the similar negative impact on health of environmental pollution; the spawning of mental and emotional disturbances by technological warfare and other forms of violence—this is a very partial listing of some of the more notable symptoms of crisis regarding the health of Americans and of their health system today.

The champions of that system are undoubtedly correct when they challenge too sweeping denunciations and doomsaying on the part of critics, and when they compare the present system, at least in certain respects, with the health picture of former days and with the situation which obtains elsewhere in the world today. That major victories have been won through science and medical technology is beyond question. Diseases like smallpox, tuberculosis, diphtheria, malaria, have been either eliminated or brought under more or less full control.[2] And there is some basis for the view that the principal malaise we are dealing with is not an objective lack of health but unhealthy demands and expectations on the part of a growing number of Americans, the assumption, for example, "that contemporary medicine is able to accomplish a great deal more than is in fact possible."[3]

Technology and Medicine

Whatever the balance of assets and liabilities, most would agree that the presence of the technological fact is an element of crucial import, that it has unquestionably brought real benefits, but that it also poses a major threat to what is distinctively human in our life. Obviously, medicine is not the only area in which the impact of technology is posing massive problems to humans. There is in fact a coalescence of pressures which makes it virtually impossible to set precise limits to what is a health problem as compared with other sorts of problems in our society. The very terms "health" and "sickness" and "healing" thus take on, not illegitimately, broader and more symbolic significations.[4] The field of health and health care thus becomes a vestibule, as it were, through which the total edifice of our society may be entered by theological reflection. Hence an effort to understand medical technology will need to draw on the extensive reflection devoted in recent decades to technology in general.[5]

In the broadest sense, the term "technology" can be used of any organized and sustained use of material resources for the achievement of pragmatic purposes involving time, space and matter. Thus, hammers and saws, wagons and waterwheels represent technologies of a more or less primitive kind. A more restricted sense of the term, however, presupposes the several revolutions involved in the Enlightenment, and refers to the organized knowledge inherent in the systematic application of scientific discovery to the solving of human problems and the achieving of human purposes. Technology is to technique as methodology is to method. *Logo*—indicates that there is question of a body of knowledge, and *techno*—indicates that there is question of a set of skills and instruments touching the pragmatic aspects of life.

So far as health care is concerned, it may be useful to distinguish technologies as: a) *physical,* which includes the use of machines and instruments such as computers and scanners; b) *pharmacological,* comprising drugs and other medicines; and c) *organizational,* the structuring and environmentalizing of human persons, relationships, and work. Technology aids in the diagnosis and prognosis of sickness, in interventions aimed at its control and cure, and in the complex supportive systems which provide appropriate environments for health care. Thus medical technology includes aids to health as diverse, for example, as the cure of TB with drugs; the use of a scanner for diagnosis of cancer; the alignments and responsibilities of a staff of nurses, attendants, technicians, physicians and others within the surgical department of a large hospital; the procedures involved in the financial reimbursement of all who contribute their services to the healing of illness.

It is roughly only since the seventeenth century that the practice of medicine has been profoundly altered through the development of physical and chemical techniques which extended the healer's eyes, ears, and hands in the diagnosis and cure of illness.[6] Instruments for registering pulse beat and body temperature came early in this development, as did incipient forms of analysis of urine and blood. The microscope was used for medical purposes in the seventeenth century, while it was only in the nineteenth century that such instruments as laryngoscopes, ophthalmoscopes, stethoscopes and electrocardiograms were developed. The development of the X-ray came later in the nineteenth century, and our own century has seen a veritable explosion of medical technology. The entry of computer science and computer technology is undoubtedly the most revolutionary factor in this development.

The major developments, and attending problems and crises, of the past few centuries in the field of health care have been closely tied in with technological development. The seventeenth century doctor relied primarily on his own senses to provide him with the basis of his diagnosis and prescription. He listened to the patient's own description of his illness, observed his appearance, and, to some degree, examined his body manually. In successive waves, the growth of medical technology brought major changes in this relationship. The gaze of the physician moved from the patient to the evidence yielded by his own instruments. He began to listen less to the patient's voice than to his body, its sounds and vibrations as mediated through his instruments. As the need of laboratories and technicians increased, and as the proliferation of specialized knowledge of health and sickness reduced the confidence of general practitioners, the modern hospital with its laboratories, its consultation techniques, and its function of training doctors and other personnel, developed. Young doctors, trained to rely on science and technology, were attracted away from rural areas to urban centers, where they could pursue increasingly specialized forms of medicine with the aid of colleagues and of more and more specialized echelons of assistants.

Such a brief description must be inadequate for conveying the scope and complexity of the impact of technology on medical practice and on human relationships surrounding health and sickness. For medical technology developed in a world where other forms of technology were likewise developing and placing profound strains on the human organism. Currents of influence met counter currents. For example, where the exhilaration of technological breakthrough by itself tended to generate optimistic visions of computer-fostered total health for all, the development of psychoanalysis was disclosing that there were hidden depths of neurotic personality not fully accessible to biochemical control, and profoundly influencing even the physical health of persons. Similarly, a technology linked to a consumerism fed by media manipulation was perceived as ravishing and polluting the human environment, promoting destructive habits of life, and substituting for the progressively vanishing infectious diseases a whole new set of diseases of civilization.

Critical Views

As with all such developments and the crises they engender, there exist the most widely divergent views regarding the present state of things and regarding the possible and desirable future. Optimists and pessimists, friends and foes of technology, health professionals and social scientists, advocates and opponents of strong governmental intervention, debate a staggering variety of issues.[7]

One of the better known viewers of the technological scene is *René Dubos,* who combines a genial humanism with biomedical expertise.[8] Acutely sensitive to the actual and potential damage of technology, he differs sharply from those who would deal with the hazards and harm of technology simply with more and better technology. Technological fixes, he says, are a jumble of procedures with unpredictable consequences. In conflict with natural forces technological magic is not much better than primitive magic and is more destructive.[9]

Dubos questions the "myth of growth," i.e., the belief that survival and the quality of life are dependent on more technical power.[10] Technology has, in fact, while raising standards of living, lowered the quality of life.[11]

The great evil to which technological development has succumbed, thinks Dubos, is the dissociation between humans and the rest of nature, especially as nature connotes "a God within," the inner form of things.[12] The transformation of technology now called for must somehow restore the organic bond of humans and nature. In this process technology must associate itself with other disciplines. Biomedical science is especially suited to be the integrating factor between science and humanism.[13]

Characteristic of Dubos' humanistic response to the technological crisis is that he considers the recent criticism of Christianity as antiecological (stemming largely from Lynn White's celebrated essay) to be at best an historical half-truth.[14] He feels that the solution of present woes is not in retreating either from the Judeo-Christian tradition or from technological civilization.[15] However serious the present crisis, humans are capable of redeeming technological society, provided they acknowledge the role of culture, symbols and imagination in making life more human, and provided they cease letting their own technological creations divorce them from their roots in nature and trap them into making technology an end in itself.

Dubos' viewpoint is congruous with the one here expressed, in its basic hope for redeeming technology through a more integral recourse to the riches of human resources and traditions, particularly as these take the form of symbolic and imaginative creations.

What is especially characteristic of Christian interest in the current technological crisis is its humanizing-dehumanizing actuality and potential. Human beings as imaging God, the dignity of human persons, the vocation to human communion—this has been at the heart of the Church's social teaching in the past century.[16] It is also the link which unites Christian concern with that of other religious believers and all who espouse human values and dignity.

The second part of this essay will seek to explore just one avenue of Christian response to this humanizing-dehumanizing issue as it occurs within our health system today. It will reflect principally on the ministry of Jesus in search of a paradigm for that response. It will then offer some theological principles for a Christian response, and, finally, will suggest how that response might be pastorally embodied.

II. ASPECTS OF A CHRISTIAN RESPONSE

Before beginning to reflect on the ministry of Jesus, there are several assumptions, well grounded in recent theology, which I shall be making:[17]

1. That the central mystery of human life is God's self-gift and

self-revelation to humans, centered in the person and mission of Jesus Christ and his Spirit, historically embodied in his Church, but verified more broadly wherever humans, Christian or not, respond in truth to human values.

2. That this divine self-gift and self-revelation are mediated principally through the self-gift and self-revelation which humans make to one another.

3. That the "speech" of both divine and human self-revelation is not limited to the narrowly empirical, pragmatic and rational, but includes the deeper dimensions of the imagination and the "heart," which find special expression in secular and religious myth and symbol.

4. That the integral appropriation of meaning in divine and human "speech" takes place through a kind of organic assimilation of hearer to speaker, a fitting of the total person of the hearer to the total person of the speaker.

5. That, if this total process of organic assimilation is identified as a process of growing in faith, theological reflection represents that aspect or element within the process which is concerned precisely with the "word-ing" of the process.

6. That, as all Christians are called to grow in faith, so all are called to theological reflection on faith. Professional theologians are not elite substitutes for other Christians. Rather, by "professing," that is, by exhibiting in the public arena of the Church's life this exercise of reflective faith common to all Christians, their role is to evoke and confirm the process as it takes place throughout the Church. Thus professional theology becomes a kind of ministerial system, complex and organic, and ultimately representative in character.[18]

What is the point of these remarks with respect to the present essay? First, they mean that when we have recourse to the life and ministry of Jesus as central mediation of God's gracious self-revelation, our gaze, our listening, must extend more widely than the rational content of his teaching. His words must be heard as conveying the insights of his imagination and the feel of his heart for human values. Secondly, we need to attend to what he "said" beyond his words, through where he chose to put his body, with whom he associated, how he dealt with his society and culture, and so forth. And thirdly, this approach implies that our exposure to the totality of his human language will have the character of organic assimilation, a fitting of our total selves to his total self to the degree to which we have access to him and permit him to have access to us. It will be, in brief, a lived, holistic experience of discipleship.

What difference does this make for perceiving and responding to our technological health system? Once again a model of organic assimilation is appropriate, and in both directions, so to speak. The Christian deeply committed to health ministry who approaches Jesus with a view to deepening discipleship to him brings something distinctive to the relationship, a gaze and a listening ear made sensitive to certain accents by engagement in the healing experience. Similarly, the Christian comes from a contemplative deepening of discipleship back to dealing with health technology enriched by distinctive habits of perception and response.

More specifically, in building on Brian McDermott's essay in this volume, this essay wishes to highlight the resources of imagination and the heart which Christian disciples can bring to dealing with the technological threat and promise in the health field.[19] Technology did not come about without these human gifts. But, once constituted, it tends to shape life on the basis of information and calculation, facts and their linear analysis. Someone has said that violence is due to a lack of imagination. Without imagination and without the engagement of the heart, technology will of necessity be destructive. What most needs healing and liberation in Christians through total exposure to Christ Jesus are these facets of their humanity. Along with his exercise of seeing, hearing, touching, it is to these aspects of his "language" that we will be paying special attention.

The Healing Ministry of Jesus

Though the world of the itinerant preacher Jesus of Nazareth is far removed from the world of twentieth century medicine, it is to the ministry of Jesus that Christians have recourse for the basic inspiration and norms of their effort to deal with the problems generated by medical technology. What can we learn for our purposes from the ministry of Jesus as portrayed in the gospels?

First of all, we see him *exercising power* and doing so quite consciously and without apology. The importance of this should not be missed by misinterpreting his directive to his disciples to exercise power humbly and in a spirit of service (Matt 20:24–28).

Secondly, this exercise of power is presented as *healing,* as *liberation,* as *restoration to wholeness.*[20] The three models intertwine, in keeping with the biblical understanding of health as wholeness, and of sickness of any kind as subjection to the power of Satan. The motif is a major one. "Hardly another image impressed itself so deeply on early Christian tradition as that of Jesus as the great physician."[21]

Thirdly, if one situates the exercise of healing and liberating power within the totality of the ministry of Jesus, there is a remarkable *consistency* and *integrity* discernible, whose central elements are the following:

1. *Teaching and preaching:* Ideology is diseased doctrine, idolatrous reliance for salvation on finite and fallible ideas, the absolutizing of relative insights into the human condition. The particular world into which the healing preacher Jesus was sent needed deliverance from specific ideologies about God, human beings, human life. Sometimes in comforting assurance and sometimes with the surgical knife of irony and castigation, but always with fidelity to what he was hearing from his Father, Jesus spoke relevantly to the ideological oppressions of his particular culture. In no way did he relieve human beings of the burden of responsibility for their own destinies; on the contrary, we find, particularly in the synoptics, a quite austere challenge to live sacrificially, precariously. But what kept this imperative from being either anxiety-ridden or arrogant was the more basic message that God was not a god demanding appeasement but a gracious Father always ready to forgive.

2. *Healing miracles:* Here is the first instance of consistency and integrity in Jesus' ministry. The exercise of power in speech was complemented by the exercise of even more manifest power in deeds of healing. Because of this intimate association of teaching and preaching with thaumaturgy, his words became deeds and his deeds

had the character of words. Together they were potent signs of the presence of God's rule.

3. *Social status:* In a sense, Jesus had no choice about the company he would cultivate. He turned no one away, but it seems that his preference was for the poor, understanding by this term not the economically deprived but the culturally/religiously disparaged. Publicans, lepers, prostitutes, tabooed women, touched and were touched, cried out and were heard, became table companions and even hosts and hostesses. How could he do otherwise? To proclaim with his lips that God had sent him to heal humans in their misery while ignoring those most wounded in society would have deprived his message and physical healings of most of their power. This physician had not come for plastic surgery for those tired of their own faces but for a deep healing of human ills that found expression, as it does in every culture, in the socially condemned.

4. *Social criticism:* Intertwined with all three of the above was another element in Jesus' ministerial strategy: his perception of and response to the positive and negative climates in the society and culture which were his as a Jew. Recent years have seen a considerable body of literature, occasioned by contemporary Church/society issues, devoted to the "politics of Jesus." As with most such major issues, conflicting positions appeal to contrasting texts. For our purposes here it is not necessary to explore the relationship of Jesus to the politics of Pharisees, Sadducees, Essenes, Zealots, and Romans. What is pertinent and what seems clear is that he did not ignore the impact that an ambivalent theocratic social system made on personal faith. At least in several instances by word and deed he taught and encouraged a kind of civil disobedience toward certain ingrained religious attitudes and practices which, in his view, were expressive of the powers of darkness and seriously hindered the coming of the reign of God. This was true in a particular way with respect to the absolutizing of ritual practices when these led to a distortion of the true image of God and placed unbearable burdens on defenseless people. Such social criticism on Jesus' part was, like his assumption of social status and associations, part of a ministerial strategy aimed at the integral healing of human persons in society.

5. *Community-building:* Any exercise of power which does not

generate discipleship and community is doomed to early extinction. One must be cautious when using the gospels in attributing to Jesus visions of an enduring Church. Still, his preaching and miracles, his life style and social criticism, when taken together, implied at least the spontaneous gathering of a community of disciples who shared in his ministry. This, too, was a work of healing, liberation, and restoration to wholeness. The stories concerning Simon Peter and the sons of Zebedee, the repeated corrections and cautions addressed to the Twelve and the Seventy-two, and the tragic failure in the case of Judas, are indicative of the presence of this dimension.

6. *Prayer:* Finally, this integral exercise of healing power found its source of strength in the relationship of Jesus to the one whom he addressed as *"abba,"* and whom he regularly sought in solitary prayer. While the Gospels nowhere suggest that Jesus the healer needed himself to be healed or liberated from Satan's power in a moral sense ("Over me he has no power" [Jn 14:30]), recent Christology has successfully dissipated the previous image of an all-knowing Jesus whose recourse to prayer would have nothing of personal need in it. The resulting Christology is more congruous with those Gospel passages where Jesus is depicted as sharing in the wonder, doubt, and anxiety characteristic of the human condition. In such a view he becomes in fact the "wounded healer" of Isaiah's fourth servant song.

There is a second way in which the ministry of Jesus was characterized by integrity. It is important for our purposes to say something about this in connection with medical technology as extension of the human senses. In each of the elements of Jesus' ministry just described, it is possible to distinguish a rational/pragmatic element from the elements of sensibility, feeling, and imagination. Our appreciation of the latter should not lead us to diminish the former. The Jesus of the gospels is a person in touch with the concreteness of human life and capable of shrewd critical analysis of his contemporary situation. With legalizers he was able to match statute for statute, and he consistently exposed the logical contradictions of those who had absolutized the logic of legal religion. It has been observed that Matthew's gospel, with its logical structure and its themes of authority and right order, faithfully reflects this rational side of Jesus, and that the terse Marcan accounts echo his attentiveness to sensate detail.

But this rational/pragmatic quality seems to be put at the service of qualities which, in a sense, are more deeply and distinctively human, namely imagination and feeling (in the sense of "the heart"), qualities which find special expression, respectively, in the gospels according to John and Luke. Brian McDermott's essay indicates how the favorite teaching genre of Jesus, the parable, was expressive of the imagination of Jesus himself and evocative of the same gift in his disciples and hearers. The same key role of imagination might be traced through the other facets of his ministry which we have mentioned. Not only his speech but his deeds, his associations, his pedagogy of community formation, manifested an ability "to look at what is and ask 'Why?', to look at what is not and ask 'Why not?' " This exercise of power gained immeasurably from its integration with feeling, tender or vehement, gentle or passionate, as the occasion demanded. One could list any number of scenes in which attention to detail, powers of rational analysis, the free play of imagination and the force of human feelings are together placed in the service of healing and wholeness. The dialogue with the Samaritan woman (Jn 3), the imaginative stroke of adding to the Mosaic prescription of stoning adulteresses (Jn 8:7) a further rule regarding the qualifications of the stoners, the "render to Caesar" line (Matt 22:21), and many others, suggest the power of a truly integrated personality to effect change in persons and in society.

Jesus' Use of His Senses

These considerations lead to that aspect of the ministry of Jesus which touches our basic suggestion for dealing pastorally with medical technology. Jesus' employment of his senses, specifically of sight, hearing and touch, offers a paradigm for an imaginative response to the threat of dehumanizing technology. The four gospels are full of interesting details regarding sense contact between Jesus and others—the sick, disciples (actual or potential), adversaries, and the great throng.

Sight: Often the evangelists are at pains to mention Jesus seeing the person in need of healing: Peter's mother-in-law (Matt 8:14); the friends of the paralytic (Matt 9:2); the woman with a hemorrhage (Matt 9:22); the widow of Naim (Lk 7:13); the crippled woman (Lk 13:12). The same is true where there is question of a less physical healing or of a call to discipleship. He notices Simon and Andrew, John and James (Matt 4:18,21), and Matthew (Matt 9:9). He looks steadily at the rich young man (Mk 10:21) and angrily (Mk 3:5) at the people in the synagogue. The pitiful crowds were likewise the object of his compassionate gaze (Matt 9:36; Mk 6:34). The sight of Jerusalem brought him to tears (Lk 19:41).

Hearing: Seeing others in misery does not necessarily involve initiative on their part. With hearing, it is different. The sick, needy one cries out, and the healer hears and heeds. The ministry of Jesus contains numerous instances when Jesus became the listener to cries or tales of human anguish. Two blind men (Matt 9:27 and again 20:30), the irrepressible Canaanite woman (Matt 15:22f.), the father of the epileptic boy (Mk 9:24), the blind men (Lk 18:39) are some examples. There are times, whether or not his attention has been caught with a cry from the afflicted, when he becomes listener and questioner. He asks the father of the epileptic boy how long his son has been afflicted, and then proceeds to lead him to a beautiful expression of faith and trust (Mk 9:14–29). He asks the blind men of Jericho, "What do you want me to do for you?" (Matt 20:34), and then heals them with a touch. No physician was ever so skillful in attracting patients into furthering their own restoration to health as was Jesus. He heard people's pleas, then encouraged them to talk, carefully listened, and bestowed on them the gift of a health that was total.

Touch: If seeing and hearing often prepared the way for healing, it was by touching (and in some instances letting himself be touched) that Jesus wrought his actual cures. Very frequently (e.g. Matt 19:13; Lk 13:13) the gospels speak of his laying hands on people to cure them, a language that will be used in the early Church also for the communication of the Spirit and commissioning for ministry.[22]

One might be tempted to wonder why so much attention is being paid here to the engagement of Jesus' senses in the work of healing. After all, seeing and hearing are ordinary conditions for human relationships, and touching the person who is being cured, while not indispensable, still is congruous with the personal help being given.

Two considerations are behind this concern. The first is that, to the eyes of Christian faith, the ministry of Jesus represents the peak of God's coming to heal his people. Throughout the Old Testament, the language of the senses is used to express the divine compassion. Yahweh is frequently being asked to see, to open his eyes, and is depicted as looking down from heaven on the plight of his chosen ones. He is also conceived as a listening God, who invites his children to call to him who promises to hear them. Sacred history unfolds under the power of Yahweh who, unlike the blind and deaf gods of idolatry, is a seeing and hearing God. The Exodus in particular is the result of the divine seeing and hearing: "God heard their groaning and he called to mind his covenant with Abraham, Isaac and Jacob. God looked down upon the sons of Israel, and he knew . . ." (Ex 2:24f).

When it comes to the sense of touch, however, the Old Testament does not present Yahweh as healing under this image. The power of his right hand, often mentioned, is certainly a saving power, but the image of deliverance from sickness by his healing touch does not occur. Nor does the Old Testament know the rite of healing by the laying on of hands. The Genesis Apocryphon of Qumran is the first known instance of this in Jewish sources.[23]

From a Christian perspective, it may be appropriate that the language of this most intimate of senses is not used in the Bible to describe God's healing power until he became present in fullness in the person of Jesus. The ministry of Jesus represents God in absolute nearness, no longer merely seeing and hearing from heaven, but close enough to touch and heal our sick and wounded humanity. One finds here, perhaps, a foundation for Irenaeus' beautiful image of the Son and Spirit as the two hands of God.[24]

The other reason for making much of the bodily senses of Jesus in his healing miracles has to do with relating his ministry as a whole to our concern with medical technology. Here recourse may be had to the Pauline observation that the Scriptures were written for our comfort and hope (Rom 15:4). That Jesus' healing exercise of sight, hearing, and touch lingered in early tradition and found its way into the recorded Gospel cannot be without significance for the process of discipleship outlined earlier in this essay. The shaping of the Christian's mind-set by Jesus calls for attentiveness to the role of the senses in Christian life and particularly in Christian ministry, modeled on their role in Jesus' own ministry. Likewise, Jesus' sensitivity in all facets of his ministry to the influence of systemic factors in promoting or hindering the healing designs of the Father will find a resonance in the disciple's sensitivity to how systems of every kind affect the embodiment of those same designs in the context of our society and culture. There is question here not precisely of a logical implication but of an effective and "iconic" assimilation, less easy to define, perhaps, but no less real and influential for an integral following of Christ.

In summary, then, what this brief reflection on the gospels discloses for our purposes is:

1. The lordship of Jesus finds a proleptic exercise of its power in his ministry.

2. The central thrust of this exercise of power is conceived as liberation from Satan, healing and restoration to health and wholeness of human beings in the totality of their lives, physical and moral, social and institutional.

3. The healing of individuals by Jesus from physical and psychic afflictions represents dramatic high points in this total ministry.

4. Jesus shows himself sensitive to the role that contemporary religious culture, the predominant social system of his milieu, was playing in perpetuating all kinds of sickness in his people. His choice of companions, his criticism and disregard of "oppressive structures" and his ways of community formation sought to liberate persons in society from such burdens.

5. In all facets of his ministry Jesus manifested, on the one hand, a hard-nosed ability to deal with the concrete and the prosaic and to engage in rational analysis of his ministerial situations, and, on the other, a remarkable power to effect change through the joined forces of imagination and feeling, exhibited notably in parabolic teaching, imaginative dealing with conflict situations and evocative formation of his disciples and the crowds.

6. In the gospels as given for Christian contemplation, the frequent mention of Jesus' seeing, hearing, touching of those whom he

healed provides for the Christian imagination and feelings a basic symbolic paradigm for understanding and developing their engagement in the work of healing today within our very complex technological health system.

Theological Axioms

Before pointing, in conclusion, to some pastoral implications of the present essay, one more task remains, namely, a summary indication of the theological principles or axioms which crystallize the biblical and ecclesial facets of the total process of discipleship. Here it will become more clear that, in my strong accent on nonrational aspects of revelation and faith, there is no intent to disparage or minimize the rational aspects. This whole essay has been, in fact, a rational reflection. The process of discipleship I am describing can be greatly helped if a broad theological anthropology is brought to bear on our current concern regarding our health system.

What religion in general and Christianity in particular have to offer in dealing with the dehumanizing threat of medical technology is primarily, I have been implying, at the level of myth, imagination, and symbol. But there are also some broad intellectual perspectives on technological society which have roots in Christian doctrine, or which have an especially close affinity with values cherished in Christian tradition. Different Christian thinkers, to be sure, offer widely divergent and sometimes conflicting views of how the Gospel relates to technology or indeed whether it has anything special to say about it. The following summary approach to technology has a predominantly Roman Catholic bias, in its accent on integration over differentiation, as well as in its optimism regarding the provisional and partial redemption of technological society within the processes of history.[25]

1. Human technology may legitimately be viewed, with support from empirical science and from philosophical analysis, as extensive of the human body and particularly of the human senses, and so as participating in the quality of humanness. As "spirit in the world" the human creature lives interdependently with cosmic processes,

and develops personally and communally through a creative interaction with matter. One important facet of this relationship is the human shaping of time, space and matter so that they become instrumental in the achievement of pragmatic human purposes. Created according to God's image, humans in turn impress the human image on the material world, which in this way participates in the quality of humanness. Analogously with the body, and extensive of it, time, space and matter cease to be mere things or elements extrinsic to persons. Keeping their intrinsic character, they become truly integral to the organic wholeness of human life. As the body is/is not the humanizing spirit, so our human technical creations are/are not our human selves, our relationships.

2. If one accepts the premise that grace and revelation are coextensive with creation, it follows that technology, participating in the quality of humanness, is a dimension of life where God manifests and gives himself to humans. Unfortunately, we are not yet as attuned to finding God in our technical constructs as in the wonders of nature or of artistic creation. Religion historically has thrived in the countryside and been threatened in the industrial cities. A classic painting or sculpture mediates transcendence more readily for most of us than does the computer at the air lines counter. But, theologically speaking, the human search for God in all things is basically incomplete as long as he is not sought and found in the world of technology.

3. Hence the basic religious response in the presence of the *mysterium tremendum et fascinans* is possible even with respect to technology. Awe and wonder, thanksgiving and *complacentia,* are not alien to an integrally human posture toward technology. Samuel Morse's "What hath God wrought," or the quasi-religious expression of wonder and hope by the first humans to reach the moon ("One small step for a man, one giant leap for mankind") conveys that, at least at peak moments of technological achievement, we are conscious of being involved in religious experience.

4. There is a truth contained in Manicheism. Human involvement with matter is replete with darkness and corruption. If there is a Manichean streak present in contemporary antitechnological currents, the element of truth in them needs to be acknowledged. But for Christians the origin of evil forces in the world of technology

does not stem from the nature of matter or from a tragic lapse of pure spirits into enslavement to matter. Neither is the human effort to develop ever more perfect techniques to be regarded by Christians as necessarily rooted in Promethean pride. On the contrary, human destiny is conceived as a call to deeper union with God in and through deeper symbiosis with the world, and as a vocation to exercise ever more intimate stewardship over the processes of creation.

The dark side of technology will be interpreted by Christian anthropology consistently with the notion of technology as extension of and participation in the human. However one interprets the myth of original sin, there is a radical flawing of our humanity which afflicts the technological endeavor as it does every other aspect of life. In the creation of technological systems we impress upon time, space and matter not only our humanity but our inhumanity; we author concupiscent instrumentalities of perverse human purposes, and in turn these dark creations, like Frankenstein monsters, tend to enslave us, to reduce the richness of our humanity to their own limits. This is the terrifying process which Jacques Ellul has described with such relentless zeal for truth. Joseph Weber's essay in this volume has shown the linkage between our descriptions of systemic evil and the mythic language of principalities and powers.

5. Though Ellul's dour prognostications are a warning against the naivete of many facile "solutions," they fall short of the promise contained in the Gospel. We have, it is true, been given no guarantee that this world will ever cease to be, in one aspect, a vale of tears, but genuine anticipations of the kingdom of peace and justice are within the scope of our responsibility and capacity. As Pope Paul's "No more war!" at the UN voiced a sound human and Christian hope that this one massive form of evil can be transcended (as slavery has been transcended) through determined human efforts, so the hope of deliverance from technologism is perfectly consistent with the Christian view of things.

6. A final point of this sketch suggests that a deeply rooted societal evil like technologism is not cast out except by enlisting the integral forces of our graced humanity. Specifically, this means that problem-solving techniques of a purely rational and pragmatic character are essentially insufficient. For the technological captivity of humans consists precisely in the confinement of the human to the ra-

tional and pragmatic, the reduction of human meaning to functional purposes and instrumentalities.

The liberation and healing that need to take place are, then, a restoration to wholeness. This means especially the reinstatement of the powers of feeling (or "the heart") and imagination to their central place in the organism of the human person and community. This needs to be done particularly in dealing with medical technology precisely as it extends the human body and senses. There is both continuity and discontinuity in this extension. There can be no question of blurring the quasi-infinite difference between the living human organism and metal or chemical or spatio-temporal organizations of matter. Still, participation and mediation (two key notions) enable us to draw these creations into the sphere of the human. Remaining what they are, our technological constructs can share in the self-transcendence characteristic of the human image of God, and can become more than they are, or better, can, to the degree that their creation is truly human, participate in a graced human condition. The imaging of human spirit by human flesh, and the imaging of the integrally human through artistic creation, are broadly paradigmatic of what is possible in the creations of technology. The Christian hope of resurrection, if it is to be fully faithful to the good news, must contain the hope of the redemption of the technological body of humanity, provisionally within history, and definitively (beyond the power of imagination to envisage) in the beyond of history which bears the names of kingdom and city.

It is in this replenishment of the imagination and the heart, in drawing the technological adventure into the basic human processes of myth and dream, that religion and particularly Christianity make their most distinctive contribution to the human journey. Social systems express themselves in the rational/pragmatic structuring of human life, and are just or unjust in their origins and in their impact. But the rational/pragmatic is essentially a derivative facet of life, and behind every structural injustice there is a distorted myth, a failure of imagination and the heart. Christianity in our day is in process of reestablishing its prophetic role of announcing justice and denouncing injustice. But unless this role is rooted in the deeper power of Christianity to heal and liberate the forces of feeling and imagination, its power to conquer demonic forces within technological society is fatally flawed. It is at the point that society meets culture that the Church needs most centrally to meet society. All this points to the crucial role of sacramental and liturgical life, devotion and spirituality, and engagement in community-building, in strategies for meeting the technological threat. For it is in these areas of the life of the Church that the healing, liberation and "wholing" of her membership is most richly advanced.

Pastoral Suggestions

There are available, then, primordially in the ministry of Jesus, traditionally and institutionally in the salvific system which is the Church, and reflectively in the main features of a Christian anthropology, rich resources for a Christian ministry to the American health system. The question now becomes a pastoral one: How can the lordship of Christ, paradigmed in the healing ministry of Jesus, embodied in the sacred institution which is the Church, and reflectively grasped in a Christian anthropology organized in sensitivity to the technological promise/threat—how can this lordship find an appropriate exercise through Christian persons, groups, and institutions?

Fundamentally, the response can only be in terms of a comprehensive re-educational effort directed not merely at Christians professionally engaged in health care but at at all members of the Church. There is probably no single institution in American life which possesses as rich resources for changing attitudes and behavior as the Christian churches. Besides the resources of a formal school system extending from pre-nursery to graduate and professional school, there is the potential (largely untapped so far as health education is concerned) of Christian education within the family, within parishes and dioceses, within voluntary associations (religious communities, groups of married people, charismatic groups, etc.), and through the printed word and other media. Because what is most in need of re-education is the life of the senses, with the life of feeling and imagination, the central areas of renewal are liturgical and paraliturgical, devotional and spiritual. For the same reason, the work of building Christian communities is at the heart of the process.

I would see four basic objectives of such an educational effort:

1. To communicate effectively that sickness and health, integrally understood (including therefore both physiological and psychic health) are not merely related to the process of salvation and to the exercise of the lordship of Christ but are contained within it as constitutive dimensions. They are integral to the healing of humanity which is the goal of God's action in Christ and the Spirit through the Church and through all the processes of humanity.

2. To generate a new and full Christian appreciation of the life of the senses (specifically sight, hearing and touch), as participating in the reality of creation and grace, sin and redemption, reason and revelation, and as gifts which mediate the bond of human charity and the exercise of human stewardship over nature and history.

3. To change basic attitudes and behaviors touching technology and its employment in the service of human healing; more specifically, to help people to view medical technology not merely as a set of tools extrinsic to the human reality but as human creations which participate in the grace and sinfulness of human persons and communities, and which in turn affect the reign of grace or sin in the totality of human life.

4. To provide a spirituality and asceticism, theoretical and especially practical, which will assist individuals and groups, particularly those engaged in the health professions, to actually grow into these attitudes and behaviors.

Conclusion

This essay has reflected on just one of the several social systems within which the lordship of Christ is exercised and to be exercised through the engagement of human beings. It has focused especially on the technological character of that system. It has been largely an exploration of methodology, theological and pastoral, toward a clear perception of and response to the technological threat contained in that system. It is obvious that, in a progressively interdependent world, our health system is interwoven with several others, no less complex and challenging, e.g., touching food and drink, work and industry, recreation and leisure, family and home, etc. To the degree that the broad lines of methodology of the present essay are valid for our health system and its redemption, it admits of application in these other areas of life as well.

It is no small part of the richness of the Gospel that it speaks to every facet of our humanity. Through the organic processes of discipleship, through the vital assimilation of the mind, heart, imagination and sensibilities of Jesus of Nazareth, Christians in the Church are enabled to transcend the barriers of centuries and of profound cultural differences. We know it to be possible because the testimony of history manifests that it is actual. The revolutionary impact of technology on human life has disturbed deep social, cultural and religious patterns as perhaps no other force in history has done. But, especially to the eyes of the Christian faith, it offers no insurmountable challenge to the power and promise inherent in the resurrection of Jesus Christ. It is part of the richness of the Gospel that it speaks to every facet of our humanity in every phase of its history. Surely Gregory of Nazianzus' axiom here finds a legitimate accommodation: "What has not been assumed has not been healed, but what is united to God is also saved. If only half of Adam fell, then what was assumed was also half, but if the entire Adam fell, then he is united to the entirety of the Son and so entirely saved."[26]

NOTES

1. A representative portrait is "Doing Better and Feeling Worse: Health in the United States," *Daedalus* 106 (Winter 1977), No. 1, pp. 1–278. See also J. Howard and A. Strauss (eds.), *Humanizing Health Care* (New York: Wiley, 1975).

2. Ivan Illich, however, claims that there is no evidence of a direct relationship between changes in the cause of death and the progress of medicine, and that environment, not medical care, is the primary determinant of general health, *Medical Nemesis: The Expropriation of Health* (New York: Pantheon, 1975), pp. 15, 17.

3. L. Thomas, "On the Science and Technology of Medicine," *Daedalus* 106 (1977) 45. He says, "There is a public preoccupation with disease

that is assuming the dimension of a national obsession" (*Ibid.* 43). Susan Sontag, in a quite different vein, has recently examined elements of myth in prevailing attitudes toward cancer, in *Illness as Metaphor* (New York: Random House, 1978.)

4. Daniel Callahan, however, views the influential definition of health given three decades ago by the World Health Organization (". . . a state of complete physical, mental and social well-being and not merely the absence of disease or infirmity") as dangerous, by making it impossible to set limits to rational discussion of the health enterprise and particularly of rights to health and health care. "Health and Society: Some Ethical Imperatives," *Daedalus* 106 (1977) 26.

5. The following writings on technology have been especially helpful: P. Bereano (ed.), *Technology as a Social and Political Phenomenon* (New York: Wiley, 1976); D. Brinkmann, "Technology as Philosophical Problem," *Philosophy Today* 15 (1971) 122–128; C. Deckert, *The Social Impact of Cybernetics* (Notre Dame: University of Notre Dame, 1966); D. Dickson, *The Politics of Alternative Technology* (New York: Universe, 1975); A. Halder, art. "Technology," *Sacramentum Mundi* 6, pp. 205–210; *Harvard University Program on Technology and Society 1964–1972* (Cambridge MA: Harvard University, 1972); R. Merrill, art. "Technology: The Study of Technology," *International Encyclopedia of the Social Sciences* 15, pp. 576–589; C. Mitcham and R. Mackey (eds.), *Philosophy and Technology: Readings in the Philosophical Problems of Technology* (New York: Free Press, 1972); A. Teich, ed., *Technology and Man's Future,* 2nd ed. (New York: St. Martin, 1977).

6. The following sketch is drawn from S. Reiser, *Medicine and the Reign of Technology* (New York: Cambridge University Press, 1978). For a dense philosophical view of the origins of modern medicine which attends especially to the gaze (literal and metaphorical) of the physician, see M. Foucault, *The Birth of the Clinic: An Archeology of Medical Perception* (New York: Pantheon, 1973).

7. See the literature cited in notes 1 and 5. For reasons of brevity, I have had to omit here a summary of the less genial but more challenging views of two other critics, Ivan Illich and Jacques Ellul. I have chosen to summarize René Dubos' position because its accent comes closer to the note of hope that I would like to sound in this essay. Illich's view of medical technology is found principally in his *Medical Nemesis* (see note 2). Ellul's principal critique is contained in *The Technological Society* (New York: Knopf 1964), and was later summarized by him in "The Technological Order," in Mitcham and Mackey (see note 5), pp. 86–105.

8. Of Dubos' many writings, the following three were utilized for this essay: *Man and His Environment. Biomedical Knowledge and Social Action* (Washington: Pan American Health Organization, 1966); *Man, Medicine and Environment* (New York 1968); *A God Within* (New York: Irvington, 1972).

9. *A God Within,* p. 41.
10. *Ibid.,* p. 268.
11. *Ibid.,* p. 272.
12. *Ibid.,* p. 14.
13. *Man, Medicine and Environment,* p. 150.
14. *A God Within,* pp. 157f. White's essay originally appeared in *Science* 155 (March 10, 1967), was included in his *Machina ex Deo* (Cambridge MA: M.I.T. Press, 1968), and is reprinted in Mitcham and Mackey (see note 5), pp. 259–265.
15. *Ibid.,* pp. 153–174.
16. See D. Hollenbach, *Claims in Conflict: Retrieving and Renewing the Catholic Human Rights Tradition* (New York: Paulist, 1979); also J. Haughey, ed., *The Faith That Does Justice* (New York: Paulist 1977).
17. The theological viewpoint followed here is especially that of Karl Rahner, expressed in many essays. A handy synopsis is his *Foundations of Christian Faith: An Introduction to the Idea of Christianity,* (New York: Seabury 1978).
18. Dorothee Sölle's distinction of representation and substitution may find here a useful application. See her *Christ the Representative: An Essay in Theology after the Death of God,* (London: SCM, 1967).
19. Among those whose views make much of imagination are Ortega y Gasset (cf. Mitcham and Mackey [See note 5], p. 21) and G. Anders, *ibid.,* p. 9. N. Berdyaev sees technology as threatening not precisely the spirit but the heart. For him technology calls for an intensification of spirituality. Only union with God makes possible a truly human engagement with technology (see *ibid.,* pp. 203–213).
20. For treatments of some of the key biblical terms, see G. Kittel and G. Friedrich (eds.), *Theological Dictionary of the New Testament* s.v. *therapeuo* (H. Beyer; TDNT 3, 128–132); *iaomai* (A. Oepke; TDNT 3, 194–215); *nosis* (A. Oepke; TDNT 4, 1091–1098); ugies (U. Luck; TDNT 8, 308–313); *cheir* (E. Lohse; TDNT 9, 424–437).
21. A. Oepke, in TDNT 3, 204.
22. On the biblical laying on of hands see E. Lohse in TDNT 9, 428 and 431–434.
23. See J. Fitzmyer, *The Genesis Apocryphon of Qumran Cave I* (Rome: Biblical Institute, 1971) p. 124, with the literature there cited.
24. Irenaeus, *Adversus Haereses* IV 34 1 (Harvey 2, 213).
25. Illustrative of these currents are the writings of Karl Rahner, Teilhard de Chardin, and representatives of the earlier neothomist revival such as Emile Mersch. For a characteristically Roman Catholic reflection, see W. N. Clarke, "Technology and Man: A Christian Vision," in Mitcham and Mackey (see note 5), pp. 247–258.
26. *Letter 101* (to Cledonius), PG 37, 177–184.

11
The Peace of Christ in the Earthly City

John Farrelly, O.S.B.

This essay raises the question of the relationship between the lordship of Jesus and systemic peace within and among political communities in the world today. It seeks to explore whether there is such a relationship and some few characteristics of this relationship.

There are many Christians who assume that there is a dichotomy between their response to the lordship of Jesus and their engagement in political life. They assume that submission to the lordship of Jesus is a matter of inner conversion and of interpersonal relations with those with whom they live day by day. And they assume that the motivations and norms for a political community's search for peace are wholly secular, pragmatic and utilitarian; it is a matter of balancing interests within and among states so that they have more to gain from the ways of peace than the ways of war.

Even among those Christians who hold that there is a close relation between the lordship of Jesus and the modern question of peace, there are great differences in their views of what this relationship is. For example, most Catholic theologians have tended to approach this question within the framework of the natural law and its application to current social issues, while most Protestant theologians in recent times have tended to approach it from a biblical perspective. Some who take Jesus' actions and words relevant to the political order as normative have interpreted his example as supporting a pacifist approach to peace in our time, while others have found in his example a support for revolutionary action for the liberation of the oppressed. In the midst of such divided views it may be helpful to explore here the relationship between the lordship of Jesus and the search for systemic peace in political communities in our time.

One way to approach this question is to ask whether Jesus in his ministry and the early Church in mediating his lordship sought the peace of Jerusalem as an integral part of their mission. An affirmative answer to this question leads to a second question: what are some of the implications of this response for the political stance of those who accept the lordship of Jesus in our time? What we offer in this is no more than an introductory answer to our questions—one that may help the reader to develop further his own study and thoughts on this subject. We shall suggest supporting sources where the reader may find a deeper study of this issue. We shall restrict our scriptural study to some central statements in Luke's gospel that the peace of Jerusalem depends upon its positive response to the ministry of Jesus or the early Church. This will be the first part of the essay. The second will ask how this example can be a paradigm for or relevant to the question of peace in the political order today.

I. THE LORDSHIP OF JESUS AND THE PEACE OF JERUSALEM

The gospel of Mark summarized Jesus' ministry by saying that he went about preaching, "This is the time of fulfillment. The reign of God is at hand! Reform your lives and believe in the Gospel!" (Mk 1:14).[1] Luke also gave similar summaries of Jesus' ministry (Lk 4:43; 9:2). And Luke asserted a connection between the Jews' acceptance of Jesus' ministry and their peace in Palestine. We recall Luke's account of Jesus' entrance into Jerusalem:

> Coming within sight of the city, he wept over it and said: "If only you had known the path to peace this day; but you have completely lost it from view! Days will come upon you when your enemies encircle you with a rampart, hem you in and press you hard from every side. They will wipe you out, you and your

> children within your walls, and leave not a stone on a stone within you, because you failed to recognize the time of your visitation" (Lk 19:41–44).

At first reading it seems that Luke is asserting—and teaching us that Jesus asserted—that the political peace of historical Jerusalem depended upon the people's response to the ministry of Jesus, their acceptance through faith of the reign of God that he proclaimed. Luke presents to us a picture of Jesus as profoundly moved by the destruction that he foresees coming upon Jerusalem because his own people did not accept his proclamation of the reign of God. This is to say that Jesus was profoundly concerned for the political peace of his people and his city. The offer of the kingdom was not irrelevant to this peace or contrary to this peace; rather this peace depended upon Jerusalem's response to Jesus' ministry.

Before asking whether this initial interpretation is supported by further analysis, we should recall two considerations that are important as context for our question. Since these considerations are developed elsewhere in this book, we need do no more than recall them. In the first place, there is a close connection in the Old Testament between Yahweh's rule in Israel and its political fortunes. The relationship of Yahweh with his people was a mutual commitment that transcended the political order (e.g., Ex 19:6). Still Yahweh exercised his lordship in part through liberating his people from Egypt, entering a covenant with them, leading them into the promised land, and raising up new leaders, particularly the Judges and such leaders as David. In fact, he exercised his lordship more directly in relation to the Israelites as a people than as individuals. And God's reign is shown not only when he saves his people but also when he judges them for their unfaithfulness to him (e.g., Amos 9:8; Jer 4:18). Within the context of the Old Testament it is not difficult to see that there is a close relation asserted in many of the prophets and in the Deuteronomic history between the people's fidelity to the covenant and God's action toward them as a people.

In the New Testament, however, the reign of God or his definitive saving intervention for his people that Jesus mediates is so transcendent that for many it is difficult to see its relation to concerns of the political order. What is offered men and women through the proclamation of the reign of God is reconciliation and communion with God and with one another,[2] and thus a victory over and liberation from all that opposes this communion. It was through the death and resurrection of Jesus, the early community proclaimed, that he mediated this kingdom. What is central in the early Church according to Luke is the proclamation made by Peter at Pentecost: "Let the whole house of Israel know beyond any doubt that God has made both Lord and Messiah this Jesus whom you crucified" (Acts 2:34–35). It is in him that the words of David are fulfilled: "The Lord said to my Lord, sit at my right hand until I make your enemies your footstool" (Ps 110:1). A number of Scripture scholars make the point that by his account of the ascension or exaltation of Jesus "in a cloud" (Acts 1:9), Luke is associating Jesus' lordship with that ascribed to the Son of Man in Daniel 7:13–14. The first Christians thought, perhaps, that Jesus would exercise his lordship when he came again at his parousia, but Luke is asserting that he is exercising it now, since this eschatological lordship was given to him through his exaltation.[3] Peter says of Jesus: "Exalted at God's right hand, he first received the promised Holy Spirit from the Father, then poured this Spirit out on us" (Acts 2:33). Jesus was given an operative share in the lordship of God, and he is exercising this through his Spirit and the community that is incorporated into him. This lordship or reign that Jesus exercises in fulfillment of Daniel's prophecy is, of course, not of this world. It comes to be through God's gift rather than the way kingdoms of this world come to be. It does not take as its central concern what kingdoms of the world do, nor is it exercised as they are. As much of Acts shows us, this lordship or reign of God that has been given to Christ is being exercised preeminently through and in his community of believers—through the proclamation of his word, through the formation of community and through the Eucharist. His final definitive reign is even now having an impact, particularly in this community and through it upon the world it evangelizes.[4]

One of the constituents of the kingdom is, according to both the OT and the NT, peace. The Hebrew word for peace was *šālōm* which meant wholeness. This meant harmony within the individual and also within the whole community, a harmony based on God's blessing and on order, and one that makes human development possible.

With the later prophets particularly, peace, the opposite of which was war, was seen to depend upon the fidelity of God's people to his covenant, or their righteousness. Peace sought or promised on other bases is a false peace (Jer 6:14; 14:13; 28; Ezek 13:16). Peace became an eschatological expectation in the OT; and as such it included paradisal fruitfulness, peace among animals, peace among persons and among nations. It expressed the ideal transformation of the world that would occur in the final age through God's gift directly or through his Messiah, "the prince of peace" (Is 9:6). This gift remains dependent upon men's response to God, but this response will be made possible since God will change man's inconstant heart (Jer 31:33f; Ezek 36: 24–7).[5]

In the Christian community, peace, *eirēnē,* is a common form of Christian greeting (e.g., 1 Cor 1:3; Gal 1:3; Eph 1:2). And Luke in particular interrelates the reign of God and peace. In the infancy narratives, we find a strong relation asserted between the visitation of God and peace. The canticle of Zechariah describes the coming saving action of God as a fulfillment of the oath he had sworn to Abraham: "he would grant us, that, rid of fear and delivered from the enemy, we should serve him devoutly" (1:74). God's visitation is "to guide our feet into the way of peace" (1:79). The multitude of angels who appeared to the shepherds chanted "Glory to God in high heaven, peace on earth to those on whom his favor rests" (2:14). Peace is an immediate consequence of salvation (7:50), and when the disciples are sent on mission to the towns of Israel, they were to call down God's peace upon the houses they entered (10:5). It would be difficult to interpret this peace as restrictedly a religious reality to the exclusion of a political reality. Luke looked upon Jesus as a prophet like Moses (Acts 3:22) as well as a Davidic Messiah, and both of these concepts have a political dimension. As Lloyd Gaston writes:

> *Shalom* is of course a religious concept, often equivalent to salvation in the broadest sense. Basically it means wholeness, not just in the sense of fullness of life for the individual but for the totality of human relationships within a community. Therefore *shalom* is equally a political concept. It is not restricted to the absence of hostility within a group, but it includes this as a matter of course. A community characterized as a perfect harmony

> of free persons with their Lord and with one another is a political as well as religious goal. This political goal of peace among the nations is an important part of the eschatological hope of Israel, in which the Messiah (Is 9:2–7; Zech 9:9f; Mic 5:5) rules over a peaceful paradise (Is 2:2–4; Mic 4:1–4). The proclamation to Israel during the first century that such a long-promised goal had become a reality could not possibly ignore the troubled political situation of the time. The redemption which the Messiah has come to bring Israel will mean peace for all Israel and peace between Israel and the nations.[6]

There seems to be a rather widespread consensus among interpreters of Luke that the reign of God and Jesus Christ's mediation thereof offered a peace that included as an integral part a peace for Jerusalem of the political order. This consensus exists in spite of varied interpretations of the pre-history of Luke's gospel and of his theology. One interpreter of Luke who affirms this quite strongly is Gaston, who relates this to the pre-history of Luke's gospel. He finds that the explicit references to the destruction of Jerusalem in Luke's gospel are found in special material in Luke (19:39–44; 21:20–24; 23:28–31, and 13:34–35—this last passage being also in Q).[7] He argues that this special material, which can be clearly distinguished from the Markan parts of Luke, represents an earlier tradition that was part of the missionary preaching of the Church to the inhabitants of Jerusalem.[8] An important part of this earlier tradition asserted that the coming of the messiah meant the offer of peace to the people of the promise. "After A.D. 70 such a proclamation would have seemed a bitter mockery, and the optimistic tone with which parts of the Lucan writing speak of peace as a real possibility is a sure sign of their early origins."[9] In early Acts (as in the early part of Luke's gospel) there is a kind of confidence that the Jews would respond to the preaching of the early Church; but in Acts there is also a growing sense of frustration in this mission (shown particularly with the incident of the killing of Stephen), as there had been in the ministry of Jesus (Lk 12:49, 51–52).

If this is the case, the predictions of the destruction of Jerusalem in Luke were not apocalyptic in the sense of a determined divine event or an event coterminous with the end of the world and the parousia. Rather they were conditioned prophecies as we find in the prophets in the Old Testament, such as Jeremiah's prophecy of the destruction of Jerusalem. If the people repented, God would not destroy the city. The promise of peace for Jerusalem and the threat of destruction were simultaneous; they were an either/or; they expressed a hope and a fear in the situation of the early Church's preaching.[10] This preaching is, Gaston holds, a faithful continuation of the preaching of Jesus himself; indeed, it reflects this teaching.[11] Although Jesus definitely centered upon a kingdom that was transcendent, he was in the tradition of the prophets; and it would be incredible that Jesus would say nothing about the burning issue for the Jews of that time—the relation of Israel to Rome.

> It is clear that Jesus did warn about the consequences of the political situation of his own time, and that like the Old Testament prophets his warning was expressed in terms of a divine judgment. If the threat of judgment does not exclude political aspects, neither does the promise of the kingdom. Put quite simply if rather naively, "if the Jewish nation had responded as a whole to his first appeal and teaching, there can be no doubt that, with all else that repentance involved, there would have been a profound modification of its actual attitude toward the rest of the world, and that the Roman power itself would not have had the excuse it actually had for being blind to the value of the Jewish faith." The kingdom of God in Jesus' proclamation was not opposite to but on the contrary must have included a solution to the political situation of Israel.[12]

This view is, we should caution, not an interpretation of the kingdom as an essentially political kingdom; Jesus did not offer a *quid pro quo* relation to God. The point is that the acceptance or the rejection of the kingdom mediated by Jesus had consequences in the political order. Jesus' interest was not exclusively man's relation to God but the relation of men and women to one another as individuals and as groups or even peoples.

The view or interpretation that Gaston offers is not dependent upon his specific stand on the pre-history of Luke's gospel. Even Conzelmann recognized that Luke held the destruction of Jerusalem to be a consequence of Jerusalem's rejection of Jesus, although he interpreted this destruction as a simply historical and not an eschatological fact.[13] Franklin and Ellis, who reject a dichotomy between history and eschatology as a correct interpretation of Luke, hold that the destruction of Jerusalem resulted, for Luke, from the fact that she "did not know the time of her visitation" (see Lk 19:44).[14] H. Egelkraut in his study of the travel narrative of Luke (9:51–19:48) interprets the dominating theme of this section to be the growing conflict between Jesus and the Jews; Israel's rejection of the kingdom brought judgment.[15] This is not to say that God brought about the destruction of Jerusalem; it was rather the enemies of the Jews who destroyed Jerusalem, but in the circumstances this destruction was divine judgment.[16]

How could acceptance of the ministry of Jesus or of the early Church have affected Israel in reference to its political relation to Rome? Without attempting to do more here than briefly indicate some few elements of an answer to this question, we can say first of all that for those who put first God's kingship over them (Lk 12:31) priorities would have changed. As followers of Jesus they would be more interested in sharing with others what they had received than in gaining more and more of this world's goods. What characterized the ministry of Jesus was this generous sharing with others. He indicated as a mark of his ministry the fact that "the poor have the good news preached to them" (Lk 7:22),[17] where the poor are not only those who had little money but all those held in contempt by the opponents of Jesus. This includes such people as publicans and sinners and all who are oppressed and who cannot defend themselves. Other chapters of this study develop this theme, and so we can restrict ourselves to recalling that Jesus' teaching was a call that, if accepted, would change the relations that the rich had to the poor, the religious authorities had to the ordinary people of the land, and that those richly endowed with God's gifts had to the needy on every level. His teaching called his followers to respect and love each other. This message and the impact of Jesus' life did, we know, through his Spirit create a human community among his followers; if accepted on a larger scale among the Jews at that time, it would have had a much wider effect upon them and their social structures and so also on their relation to Rome. At the least it would have placed the political domination they experienced from Rome in a different perspective. Though painful to the Jews, it would perhaps not have been so to the extent that it would provoke them to a suicidal military uprising against Rome.

Gaston points out that central to the Jews' self-understanding from about 168 B.C. to 135 A.D. was a "theology of martyrdom."[18] In their situation as a small community amid the powers of their time, their alternatives were armed resistance to the Hellenistic world or accommodation to it. In the book of Daniel they were directed to a path that lay between these two extremes. Daniel called the people to a confidence that God would save them and that they would be vindicated; on the basis of this hope, they were called to continue faithful to their covenantal relation to God and by this fidelity witness their faith to the world. Jesus' answer to the question about taxes to Caesar—"Give to Caesar what is Caesar's but give to God what is God's" (Lk 20:25)—was consistent with this attitude.[19] We know, however, that, contrary to this, provocations by Roman officials in Palestine and acceptance of violent means of revolution by the Zealot party resulted in uprisings among the Jews that led to the destruction of Jerusalem itself.[20]

We have suggested in this treatment that the reign of God and the peace that it offered, according to Luke and Jesus himself are eschatological but have an impact on the present, not only in reference to man's relation to God and the personal reconciliation among men and women that it brings about, but in reference to the relation among peoples in the political order. At least it was meant to have that impact for the people of Jerusalem. Similarly, God's eschatological judgment can have an impact in the historical and specifically political order, and does have this for those who reject the reign of God. At least it reached the city of Jerusalem in the destruction it experienced in A.D. 70.

II. The Reign of God and Peace on Earth Today

If one grants the basic validity of our interpretation of Luke's theology of the reign of God and its implications for the peace of Jerusalem and the rootedness of this theology in the ministry of Jesus, does the relation of the reign of God to the peace of Jerusalem revealed there constitute something of a paradigm or symbol for political communities in our time? What are the implications of this for Christians today in their relation to the political communities of which they are a part? In this part we shall briefly examine this question by (1) expressing our difference from some views of this matter which seem extreme; (2) placing this matter in the general context of the relationship between the reign of God or redemption through Christ and creation in its present state; (3) more specifically indicating some norms that are implied in this viewpoint for mankind's construction of peace in the political order.

1. Some Dualistic Views

We propose that the relation between the reign of God or lordship of Jesus and the peace of Jerusalem that we analyzed above is in some way paradigmatic or symbolic for us today. St. Paul tells Christians of his time:

> Consider the kindness and the severity of God—severity toward those who fell, kindness toward you, provided you remain in his kindness; if you do not, you too will be cut off (Rom 11:22).[21]

What Paul says more generally here in reference to the implications of the Jewish experience for Christians, Luke's theology extends to the political order. But there are Christian theologians who seem to totally sunder the reign of God and the political order at least in the sense of denying that the reign of God can ever find partial and temporary manifestation or expression in political activity. For example, some of Jürgen Moltmann's statements seem to reflect this viewpoint:

> Jesus' eschatological message of freedom was implicitly a total attack on the very existence of the religious state...
>
> Those who recognize God in the Crucified one see the glory of God only in the fact of Christ crucified and no longer in

> nature, reason, or political achievements. Glory no longer rests upon the heads of the mighty. For believers, Christ crucified was made the righteousness of God, and for them political authority was deprived of its religious sanction . . .
>
> Here the political theology of the cross is a critical and theoretical instrument for freeing men from political idolatry, paternalism, and alienation.[22]

We can acknowledge that the association of the "German Christians' Faith Movement" with Hitler's National Socialist party in the early years of the Third Reich gives good grounds for Moltmann's view that the Church should take a critical stance toward the State. There have been overidentifications of Christianity with the State in the history of our own country,[23] and another essay in this volume analyses an instance of this overidentification in the history of the Church under Constantine. But for a theologian to virtually restrict the attitude of the Christian as Christian to the State to the negative character outlined by Moltmann seems to be narrower and harsher than the example of Christ or the early Christians. In his ministry the basic attitude of Jesus, which symbolizes the reign of God and its present impact, was to reconcile man to God and men and women to one another. His physical healings and his parables, examined elsewhere in this volume, are symbols of this. These healings cannot be interpreted only individualistically. They indicate symbolically Christ's mission to save or heal not only individuals but to heal even the relations among men and women and specifically those in the social, economic and political dimensions of life. They show that God's eschatological reign is already having an impact and that the power of this reign is to transform individuals and societies, beginning with the present. The fact that tares remain among the wheat is not evidence against the operation in the present of the reign of God in the life of an individual, of the Church, or even of a society. Jesus was a Jew and he identified with his people and, as we have shown, took the construction of peace in his own country as a part of his mission. We are told in Scripture, "One who has no love for the brother he has seen cannot love the God he has not seen" (1 John 4:20). It would seem to follow from this as well as from the example of Christ that one who does not love the country of which he is a part physically cannot love the reign of God. Though it may seem more Christian to totally relativize our adherence to every political community because of how far it falls short of the reign of God, the example of Christ would show us that this is a false universalism—as reprehensible as a false particularism.[24] Early Christians did in fact find a way to relate the State positively to God, as we see in Paul's famous passage:

> Let everyone obey the authorities that are over him, for there is no authority except from God, and all authority that exists is established by God. As a consequence, the man who opposes authority rebels against the ordinance of God. . . . You must obey, then, not only to escape punishment but also for conscience' sake (Rom 13:1–2a, 5).[25]

We shall offer reasons below for viewing the State within a moral and religious context in a way that is not idolatrous, and in a way that offers us criteria for evaluating the actions of a political community within this context.

Moltmann's view may well be in part derivative from a Lutheran interpretation of grace that has difficulty in asserting that the reign of God comes about at all through human activity or causality. To assert this may seem to take the glory of the kingdom away from God to give it to man. This is a large issue, but it is important for us at least to point out that the view we are proposing rests on a theology of grace which affirms that God's glory in bringing about the reign of God is enhanced rather than diminished through his use of human agents. We are agreed that he used the human activity of the man Jesus, who, when his healing of a demoniac was ascribed to Beelzebub, replied, "If it is by the finger of God that I cast out devils, then the reign of God is upon you" (Lk 11:20). It would seem that we must acknowledge in our own time that physical and spiritual healings of individuals and, at times, of social and political divisions occur, and occur through human agents. Injustice is replaced by justice, strife by love, disunity by unity, in a way that, at times, reflects moral and religious values and concerns. It would also seem that if we are to give God his due we must at times ascribe this to his operating in history—to the finger of God or, as Matthew puts it, to "the Spirit of God" (Matt 12:28). If this is the case, human agents not only announce the reign of God but have a causal influence in making it present, not by their own power but through the power that God gives them by his Spirit.

A dichotomy between the reign of God as understood by these Christians who think it has implications for political activity and action by governments in our time is also asserted by many contemporary politicians and students of politics. For example, Hans J. Morgenthau writes:

> The natural aspirations proper to the political sphere—and there is no difference in kind between domestic and international politics—contravene by definition the demands of the Christian ethics. . . . It is *a priori* impossible for political man to be at the same time a good politician—complying with the rules of political conduct—and be a good Christian—complying with the demands of Christian ethics. . . . The gap between the rational postulates of natural law and the contingencies of the concrete situation within which man must act and judge is just as wide as the gulf which separates the demands of Christian ethics from the rules of political action. In truth . . . both gaps are identical.[26]

We find, for example, that in the United States many have held that in the political order what is at stake is the national interest or the balancing of interests within the country in a utilitarian and pragmatic way, divorced from a moral order that controls personal behavior in the lives of individuals. Of course, this view of a dichotomy between the interests of a political community and the implications of Christian ethics and the natural law is understandable if some interpretations of these implications are accepted as legitimate. But the view that this dichotomy exists in principle is not an adequate interpretation of the actions of the political community. It is thus not a good empirical theory. As T. A. Spragens writes:

> It seems fairly clear that the idea of natural rights has had a very profound operational significance in the context of limitation on governmental power, civil liberties, and so on which

> American courts have imposed and guaranteed. It also has had operational significance in the nation's political culture. Any empirical theory of democracy which does not incorporate such realities would strike many of us as rather inadequate.[27]

The view that men have natural rights which are God-given and that the political community has a moral obligation to recognize these was expressed in the founding documents of the United States.[28]. Many of the early settlers in what was to become the United States viewed themselves as covenanted people on the model of the ancient Israelites.[29] Thus, Morgenthau's interpretation of the bases of political action within a liberal utilitarian model is not sufficient for guidance of a State in our time, for a pragmatic attitude divorced from considerations of morality results in an inadequate moral context for the actions of a country, and one that loses the loyalty and respect of its own people and other peoples.[30]

2. Creation and redemption

The basic reason why the eschatological lordship and reign of Jesus Christ has implications for the political order is the relation this reign or lordship has to that of the God of creation and history. The Judaeo-Christian understanding of God is that he created the world and mankind for a purpose that he will realize without fail through his own providential guidance of mankind in history and through mankind's response to that guidance. Mankind has opposed God's purposes by sin from the beginning and in the process has seriously harmed itself as well as its religious relation to God; it has become subject to powers opposed to God's purposes. The eschatological kingdom given to Christ through his death, resurrection and ascension is a share in the lordship God has as creator and Lord of history, and it is given to him to realize God's purposes in history and overcome all that stands in the way of their realization. These purposes are human as well as transcendent. Of course, they will not be realized fully within history, but only in that "new heaven and new earth" (Rev 21:1), in "the holy city Jerusalem coming down out of heaven from God" (Rev 21:11). But this eschatological reign of

Christ is already having an impact, as we have found, here and now not only in individuals but in the human community.

This is found preeminently in the Church which is the sacrament of the kingdom present in mystery, though even there we know that this kingdom is only partially realized and expressed. The presence of this kingdom is realized within the Church by the proclamation of the word, the celebration of the Eucharist, the formation of community and other ways analyzed in other chapters of this book. This has an impact not only within the Church but within the human communities from which its members are drawn. Like Christ, the Church is concerned for justice and peace. As the Synod of Bishops stated in 1971:

> Action on behalf of justice and participation in the transformation of the world fully appear to us as a constitutive dimension of the preaching of the Gospel, or, in other words, of the Church's mission for the redemption of the human race and its liberation from every oppressive situation.[31]

This is in accord with the statement of the Second Vatican Council in its decree on the apostolate of the laity:

> Christ's redemptive work, while of its nature directed to the salvation of men and women, involves also the renewal of the whole temporal order. The Church has for its mission, therefore, not only to bring to men and women the message of Christ and his grace, but also to saturate and perfect the temporal sphere with the spirit of the Gospel. The two spheres [spiritual and temporal], distinct though they are, are so linked in the single plan of God that he himself purposes in Christ to take up the whole world again into a new creation, initially here on earth, completely on the last day.[32]

By the Church's very expression of a degree of unity among men, it can offer men and women an image of what is possible in the social, the economic, and the political spheres of their lives; this constitutes a great responsibility for the Christian community in the present age. Moreover, through helping men and women to overcome alien influences in their lives and center on the kingdom of God first of all, the Church can help them to take the risks with their physical and temporal welfare that are necessary to promote and defend a truly human peace—risks they would not be likely to take if their interests were exclusively secular. They are enabled to overcome the influences of individual and social sin that are at the roots of injustice and false peace. Conversely we can say that if men and women think that they can achieve a truly human peace by their own unaided human efforts and insights, we may be sure that they will reduce peace to a dimension that is less than fully human. Perhaps they will prefer lack of tension to peace, or peace simply for themselves or their sector of the world or social class rather than peace built upon a more universal justice. It takes more than human resources to patiently accept the sustained effort and endure the frustrations that are the costs of contributing to a true peace in the world.

We cannot then think that the only anticipations within history of the eschatological reign of God are to be found within the Church. They are being effected as well by Christ through men and women in the human communities or societies that constitute the world. Jesus said that "Full authority has been given to me both in heaven and on earth" (Matt 28:18), and judgment of all men's actions is given to Christ (Rom 2:16). When in political or social communities injustice gives way to justice, disunity to a unity that is of a moral order and that manifests a real compassion for the disadvantaged, we may well have to acknowledge that even now the powers that oppose God's rule are being overcome through human agents and thus that Christ's reign and redemptive work is operative in part. There is, however, no promise of a millennium within history; and attempts to bring this about within history at the cost of any violence result, we know, not in a millennium but in making an idol of the temporal and political order.[33] We must, similarly, acknowledge that when justice gives way to injustice, unity to disunity, and a broader concern for the human community to an excessively particularistic one, then it is the lordship of Christ as well as human welfare that is being resisted. And we can expect that God's judgment will reach such societies as it reached even Jerusalem, for as God's kingdom has its anticipations in this world so too does God's judgment. Even in these circumstances there is a kind of peace, the deeper peace that those who share fellowship with Christ can have in this world, for he told his followers: "My peace is my gift to you; I do not give it to you as the world gives peace" (Jn 14:27).

3. Christian norms for peace today.

How can the Christian imperative present in Christ's concern for the peace of Jerusalem in the political order be made concrete and relevant to the changed conditions of today's complex and conflictive world? Is this symbol to be subject to each Christian's personal interpretation of what it means? Or is it to be presented to modern men and women deeply concerned with peace outside a Christian context in a way that seems alien to them and an imposition from without? I suggest that the recent social teaching of the Catholic Church goes far to making this Christian symbol operative today in a way that is neither arbitrary nor alien to modern secular concerns and approaches. Here we can do no more than indicate a method of approach which the reader can find spelled out in the documents we refer to. But this restricted purpose can point to a human and Christian framework for thinking about peace and for constructing systemic peace within and among political communities, and it is this that is perhaps most important for the realization of peace in our time. What must be changed is the "mind-set" of approaching the question of peace from a too narrowly conceived pragmatic context or a too narrowly conceived Christian context. If we Christians can objectify in our lives and political activity an approach to the problem of peace that is fully Christian and fully human for our time then perhaps we can contribute effectively to a transformation of the world in which we live; at least we can come closer to the model of Jesus' concern for the peace of this world. We shall reflect briefly on Pope John XXIII's encyclical *Pacem in Terris* (1963) and then on the document written by Cardinal Maurice Roy to commemorate this encyclical on its tenth anniversary. This will help us to see the direction of the development of the Church's teaching on the issue of peace in the changing circumstances of our time.

The Teaching of John XXIII

How does Pope John understand the Christian attitude toward the construction of peace in our time? He clearly identifies with the concern for peace felt so widely in our time, and he contributes to the realization of this peace by pointing out:

> Peace on earth, which men of every era have most eagerly yearned for, can be firmly established only if the order laid down by God is dutifully observed (1).

Peace within societies and among societies is indeed a pragmatic interest of individuals and political communities, but more than this it is a human value and goal intended by "God, the provident Creator of all things" (50). In fact, God has established an order on which the achievement of this peace depends, an order that is shown to us in ways that are accessible to "all men of good will" (166), namely, in "the requirements of human nature itself" (157)[34] and in the signs of the times. Peace is one of the conditions for human fulfillment, and thus it is a value that God sanctions, since as provident Creator he wants what is necessary for human fulfillment; peace is a value that has God as its source and foundation. God gives to men the "task of bringing about true peace in the order established by God" (163), a task that is a moral exigency and, indeed, implicit in man's relation to God and his fellow men. In his encyclical Pope John spells out some of the implications of this "task of restoring the relations of the human family in truth, in justice, in love and in freedom" (163)—characteristics of a fully human peace, We shall restrict ourselves to indicating some criteria or foundations for human peace today and representative aspects of systemic peace that our own age calls for.

In continuity with earlier social teaching of the Church, John identifies the dignity of the human person as the criterion for a relationship among individuals and their political community that can truly be called a human peace within a society.

> Any human society, if it is to be well-ordered and productive, must lay down as a foundation this principle, namely, that every

> human being is a person, that is, his nature is endowed with intelligence and free will. By virtue of this, he has rights and duties of his own, flowing directly and simultaneously from this very nature. These rights are therefore universal, inviolable, and inalienable (9).

John spells out a charter of human rights on this basis that includes both political and economic rights and the right to juridical protection of these human rights. With each right man has correlatively a duty to recognize that others possess the same rights and to contribute generously "to the establishment of a civic order in which rights and duties are progressively more sincerely and effectively acknowledged and fulfilled" (31). It is for this purpose that men and women establish civil communities. As the Second Vatican Council was to state in *Gaudium et Spes:*

> Individuals, families, and various groups which compose the civic community are aware of their own insufficiency in the matter of establishing a fully human condition of life. They see the need for that wider community in which each would daily contribute his energies toward the ever better attainment of the common good. It is for this reason that they set up the political community in its manifold expressions.
>
> Hence the political community exists for that common good in which the community finds its full justification and meaning and from which it derives its pristine and proper right. Now, the common good embraces the sum of those conditions of social life by which the individuals, families, and groups can achieve their own fulfillment in a relatively thorough and ready way (74).

John commends as in accord with human nature and the common good such aspects of modern political communities as the division of government into legislative, judicial, and executive branches, and the practice of spelling out in a constitution fundamental human rights, procedures for appointment of public officials, and the scope and term of their office. At the same time he explicitly separates himself from those who say that the only source of civic rights or the binding force of the constitution is "the mere will of human beings, individually or collectively" (78). Counter to this, "it is divine wisdom, and not mere chance, that has ordained that there should be government, that some should command and others obey" (46).[35] In their social and political lives men and women are related not only to their own societies but to God himself, the source and guarantor of human values. By recognizing this, they make the ties that bind them to God the solid foundation of their lives, both of that life which they live interiorly in the depths of their own souls and of that in which they are united to other men in society (45).

God's providential concern in history for fulfillment for men and women that accords with their human dignity is the ultimate source of the responsibility men and women have of helping to create in their societies political and social orders that support such fulfillment. To work for peace is to cooperate with God, and to cooperate with God is to work for peace.

In our period of history the genuine needs of men call for relations of solidarity among states. John insists that political communities as well as individual human beings are "reciprocally subjects of rights and duties" and that "the same moral law which governs relations between individual human beings serves also to regulate the relations of political communities with one another" (80). Active solidarity among states is particularly important in our age, in which one sign of the times is that the common good of one state "cannot be divorced from the common good of the entire human family" (98). It is in this context that such modern questions as disarmament, the treatment of minorities, and the evolution of developing countries should be approached. No state in our time is capable on its own or simply by acting reciprocally with some other states of assuring its own peace or development. Hence the signs of the time show that:

> At this historical moment the present system of political organization and the way its principle of authority operates on a world basis no longer corresponds to the objective requirements of the universal common good (135).

There is a "structural defect" (134) in the organization of authority in the world today, for there is a need for worldwide public authority. "The moral order itself, therefore, demands that such a form of public authority be established" (137). John spells out some of the characteristics and limits of such authority, commends the United Nations and its "Universal Declaration of Human Rights" (Dec. 10, 1948) as "an important step on the path toward the juridico-political organization of the world community" (144), and expresses the hope that it may quickly develop into an effective safeguard for "the rights which derive directly from man's dignity as a person" (145).

Pope John then tells us that the task of constructing a truly human peace according to the exigencies of our time is not only a human interest; it is a task committed to men by God himself, and men's activity for this goal is a cooperation with God in his historical purpose in our time. This is a task that calls for technical competence as well as an inner attitude in accord with the moral order; it is a task possible for men not by human resources alone but by the aid of "help from on high" (168). While "it must be borne in mind that to proceed gradually is the law of life in all its expressions" (162) and so too in this work, we can conclude that to reject this task out of attachment to some more immediate good such as peace conceived as absence of tensions or simply as individual, group, or national interests is a rejection of an order established by God.

Reflections of Cardinal Roy

For an adequate answer, within the limits we set ourselves, to the question of how the symbol of Christ's concern for the political peace of Jerusalem may be made relevant today, we must also refer briefly to the Church's social teaching in the years since Pope John's encyclical. As effective and well received as John's encyclical was, there was need for the Church in its social teaching to encourage an attitude to the construction of systemic peace that took even more account than he did of the dynamism of history and the conflicts within it, the brokenness of man and the primacy of love over justice for addressing the problems of our time, and the integration of Christian symbols and human reflection. We can see some representative ways in which the Church built on John's encyclical to integrate these dimensions more fully into the Christian attitude toward peace if we look to the document written in 1973 by Cardinal Maurice Roy, namely, his "Reflections on the Tenth Anniversary of the Encyclical *Pacem in Terris* of Pope John XXIII (April 11, 1973)."[36] We shall refer briefly to the way Cardinal Roy, with the help of the Church's social teaching since John, describes the world scene in 1973, speaks of the matters and subjects of peace in these changed circumstances, and discusses a methodology for reflection on peace.

There were such changes in the decade after 1963 that Roy could say, "It is a different universe from that of John XXIII" (90). For example, while the earlier model of the world was dominated by the split between the Western industrialized democracies (first world) and the Communist bloc (second world), at the later period the countries of the Southern hemisphere were asserting themselves and had to be taken into account. In 1973 there was a greater awareness of the needs and demands of the countries of the third and fourth (marginal) world. While there had been a degree of thaw between East and West (due more to a balance of terror that brought peace of a sort than from a positive movement to that vision of peace put forward by John), this improvement was not found in the relations between North and South. Economic competition increased and created its own divisions and tensions. While the probability of nuclear holocaust may have diminished, local conflicts within particular regions and countries remained and terrorism increased. In fact, violence and the awareness of violence grew so much that in 1973 what was evident was a widespread society of protest:

> Conflict, expressed by violence, is a fact, a new fact, in all its breadth: this violence is everywhere, in countries that are not at war and in all social bodies, to the extent that a new chapter would have to be added to the Encyclical: *Bellum in Terris* (92).[37]

This violence was physical, but also structural (e.g., economic) and cultural (e.g., pressure exerted by public media). New rights were being pressed by violent and non-violent means, e.g. the right to dissent—a civil variety of conscientious objection. Many saw in violence a condition for the dialectical development of history. All of this is very different from John's vision of an ordered and somewhat hierarchical society.

In these changed circumstances, Roy considers a few of the *things* we must do to construct peace as well as the *subjects* of peace. For example, the elimination of war calls for a cessation of the arms race, an injustice and indeed a theft against the needy of the world as well as a danger and a tragic mistake (106). He is calling for that kind of disarmament that is in accord with Vatican II's call: "not indeed a unilateral disarmament, but one proceeding at an equal pace according to agreement, and backed up by authentic and workable safeguards."[38] While calling for the construction of peace, Vatican II recognized that:

> As long as the danger of war remains and there is no competent and sufficiently powerful authority at the international level, governments cannot be denied the right to legitimate defense once every means of peaceful settlement has been exhausted.[39]

The construction of peace also calls for changed economic relations between the industrialized and the poorer countries of the world. Pope Paul VI had treated these at length in his encyclical *Populorum Progressio* (1967) where he gave such great emphasis to building a peace day by day in a spirit of brotherhood, a peace that goes by the new name of development.[40] The Church is placing a greater emphasis on brotherly and Christian love as a key attitude necessary for the construction of peace, and is accepting a more dynamic conception of the peace of the world, which it expresses by speaking of integral human development to which all human beings have a right.[41] Within individual countries there must be more recognition of people's right to dissent and even to disobey civil laws when this is "moral resistance to unjust and qualified oppression, such as religious, moral, civic or racial intolerance" (113). Because of the rapidly changing character of the world, there must be constant reexamination of the goals of national and international political communities in their relation to the rights of the men and women they serve.

Of course the construction of peace depends also upon the "subjects of peace." There were such changes in the people upon whom the construction of peace depends in the decade after John's encyclical that Cardinal Roy felt compelled to ask about the subject of peace: "But does he want it [peace]? And can he achieve it? In 1973, the answer is no longer that of 1963; at the very least it is ambiguous" (120). Some dissents in our time represent "nihilism, which is so contrary to reason and to the common good" (113). We must examinine not only the objective conditions necessary for peace, but the psychological sources of conflict and general dissatisfaction in people today:

> Among these sources, reference is made to the traditional conflict between the generations and the sexes, the Oedipus complex, the absence of great causes that arouse incentive, the projection on to the collective body of individual ills and resentments, the intensification of distrust, etc. In addition, the list of the frustrations that are at the root of social explosions grows longer every day. . . . In order to be an "agent of peace," one must achieve peace within oneself. The peace of the world depends upon the conversion of the subject (123).

Peace is the act of a collective subject; it is attained only by the efforts of all. It is only when humanity consciously recognizes and accepts its unity that peace can come, and this calls for conversion.

The third major reflection of Cardinal Roy is on the question of *methodology*. There were two principles central in Pope John's appeal to all men of good will in *Pacem in Terris*—an understanding of the unity of humanity and a discernment of the signs of the times. These two principles are still appropriate, but both have seen development in the Church's teaching. For example, it is recognized that the demands of human dignity are historically conditioned and that we must go beyond respecting an order in society to the creation of one in a world in flux. Man:

> must achieve the creation of society.... Peace therefore is an order to be created, a future to be brought into being....
>
> In view of the ever more rapid changes of the last ten years, this idea of a history to be brought to successful realization according to the pace of the present time presents itself with ever increasing urgency. It is a question of successfully accomplishing the transformation and so to speak the cultural revolution of these decisive years (134, 136).

This demands that we plan for the future and that we adopt strategies to bring this future about.[42] Pope John's second principle, the signs of the times, has been much used and indeed misused since his time. We want to point out that, as this is a phrase taken initially from Scripture, so the Church is making more use than it did earlier of Christian symbols to envisage the social future and to motivate Christians to bring it about. For example, the bishops assembled together in the Second Synod (1971) wrote in their document *Justice in the World:*

> Listening to the cry of those who suffer violence and are oppressed by unjust systems and structures, and hearing the appeal of a world that by its perversity contradicts the plan of its Creator, we have shared our awareness of the Church's vocation to be present in the heart of the world by proclaiming the Good News to the poor, freedom to the oppressed, and joy to the afflicted....
>
> The uncertainty of history and the painful convergences in the ascending path of the human community direct us to sacred history; there God has revealed himself to us, and made known to us, as it is brought progressively to realization, his plan of liberation and salvation which is once and for all fulfilled in the Paschal Mystery of Christ (5, 6).[43]

We need Christian symbols to understand not simply our personal lives but the social lives and the political lives we have together and the demands they place on us. What we face in attempting to create systemic peace is not simply an expansion of achievements already evident, but also a conversion of a world moving in a direction opposite to a human peace that is truly appropriate for societies in our time. In this context, we have in this essay centered on the symbol of Christ's concern for the peace of Jerusalem in the political order as an integral part of the reign of God he announced and sought to bring about. The recent social teaching of the Church shows us some major ways in which this symbol has significance for Christians and all men and women of our time.

The Church's use of Christian symbols is not an abandonment of the human norms that John presented for the peace appropriate for our time. Reading the signs of the times is not a monopoly of Christians: "It is the right and duty of every man and of all men to carry out this discernment between events and the moral good that they know through their consciences" (152). One cannot draw immediately from Christian symbols one political strategy to set at rights some evil afflicting a society, rejecting all other strategies solely on the basis of these Christian symbols.[44] But, as we have suggested in this paper, the Christian symbols are essential to our understanding of and attitude toward peace in the political order. As gifted with the kingdom we have the mission and responsibility to do what we can to create such peace since it is meant to be an integral part of the expression of the kingdom in history.

NOTES

1. Quotations from Scripture are according to the New American Bible.

2. A recent study of the reign of God in the New Testament may be found in Edward Schillebeeckx, *Jesus. An Experiment in Christology* (New York: Seabury Press, 1979) pp. 140–154.

3. See E. Earle Ellis, *Eschatology in Luke* (Philadelphia: Fortress Press,1972) pp. 16–20; Eric Franklin, *Christ the Lord. A Study in the Purpose and Theology of Luke-Acts* (Philadelphia: Westminster Press, 1975) pp. 40–43.

4. Hans Conzelmann, in *The Theology of St. Luke* (New York: Harper and Row, 1960; originally published in 1953) had proposed that the central problem for Luke was the delay of the parousia, and that in answer to this he developed a theology in which the end was not so important; what

took its place was a salvation history in three stages, the period of Israel, the period of Christ, and the period of the Church. Both Ellis and Franklin, along with others, contest this interpretation. They hold that the unbelief of the Jews was a more serious problem for Luke than the delay of the parousia, that what he opposed was an attempt to calculate the time of the parousia, and that Luke does not dissociate history from eschatology. See Franklin, *op. cit.,* p. 43: "History in Acts does not embrace eschatology, neither does it deny it. It rather proceeds from the eschatological event and bears witness to it." History proceeds from eschatology, because the crucial eschatological event has occurred; Jesus is Lord at present through his resurrection and exaltation. See Ellis, *op cit.,* pp. 19–20:

> The whole of Lukan eschatology is within the context of a two-stage manifestation of the kingdom of God, present and future. But *how* is the age-to-come present? It has been observed that Matthew couples future eschatology and the Church. Luke, on the other hand, combines future eschatology and the Spirit of Jesus. Jesus, who gives the Spirit (Luke 3:16; Acts 2:33), represents in his resurrection an individual fulfillment of the age to come. His followers not only manifest the same *eschatological powers of the Spirit* as he does, but they also have a *corporate identification with the (risen) Lord.* In both ways Luke sets forth the new age as a present reality.

Further analysis of the kingdom, and specifically such questions as the relation between the future and the present and between the kingdom of God and the kingdom of Christ, may be found in R. Schnackenburg, "Kingdom of God," *Sacramentum Verbi* (ed. J. B. Bauer; New York: Herder and Herder, 1970) 2: 455–470. On this latter point, we may quote Schnackenburg (467):

> Since from the point of view of Jesus the coming kingdom of God was also his kingdom (see Lk 22:30) insofar as he would bring it about and he and his disciples would be assembled together in it, the early Church can already in the interim period speak of a kingdom which belongs to him who has been exalted to the right hand of God and even speak of itself as being "the kingdom of the Son of Man" (see Mt 13:41).

5. See H. Gross, "Peace," *Sacramentum Verbi* 2:648–651.

6. Lloyd Gaston, *No Stone on Another. Studies in the Significance of the Fall of Jerusalem in the Synoptic Gospels* (Leiden: Brill, 1970) p. 244. We should note that Gaston wrote this book largely out of a desire to improve Jewish-Christian relations. He traces their bitter relations all the way back to different attitudes taken to the fall of Jerusalem; but he distinguishes the destruction of the temple from that of Jerusalem and notes that it is only with the latter that Luke is concerned. The destruction of the city did not

imply God's rejection of Israel. We need not follow Gaston's interpretation of the negative attitude of some Christians toward the temple (see p. 472), since that is not our theme.

7. Gaston, *op. cit.,* p. 244.

8. *Ibid.,* p. 214.

9. *Ibid.,* p. 256.

10. *Ibid.,* p. 368.

11. *Ibid.,* p. 423.

12. *Ibid.,* pp. 425–426. The enclosed quotation is from S. Liberty, *The Political Relations of Christ's Ministry* (Oxford, 1916) p.14.

13. Conzelmann, *op. cit.* , pp. 133–134.

14. E. Earle Ellis, *The Gospel of Luke* (London: Nelson, 1966) pp. 227–228; see Franklin, *op. cit.,* p. 89.

15. H. Egelkraut, *Jesus' Mission to Jerusalem: A Redaction Critical Study of the Travel Narrative in the Gospel of Luke, Lk 9:51–19:48* (doctoral dissertation, Princeton Theol. Seminary, 1973, unpublished).

16. See J. Comblin, "La paix dans la théologie de s. Luc," *Ephem. Théol. Lovan.* 32 (1956) pp. 439–460, esp. 453; Franklin, *op. cit.,* p. 89.

17. See J. Jeremias, *New Testament Theology. The Proclamation of Jesus* (New York: Scribner's, 1971) pp. 108–118.

18. Gaston, *op. cit.,* p. 382.

19. See Charles Giblin, " 'The Things of God' in the Question Concerning Tribute to Caesar," *Catholic Biblical Quarterly* 33 (1971), pp. 510–527. Also see R. Cassidy, *Jesus, Politics and Society: A Study of Luke's Gospel* (Maryknoll, N.Y.: Orbis, 1978).

20. See, e.g., E. Lohse, *Le Milieu du Nouveau Testament* (Paris: Les Editions du Cerf, 1973) pp. 48–65, 101–103.

21. On this whole section of Paul (Rom 9–11) see L. de Lorenzi (ed.) *Die Israelfrage nach Röm 9–11* (Rome: St. Paul's, 1977); I have treated this section in *Predestination, Grace and Free Will* (Westminster, Md.: Newman Press, 1964) pp. 63–69.

22. J. Moltmann, "The Cross and Civil Religion," *Religion and Political Society* (New York: Harper and Row,1974) pp. 343–35. John Yoder offers a negative view of the state in *The Politics of Jesus* (Grand Rapids: Eerdmans, 1972). Richard Mouw presents a critique of this viewpoint in *Politics and the Biblical Drama* (Eerdmans, 1976).

23. See Conrad Cherry (ed.), *God's New Israel* (Englewood Cliffs: Prentice–Hall, 1971).
Theology (Maryknoll: Orbis, 1976) pp. 140–145. Segundo's own view that Jesus was touched by nationalism because he wept over Jerusalem ("How could Jesus have wept over Jerusalem if there had been no trace of nationalistic prejudice in him?" p. 164) seems to lose the distinction between love of one's own people or country and nationalism.

25. In view of widespread Protestant treatment of the Christian attitude to the state in the context of "powers and principalities," we should re-

fer to the treatment of this in Mouw, *op. cit.,* Ch. 5, "Confronting the Powers" pp. 85–116. His view seems close to that of Joseph Fitzmyer who comments on Romans 13:1–2a, 5 in the *Jerome Biblical Commentary* (Vol. II, 326) as follows:

> What is primary in Paul's affirmation is the relation of the Christian to the secular government, whether this be regarded as entirely human or as controlled by angelic spirits. . . . Even Rome's imperial authority comes from God, although it may be reluctant to admit it. Paul indirectly acknowledges the Father as the source of all the welfare and peace brought about by imperial Roman rule. . . . Obedience to civil authorities is a form of obedience to God himself, for man's relation to God is not limited to a specifically religious or cultic sphere. . . . His appeal to conscience suggests a moral obligation for obedience to civil laws, and not one that is just legal or penal. It links man's reaction to civil rulers with the divine origin of civil authority itself.

Of course, Paul is supposing in this that a civil government is basically fulfilling its responsibilities. Elsewhere in the New Testament (e.g., Rev 18) we have a veiled reaction to a government that is tyrannical and oppressive.

26. Hans J. Morgenthau, "The Demands of Prudence," *Worldview 3,* No.6 (June 1960), pp.6–7. This is quoted in Paul Ramsey, *The Just War. Force and Political Responsibility* (New York: Scribner's, 1968) p. 152. Also see Jerome Dollard, *Ethics and International Relations in the Realist School of International Relations and the Teachings of Vatican II and Pope Paul VI A Critical Comparison* (unpublished doctoral dissertation, Catholic University of America, 1974).

27. T. A. Spragens, *The Dilemma of Contemporary Political Theory: A Post-Behavioral Science of Politics* (New York, 1973) pp. 105–106.

28. See for a recent controversy over the sources of Thomas Jefferson's thought, Gary Wills, *Inventing America* (New York: Doubleday, 1978) and a review of this book by Kenneth Lynn, "Falsifying Jefferson," *Commentary* (October 1978) pp. 66–71.

29. See Robert Bellah, *The Broken Covenant. American Civil Religion in Time of Trial* (New York: Seabury, 1975) pp. 14–15.

30. For critiques of pragmatism, utilitarianism and relativism as forming an adequate political philosophy in the United States in the twentieth century, see Edward Purcell, Jr., *The Crisis of Democratic Theory. Scientific Naturalism and the Problem of Value* (University Press of Kentucky, 1973), and Victor Ferkiss, *The Future of Technological Civilization* (Braziller, 1974).

31. Second Synod of Bishops, "Justice in the World," 6. This and other documents of the Catholic Church are, unless otherwise noted, cited according to the translation found in Joseph Gremillion, ed., *The Gospel of Peace and Justice. Catholic Social Teaching since Pope John* (Orbis Books, 1976).

Our references will be to the paragraph of the documents, the number of which we shall place in the text.

32. *Apostolicam Actuositatem,* 5, as quoted in International Theological Commission, "Human Development and Christian Salvation," translated by Walter Burghardt, *Origins*, vol. 7 (Nov. 3, 1977) 311.

33. See Joseph Cardinal Ratzinger, "Eschatology and Utopia," *Communio* 5 (1978) 211–227.

34. In his "Reflections on the Occasion of the Tenth Anniversary of the Encyclical *Pacem in Terris* of Pope John XXIII" (April 11, 1973), Cardinal Roy states:

> Although the term "nature" does in fact lend itself to serious misunderstandings, the reality intended has lost nothing of its forcefulness when it is replaced by modern synonyms (almost all of which moreover are to be found in the Encyclical). Such synonyms are: man, human being, human person, dignity, the rights of man or the rights of peoples, conscience, humaneness (in conduct), the struggle for justice, and, more recently, "the duty of being," the "quality of life." Could they not all be summarized in the concept of "values," which is very much used today? (129)

35. This is a quotation from John Chrysostom. For an analysis of how the Church's interpretation of human rights fits into current secular interpretations by Marxism, liberal democracy and the United Nations see David Hollenbach, *Claims in Conflict. Retrieving and Renewing the Catholic Human Rights Tradition* (New York: Paulist, 1979) Chapter 1, "The Human Rights Debate," pp. 7–40.

36. Hollenbach's book analyzes the development of the Church's social teaching, particularly that since John XXIII through the early 1970's.

37. Perhaps the greatest violence in the Western world today is found in widespread legalized abortion. See John T. Noonan, *A Private Choice: Abortion in America in the Seventies* (New York: The Free Press, 1979).

38. *Gaudium et Spes* 82.Bishop Agostino Casaroli gave a recent analysis of the subject "The Holy See between Tensions and Détente", *L'Osservatore Romano,* March 2, 1978.

39. *Gaudium et Spes* 79. The Council condemns total war and declares that

> any act of war aimed indiscriminately at the destruction of entire cities or of extensive areas along with their population is a crime against God and man himself (80).

It recognizes the deterrent value of weapons at the present time (81) and does not judge whether there are legitimate targets for nuclear weapons in accord with the traditional just war theory. On this latter subject, see Thomas Aquinas, *Summa Theologica* II–II, 40,1, and James Childress, "Just War Theories: The Bases, Interrelations, Priorities, and Functions of Their Criteria," *Theological Studies* 39 (1978) pp. 427–445, and Paul Ramsey, *The Just War*. In reference to the latter one should also consult James Johnson and David Smith (ed.), *Love and Society: Essays in the Ethics of Paul Ramsey* (Missoula, Montana: Scholars Press, 1974), Part II: "War and Political Ethics," pp. 91–184. Also see J. O'Rourke, "The Military in the NT," *Catholic Biblical Quarterly* 32 (1970) pp. 227–236.

40. See *Populorum Progressio,* 76, 87.

41. See *ibid.,* 14–16.

42. See Hollenbach, *Claims,* Ch. 5, "Toward Policy," pp. 187–210.

43. This is a theme continued in Pope John Paul II's first encyclical, *Redemptor Hominis,* 16.

44. See John Paul II's "Address to the Third General Assembly of Latin American Bishops at Puebla," III, 2 & 3, *Origins* 8 (1979) 536. The whole of John Paul's "Address to the United Nations General Assembly," *Origins* 9 (1979), pp. 258–266, is devoted to the requirements for the construction of peace in our time.

Epilogue

In the foreword to this volume, we mentioned several classes of readers who we hoped would profit by our effort to relate the lordship of Christ to social systems. Inevitably, different readers will have been drawn to different essays, and will already have come to new insights into their own situations, problems and opportunities. But there are some common fruits of our work which, in retrospect, we ourselves can observe. In concluding with a word about these, we will at the same time be pointing to some of the ways in which the experience of reading this book might affect the attitudes and practice of our readers.

First, in countering a "privatizing" interpretation of the Gospel, one which would limit the power of its word to the realm of the personal, we have had numerous occasions to speak of the way in which persons and systems, consciousness and structures, are touched in their interaction by the Gospel. Our several reflections, then, have challenged the reader to develop what for many Christians is a new habit—the habit of attending to what happens to people, ourselves and others, as we affect and are affected by our social systems. The lordship of Christ over social systems is not to be separated from his lordship over human hearts. As persons and their societal creations are never adequately distinct, Christian mission and ministry can never address one without somehow touching the other.

How, for example, has my family's life been changed by moving from a city apartment to a suburban home? What difference has the demise of the neighborhood grocery and the coming of the shopping mall made for the patterns of our consuming? How do we experience the difference between visiting a small nursing home down the street and visiting a new 300-bed suburban hospital? And when we perceive that this or that system within our experience is proving hurtful to people, destructive of values that we cherish, what sense do we have that these systems might be changed for the better? How indeed would we go about instituting systemic change in the various contexts of our busy lives? The present volume has offered those concerned with such questions the conviction that they are Christian and theological questions, and that whatever efforts Christians make to improve the condition of society are a pilgrimage—a going forth in faith—to find the Christ who meets us in society no less than in the more contemplative aspects of our life. And so this is the first impetus which the essays in this volume would like to give—or confirm—in the lives of its readers: to cast upon our society the same critical/creative gaze which Jesus cast upon his, to acknowledge the legitimacy of extending the language of sin and grace to structures secular and sacred, and hence to let our zeal for his lordship in our lives range beyond our personal hearts to our systemic world.

Second, our essays will have been useful if, even as they impel to commitment to the healing and transformation of social systems, they also caution against every naive or absolutizing utopianism, Constantinian or other. God's kingdom can be anticipated and prefigured in history, through the persevering effort to create structures of peace and justice. But no historical embodiment will ever flawlessly realize the human and Christian dream of peace on earth, the new heavens and new earth where justice dwells. No politico-economic system, whether bearing the name of capitalist, socialist or distributist, will ever constitute a definitive *status quo* beyond the need of criticism and reform. Hence the "eschatological proviso" must be kept ever in readiness to challenge the perennial tendency to absolutize particular systems.

Such a proviso, however, must not be construed as a cynical or passive surrender of social systems to the principalities and powers which block the victory of Christ's lordship. Whatever theological links are to be affirmed between present efforts and the "absolute future," between the time of pilgrimage and the definitive entry into the kingdom, we need to insist on a basic axiom: the Christian commitment to struggle for peace and justice exists not in spite of but precisely because of the Christian expectation of ultimate salvation coming as sheer gift of God.[1] It would seem to be only paradoxically and/or dialectically that the posture of Christian hope, which escapes all clear definition, can be described.[2] The Second Vatican Council alluded to this characteristic of Christian hope when it declared that "... the expectation of a new earth must not weaken but rather stimulate our concern for cultivating this one."[3]

Such a posture of hope will find support in a *third* conviction fostered by this volume, namely that the lordship of Chrıst over social systems is both an "already" and a "not yet," both indicative and imperative, or, in Dietrich Bonhoeffer's statement, a call for both believing and obeying. "Only he who believes is obedient, and only he who is obedient believes."[4] This conviction is really the assertion of the mystery of grace/freedom applied to the flow of human history. In terms of the lordship of Christ, it is grounded in the affirmation that, even prior to the free engagement of Christians in any given age, and thanks precisely to the free engagement of Jesus of Nazareth in his life, passion and death crowned by the gift of his exaltation, Jesus is *already* Lord; but, at the same time, that lordship becomes more fully actualized and manifest through the free initiatives of Christians and others. From this standpoint the Church witnesses, in the very effort to evangelize within the reality of social systems, to a Lord who, so to speak, arrived there ahead of her, especially in the hiddenness of his Spirit poured forth on all that is human. On such a foundation Christians will labor zealously, but without anxiety. They will "act as if everything depends on God, and pray as if everything depends on us."[5] Here again, the "not in spite of, but precisely because of" is operative. The paradox needs to be experienced, in oneself or in others, to be cogent and real.

Fourth, the two preceeding considerations lead to another conviction which emerges from our reflections on the lordship of Christ—that is only in conflict and in and through the suffering which it brings that the lordship of Christ becomes progressively realized in Christians and in the world. The biblical rendition of that lordship presents it clearly as a victory over principalities and powers. The insights of recent theology have yielded the concepts of societal sin, unjust structures, and the like, together with what we have said under the third point, give to the notion of lordship a strongly conflictual tone. If in some Christian circles there is a facile recourse to the language of Jesus as Lord in a mood which seems to suggest a "social quietism," this is far from being an authentic version of that lordship as it is disclosed in the Gospel. The crucified One is the risen One. The Lord (*Kyrios*) is no other but the one who willingly became Servant (*diakonos*), and even slave (*doulos*). If our essays have been effective, no small part of this effect has been to reduce in the minds of readers the illusion that recourse to Jesus' lordship offers an escape from the trials of Christian discipleship. It does, however, offer comfort in those trials. In faith we affirm that the failures and defeats of those who suffer persecution for righteousness' sake will be transformed into victories, for it is the crucified Jesus who reigns, Lord without end. If this book has any one message, it might be that the principalities of evil and the forces of death can have no ultimate power against those who submit to the glorious power of Christ's name.

Fifth, one of the principal areas where such conflict will be experienced is the one where charismatic and institutional facets of the Church, and also, we have suggested, of secular society, must be maintained in a basic harmony that is never without tension. From this point of view, both "enthusiasm"—here in the pejorative sense of the illusion of a spontaneous following of the Spirit without the need of institutions—and institutionalism—the quenching of the movement of the Spirit in the community through the absolutizing of the system—represent basic deviations from genuine obedience to the Lord. And it is precisely the goal of the spirit of darkness to produce division between two indispensable aspects of human and Christian community, charism and institution, and between those who are drawn to champion or represent one or the other. Our volume has offered some guidelines for dealing with this kind of conflict, but sees no escape from the struggle. Where the law of the cross is permitted to prevail, the tension can become not merely bearable but a creative source of growth. Since the struggle takes place in the flow of history, discerning the signs of the times, knowing when the moment has come for accenting charismatic or institutional structures, or for bearing patiently with the tensions between them, is the crucial grace to be prayed for by Christians.

We cherish the hope, *sixth,* that what has been written here about the life and ministry of Jesus will stimulate many to read the gospels with new eyes. The theme of lordship, viewed in the three stages of its development, can give to the prayerful study of the parables and miracles of Jesus a fresh perspective.[6] The exercise of power in the conditions of powerlessness, the anticipation of lordship in faithfulness to the role of servant, and the contagious power of Jesus' imagination as it frees the enslaved imaginations of his disciples—all of these offer to today's disciple both paradigm and inspiration for sharing the prophetic and servant role of Jesus through various kinds of engagements within social systems. Several of the essays in this volume have likewise encouraged a reading of the gospels which fully attends to the way in which Jesus, while refusing to be captured by any political faction, set forth the revolutionary challenge of the kingdom with a creative critique of his contemporary religious culture. In this restricted sense, the Jesus we have offered for homage and imitation has been the political Jesus.

And *finally,* the deepest and most comprehensive impact we have desired to have on our readers touches the heart of their Christian faith, the crucial response that each is called upon to make to the question, "Who do you say that I am?" The New Testament itself witnesses abundantly to the development of understanding within the first generations of Christians, which made the confession, "Jesus is Lord," a very privileged credal identification of what it means to be Christian. It also witnesses, of course, to the emptiness of saying "Lord, Lord," unless confessional orthodoxy generates and is penetrated with the orthopraxy of deeds of love and justice. Today, in the current of theological reflection of which this book is an example, this most honored formulation of Christian commitment has found a new kind of expression. Unless our confession of Jesus as Lord includes in its scope the social systems for which we accept human and Christian responsibility, it becomes a vain and empty refuge. But when this inclusion is made, the power of the Name that is above every name is made available for the struggle to create a world of justice and peace, a world where his lordship is more fully achieved and acknowledged.

NOTES

1. This formulation echoes that of Karl Rahner touching the human/divine relationship in creation and Incarnation. See Karl Rahner, "Current Problems in Christology," *Theological Investigations* (Baltimore: Helicon 1961), vol. 1, p.162; see also his *Foundations of Christian Faith* (New York: Seabury, 1978), pp.75-81.

2. Gustav Wetter, *Dialectical Materialism* (New York: Praeger, 1958), pp. 386ff., interestingly portrays a comparable dialectical approach in the thought of the Russian Marxist philosopher, G. V. Plekhanov, who, in relating necessity and freedom, appeals to the example of such figures as Mohammed, Luther, and the Calvinists and Puritans. For all of these, it is maintained, "fatalistic" doctrines, far from generating social quietism, provided a psychological basis for energetic action.

3. *Gaudium et Spes* 39; E. T. Joseph Gremillion, *The Gospel of Peace and Justice: Catholic Social Teaching Since Pope John* (Maryknoll: Orbis, 1976), p. 273.

4. Dietrich Bonhoeffer, *The Cost of Discipleship* (New York: Macmillan, 1963), p. 69.

5. This is an abbreviated form of the more dialectical version of the aphorism of an unknown follower of St. Ignatius of Loyola. See Gaston Fessard, *La dialectique des exercises spirituelles de Saint Ignace de Loyola* (Paris: Aubier, 1956), pp. 305-363.

6. For the three phases, see above.

Biographical Data

FRANCINE CARDMAN (Ph.D. Yale University), associate professor of historical theology, Weston School of Theology.

THOMAS E. CLARKE, S.J. (S.T.D. Gregorian University), research associate, Woodstock Theological Center.

AVERY DULLES, S.J. (S.T.D. Gregorian University), professor of systematic theology, The Catholic University of America; research associate, Woodstock Theological Center.

JOHN FARRELLY, O.S.B. (S.T.D. The Catholic University of America), professor of systematic theology, De Sales Hall School of Theology.

JOHN C. HAUGHEY, S.J. (S.T.D. The Catholic University of America), research associate, Woodstock Theological Center.

MONIKA K. HELLWIG (Ph.D. The Catholic University of America), professor of theology, Georgetown University.

OTTO H. HENTZ, S.J. (Ph.D. University of Chicago), associate professor of theology, Georgetown University.

PHILIP LAND, S.J. (Ph.D. St. Louis University), staff associate, Center of Concern.

BRIAN O. MCDERMOTT, S.J. (Dr. Theol. University of Nijmegen), associate professor of systematic theology, Weston School of Theology.

J. P. M. WALSH, S.J. (Ph.D. Harvard University), assistant professor of theology, Georgetown University.

JOSEPH WEBER (Ph.D. Boston University), professor of biblical theology, Wesley Theological Seminary.